Productivity in Public Organizations

Marc Holzer is Editor-in-Chief of the *Public Productivity Review* and Director of the Center for Public Productivity at John Jay College, New York City. He has published several articles about public productivity and the general field of public administration.

Productivity
in
Public
Organizations

EDITED BY MARC HOLZER

KENNIKAT PRESS
Port Washington, N. Y. • London
A DUNELLEN PUBLISHING COMPANY BOOK

TO MADY

© 1976 by the Dunellen Publishing Company, Inc. and
Kennikat Press Corp.

Printed in the United States of America

Distributed in United States and Canada by
Kennikat Press, Port Washington, N. Y. 11050

Distributed in British Commonwealth (except Canada) by
Martin Robertson & Company Ltd., London

Library of Congress Cataloging in Publication Data

Main entry under title:

Productivity in public organizations.

 Includes bibliographical references.
 1. Civil service–United States–Labor
productivity–Addresses, essays, lectures.
I. Holzer, Marc.
JK768.4.P76   353.001'47   76-8432

ISBN 0-8046-7102-8 (Hard cover)

ISBN 0-8046-7108-7 (Paperback)

CONTENTS

Productivity in Public Organizations

INTRODUCTION

PUBLIC PRODUCTIVITY: DEFINING A MANAGERIAL FRAMEWORK

A major public administrative theme of the seventies will be "productivity." As that term gains favor, with good reason, among top management, chief executives and legislators in the public sector, it may at the same time gain equal disfavor among middle and lower level administrators, employees and union officials. Those individuals—the very ones who must be relied upon to achieve significant increases in output—are likely to criticize the "productivity push" out of sheer frustration . . . frustration with the barrage of concepts they are supposed to assimilate, with no clear framework for assimilation and situational application; with the organizational complexities they recognize, but which particular statements, reports or memos on productivity fail to acknowledge; with an effort that may appear to be only a "speed-up," but which is actually an honest attempt to develop and apply fair work standards; and with a quantitative measurement emphasis that may unduly preclude the consideration of qualitative factors in managerial decision-making.

The literature on public productivity, burgeoning since President Nixon's appointment of the National Commission on Productivity, unintentionally fosters those frustrations. But those errors are matters of omission, not commission. In the necessary process of generating new ideas and exploring promising concepts and innovations, investigators and commentators are often so preoccupied with relatively specific "solutions" to productivity problems that few pause to place those specifics in perspective. Even the infrequent attempts at overviews are not systematically comprehensive, are too technical or are too esoteric to facilitate comprehension by busy managers, workers and union leaders. Perhaps the size and complexity of the literature did not, until recently, demand a clear, conceptual overview. That overview can simplify an increasingly intricate and varied set of terms and concepts, thereby dispelling the technical and mysterious aura of productivity management.

This collection of readings is structured around a specific framework for comprehension and analysis (Fig. 1). By delineating the framework we have attempted to categorize the various concepts developed in the literature in terms that administrative practitioners, academics and politicians alike might find useful. (In contrast, economists and statisticians will find our framework unabashedly simple.)

Basic Relationships

Although most of the literature specific to public productivity has appeared within the last two years, the outline of those concerns was sketched almost a decade ago by a Bureau of the Budget (BOB) study, *Measuring Productivity of Federal Government Organizations.*[1] As defined by that study, and others since, productivity in public organizations, as in private organizations, is simply the relationship between inputs and outputs. Inputs are basically resources such as labor, materials and capital. Outputs are such accomplishments as the work done, products distributed and services

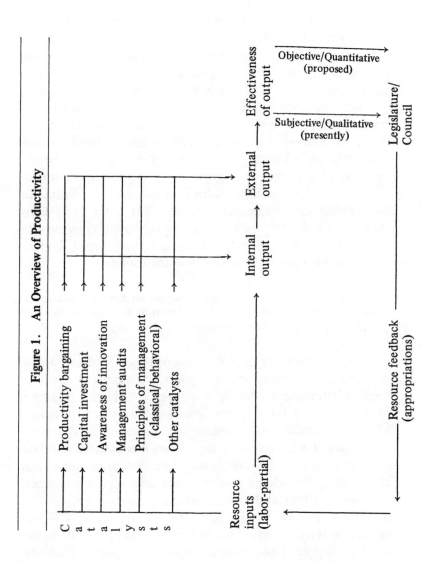

Figure 1. An Overview of Productivity

rendered. Indexes of productivity are the ratios of outputs to inputs.

Thus, increased productivity can occur in four general situations. The output to input ratio improves over time if resource inputs diminish while organizational input remains constant, consistent with President Kennedy's call for improved manpower utilization to insure that public programs are carried out with the minimum number of employees. Second, it improves if output increases, but resource inputs remain constant, exemplified by President Johnson's emphasis on a dollar's worth for a dollar spent. Third, output may increase while inputs decline. And, fourth, although both increase, output may grow at a faster rate than inputs.

Any one of those relationships, of course, is applicable to both public and private organizations. But as the 1964 BOB study also indicates, they are more easily applied by private than public enterprises because the latter are forced to more amorphous measures of output than the former:

> ... managers of government agencies have no general indicators of their choices or the efficiency of their performance comparable to the profit-and-loss statement.[2]

As a substitute for quantitative profit-loss feedback about output-input relationships, the study discusses the development of alternate productivity indexes as objective measures of output. Three types of resource-oriented indexes, based on physical or dollar measurements, are suggested. First, assuming output is measurable, in some cases it is possible to relate an output to total resource inputs. In other cases, output can be meaningfully related to only some resources, a combined measure. And in still other instances, perhaps most, it is useful to view output in relation to only one type of input, usually units of labor. This last relationship, keyed to the most expensive, most complex resource inputs and usually termed "labor productivity," is the most frequently utilized data base for public productivity analyses. Our own reference to that labor-based ratio will be "labor-partial productivity," a designation that may distinguish it from less common partial ratios based on capital, energy or other resource inputs.

Measurement of Output

As in private organizations, public sector inputs are measurable in terms of the common denominator of dollars, or man-hours in the case of labor resources. The basic data for the measurement of output and output-effectiveness in the private sector is sales; the profit-loss statement is also a rough index of productivity. Similar measures, however, are not generally applicable to the public sector. Thus, the major obstacles to efforts to gauge public productivity are often measurements of output, not input.

As a means of encouraging the types of analyses that private sector output and output-effectiveness measures facilitate—such as forcing product comparisons and public scrutiny, indexing progress, developing standards of performance, identifying reasons for success, delineating bases for performance incentives and reallocating resources—our analysis of the literature identifies three measurement categories. We suggest that those bases for public productivity indexes be termed "internal output," "external output," and "effectiveness of output," categorizations that can reconcile the wide variety of terms in the literature.

Perhaps the best standard for the utility of such measures, specified by the Civil Service Commission-General Accounting Office-Office of Management and Budget Joint Project on Productivity (referred to below simply as the Joint Project), are those ". . . which are quantifiable and measurable over a period of successive years in terms of their number and qualitative composition, and for which the labor consumed in their production can be identified."[3]

Internal Output

The first category, work as an internal (or intermediate) product, includes activities of a work center within an organization ranging from investigatory and clerical to transportation and training. Measurements of letters typed, freight moved, vehicles serviced, or employees trained represent, therefore, measures of internal outputs or of activities that the organization performs for itself. Those quantifications, however, should only be utilized to improve productivity if they are complemented by corresponding qualitative analyses. The analysis of some internal activities that are not reasonably quantifiable must rely wholly on qualitative analysis.

As indexes of labor-partial internal productivity, each measurable output can be divided by units of time such as man-days, man-months, or man-years. Examples of such ratios would be letters typed per man-hour, freight moved per man-day, vehicles serviced per man-month or employees trained per man-year. Alternatively, internal outputs can be gauged against costs. Instead of the time-based labor-partial productivity measure, output can be divided by the cost of labor inputs or the cost of any important set of resource inputs to produce a monetary measure per unit of internal output. Corresponding "unit cost measures" would be the dollar expenditure for each letter typed, ton of freight moved, vehicle serviced or employee trained.

In either case, such data—work units per unit of time or cost per work unit—can supply managers with some of the facts necessary to make better decisions. Comparing internal output indexes over a period of time, and complementing that data with relatively subjective or abstract management knowledge, a manager might find it easier, for instance, to attain performance goals for an individual employee or group, project future work force requirements, judge labor efficiency against a standard, or schedule work. And important questions, previously overlooked, might now be evident.

The quantification of internal products is relevant to, but is not limited to, work measurement, a process of comparison elaborated upon by the Joint Project's *Guidelines for Evaluating Work Measurement Systems in the Federal Government*. Work measurements, as measures of internal output, are described in the *Guidelines* as

... measuring the physical work units produced by individual work centers [within an organization or a component] and comparing them to an objectively derived standard of performance to obtain current efficiency.[4]

Further, a summary of that study in the overall Joint Project report indicates that

... work measurement data consists of stating quantities of work performed in terms of hours consumed as compared to a standard. For instance, if the standard for reproducing pages of photo copy is 50 per hour, and the operator produces only 47 per hour, he is working at 94 percent of standard.[5]

External Output

The second measurement category, external (or final) output, is defined by the 1964 study as the "end-products of the organization, that is . . . goods produced or services rendered for use outside the organization itself."[6] For example, the intermediate, internal process of sorting mail contributes to the external service of delivering mail; the activity of making photocopies may help a caseworker place a client in a job; training building inspectors may help each issue a greater number of citations for code violations.

Although indexes of external output productivity are often conceptualized as the ratio of all outputs to all inputs, or just to physical inputs, the computation of comprehensive output-based indexes is not always feasible; raw units of various outputs, such as social service referrals and home visits, cannot usually be combined. It is even difficult to assign dollar values, as a common yardstick, to many such services. Thus, external output indexes of actual use to managerial decision-makers will usually represent only partial measures. In terms of raw scores, only one output may be related to labor input; for instance, the number of felony arrests per man-month. Or, as is the case with internal output ratios, labor-partial productivity measures can be supplemented by unit cost measures. Moreover, other useful productivity indexes could be developed by treating internal outputs as inputs into the production of external outputs. Are the number of citations a building inspector issues (external output) related to the extent of his training (internal output)? Are the number of clients a caseworker places in jobs (external output) at all related to the intermediate, internal output of completed forms?

Effectiveness of Output

Advocates of effectiveness measurement acknowledge the value of internal and external output measures, but argue that meaningful attempts at productivity analysis must also consider such analyses as "the measurement of agencies' success in accomplishing assigned missions" or the quantification of "whether government programs and activities are achieving the objectives established for them, with due regard to both costs and results."[7]

Furthermore, they suggest that public organizations attempt to gauge the impact, in terms of quality, utility, social benefit or client satisfaction, derived from the monopolistic public organization's external outputs of goods and services. Such data would be analogous to the sales and profit data that has a direct impact in competitive, private organizations. Sales quantifications used by organizations in the private sector are, after all, rough measures of client satisfaction. Public sector monopolies have not had similar feedback quantifications; rather, their resource feedback has usually been dependent upon subjective, qualitative perceptions of client satisfaction by elected officials. Do community leaders "feel" the schools are doing a "good" job? Does the mail "seem" to be delivered "efficiently"? Does a social service program "appear" to be run "well"? But those value judgments may not be satisfactory, even to legislators. After all, as some authors indicate, legislators themselves are accustomed to quantitative defenses of their accomplishments—terms served, bills introduced, record of attendance—and elections as quantitative expressions of voter perceptions about their competence.[8] Might they not also respect quantified evaluations of administrative outputs?

The Urban Institute suggests several effectiveness-measurement mechanisms, such as scientifically designed sample surveys to gauge consumer perceptions of an agency's effectiveness in achieving stated objectives.[9] Effectiveness measurements other than sample surveys have also been applied to varied program bases. For instance, the General Accounting Office has reviewed the objectives of Federal Work Incentive Programs, construction grant programs for abating, controlling and preventing water pollution, and other areas ranging from narcotics addiction rehabilitation to sanitary inspections of food processing plants. The Department of State has developed a Policy Analysis and Resource Allocation System by which it assesses attainment of objectives, related to a specific budget year, and goals, relevant to longer periods of time. Similarly, the Department of Health, Education and Welfare, an organization with many intangible outputs, has begun to utilize an Operation Planning System keyed in part to the management by objectives concept. In terms of the potentially broadest applicability, the Office of Management and Budget has also incorporated the management by objectives concept into a Performance Management System (PMS) as an aid to line managers in almost any federal program.[10]

Effectiveness measurement has also been applied to problems confronting smaller, local units of government. In California, selected programs were asked to develop "program effectiveness measures," a request to which the state Social Services Program responded by constructing a "service contract" measurement device.[11] And the Urban Institute's consumer-oriented work deals with such measures as citizen feelings of security in terms of law enforcement, street cleanliness as a function of solid waste collection, "bumpiness" as a measure of maintenance activities, and noninstitutional placements as at least a rough measure of care for neglected and dependent children.[12]

If effectiveness can be quantified, then potentially useful productivity indexes can be derived by plotting that type of measure against the cost or amount of resource inputs, internal outputs or external outputs. For instance, as a measure of effectiveness, citizen feelings about the adequacy of a public transportation system could be plotted against the number of buses on the street; presumably, at some point there would be only an insignificant increment in perceived transportation adequacy as the number of buses increased, thus indicating a need for different types of resource expenditures to further increase that effectiveness measure. If that type of resource-oriented relationship is considered relatively crude and hard to interpret, then it might be more meaningful to relate adequacy to an intermediate output such as number of newer vehicles in service. Even better indexes may be the relationship of effectiveness to the salient concern of number of modern vehicles per thousand rush-hour passengers.

Enhancing Productivity

The quantifications of output and input delineated above are measures of the relationship between outputs actually produced and resources, particularly labor resources, actually utilized. The managerial utility of that information is not as measurement merely for the sake of measurement, although the quantitative emphasis evident in the productivity literature might convey that impression to some practitioners. Admittedly, the Joint Project staff originally "supposed that productivity indexes would be of use primarily to historians and economists at higher levels of government; the data would be too late and too general to be helpful in internal management."[13] But the project staff's report does acknowledge a substantial potential for management utilization of such data in planning and decision-making.

Despite that realization, the emphasis in the literature so far is how to measure, rather than enhance, the output-input ratio in public organizations. The 1972 Joint Project report devotes a chapter to enhancement, but even that chapter's emphasis is largely "the use of better measurement systems," still a step short of improving productivity.[14] In a sense, if the improvement of productivity ratios is a measure of the effectiveness of inquiries into productivity, then those inquiries themselves have not yet exhibited reasonable productivity. Five interrelated catalysts, broadly defined, however, are objects of some exploration. Of the five (which are discussed below), our review indicates that productivity bargaining has received the most extensive treatment. Two others, the consideration of capital investment and the awareness of innovation, are the objects of at least limited attention. But management auditing and principles of management are only cited infrequently in recent publications on public productivity.

Productivity Bargaining

The process of negotiating increased productivity with public employee unions is usually termed "productivity bargaining." It is not, as some authors suggest, the solution to productivity problems, but it is a potentially effective means for improving low output to input ratios.

A study of the New York City experience, prepared by the Labor-Management Relations Service, outlines characteristic obstacles that effective productivity bargaining might help remove. The underlying premise is that "far-sighted union leaders, while fighting hard for higher wages and benefits, recognize that the interests of the workers that they represent are best served if they are in the forefront of the drive to make comparable increases in productivity." If a joint union-management atmosphere of concern is seriously established, if union leaders perceive "productivity" as an advantage rather than a threat, then even militant unions might accept certain organizational changes.[15]

Further, restrictive work rules and traditions might be abolished in favor of flexible uses of manpower and the introduction of labor-saving equipment. The virtual tenuring of incompetency—work situations in which employees are fired only for serious breaches of the law—might no longer be tolerated. Unconscionably low workloads could be supplemented. And specific mention of productivity could be written into every negotiated contract.

Capital Investment

According to Kendrick, his own research (confirmed by others) indicates that the most important long-run effect on productivity is investment: "Increases in productive efficiency over the long run largely reflect cost-reducing technological advances."[16] Those advances can include research, development and tangible capital goods, as well as "intangible" human investments in education and training (also discussed separately below in terms of management principles).

The projected utility of investments in labor-saving equipment is explicitly being addressed by the Productivity Commission. And the Joint Project team reiterates that concern, citing the utility of such purchases as "automated equipment to reduce the cost of disbursing federal checks, modernization of buildings and equipment to reduce the cost of jet engine overhaul, and the replacing of existing reproduction equipment with more sophisticated equipment [to] reduce the amount of waste and increase the output per man."[17]

The 1973 Joint Project report identifies four major obstacles to capital investment. Present modes of financing constrain capital investment; alternate financing techniques, such as a capital budget, revolving funds, a productivity bank, or agency omnibus funds, are advocated. The team also recognizes pervasive failures to undertake adequate analyses of potential productivity investment programs. It recommends that managers be instructed and trained in the preparation of those economic analyses.[18]

Awareness of Innovation

A constraint on productive capital investments or on the advantageous application of other catalysts such as productivity bargaining is simply inadequate information about similar efforts. According to a recent, extensive study by the Urban Institute and the International City Management Association, we do not now have adequate mechanisms to identify existing local government innovations, evaluate their productivity potential and rapidly disseminate such findings to other governmental units.[19] Although that type of information exchange does take place informally, it is usually ill-defined and incomplete, and therefore largely ineffective. Even the formal published material lacks important evaluative information. An adequate awareness of what other jurisdictions are doing, therefore, can be a substantial catalyst to the productivity of almost any public organization.

Management Audits

As an impetus to goal attainment, the Joint Project proposes management auditing as a means of effectiveness measurement.[20] Although that type of examination is not a financial audit, its synonymous descriptions as "effectiveness," "program" or "operational" audit indicate that it is as much concerned with process as effectiveness. Indeed, its range of concern is broadly defined as the three E's—efficiency, economy and effectiveness—or as a general means of improving an organization's operations.

The "how" of management auditing may be relatively simple, although perhaps expensive. It seems only contingent on management's willingness to commission a skeptical, systematic and relatively independent examination of the organization's process and goal-oriented effectiveness. There is probably so much under-utilized productive capacity in most public organizations that effective management auditors need not even have administrative or substantive training, only "common sense, alertness, imagination, initiative, inquisitiveness, persistence, sensible degree of skepticism, objectivity and an educated curiosity."[21]

Principles of Management

The public productivity literature has afforded some attention to the application of private sector models in terms of measurement of output and input, productivity bargaining, capital investment, awareness of innovation and even management auditing. The factor that may be the most direct means of enhancing productivity, which may be the most basic element or denominator of efficiency, however, is the comprehension of those qualitative management principles that can help administrators maximize the advantages of quantitative findings.

Frankly, it is an enigma that the private sector is so highly touted as a model of productive competency, but that the more qualitative management skills—the skills acquired by the intangible human investments in education and training that Kendrick and others allude to, that many firms use to improve output-input ratios and that an ever greater percentage of public administrators are also aware of—are not yet afforded systematic attention as elements of public productivity.

Why do we give only superficial attention to such basic elements of productivity? Perhaps management competency is generally assumed, although it would certainly be a mistake to conclude that even most occupants of managerial positions are adequately trained to be, or have the intuition to be, competent managers; the prerequisites for management should certainly be more complex and stringent than for management auditing. Perhaps we only presume, although incorrectly, that the public sector widely recognizes and has adopted principles of management as catalysts to productivity. Or our error of omission may occur because the development of quantification has an innovative appeal, but teaching established management techniques is a less exciting task.

As an element of productivity, "management competency" is a conceptual umbrella for a host of prerequisites to enhanced production. If an organizational unit is to achieve its productivity potential then the management of that unit must understand not only techniques of quantitative analysis or Taylor's scientific management, but perspectives ranging from Fayol's functions of management and Gulick's PODSCORB to concepts of the organization as a system, decision-making, and the management of change. Those are, after all, fundamentally attempts to improve productivity. The umbrella of competency also extends to an awareness of production incentive systems and manpower planning to meet changing workforce requirements.

If many statements on public productivity communicate little about such elements of management, then most evidence virtually no knowledge or appreciation for behavioral aspects of administration. Although humanizing the work place, adding variety to tasks and increasing employee participation will not always lead directly to quantum advances in productivity, they will increase employee satisfaction, morale and motivation. There is a vast body of knowledge on the role of employee morale and motivation in improving productivity in a variety of organizational contexts. Yet, as Newland indicates, "while most basic to productivity improvement, behavioral science and technologies [organizational design] have been relatively neglected in current public sector efforts."[22] One of the few determined efforts to remedy that neglect is Wisconsin's productivity program, which seeks to establish

> a humanizing force in government, providing job enlargement for those trapped in tedious positions, offering new challenges to both administrators and workers, facilitating participative management, taking greater account of the individual capabilities of employees.[23]

Similarly, the Joint Project's 1972 review of private sector productivity

> discovered a number of situations in which quantum improvements in productivity have apparently resulted from employee involvement in the management process: participation in decision-making, sharing in the fruits of company success, and so on.[24]

The Joint Project subsequently undertook several intensive explorations into the effective use of human resources. Although it found that "organizational development" or "productivity motivation" concepts were often only inconclusive enhancement techniques, further investigative efforts were strongly recommended.[25]

Other Catalysts

Our overview of catalysts is by no means exhaustive. Others which are sometimes proposed, but which are not as frequently pursued in discussions of productivity, include mergers to effect economies of scale, the use of citizen volunteers, improved legislative capability and the elimination of legal constraints.

Limiting Factors

Admittedly, there is an unevenness to productivity measurement. Some measures are relatively sophisticated, others crude. But in the common absence of any yardstick of productivity, even crude information is of value. At least it is a means of introducing systematic quantitative analysis into the decision-making process. Once that precedent is established, incremental refinements will undoubtedly lead to more sophisticated measures. Quantifications should only be attempted, however, if the organization has the qualitative and technical capacity to interpret and apply data meaningfully.

No matter what level of measurement sophistication we achieve, no one productivity measure is likely to be "the" measure. Attempting to meet an organizational goal is such a complex, causal process that managers will probably find many types of comparisons useful. For instance, they might focus on a set of sequential outputs in terms of internal, external and effectiveness indexes. They might compare the productivity indexes exhibited by different outputs at any one output stage—internal, external or effectiveness. And they might examine index trends over time.

Although competent measurement is an important element of productivity, production averages are easily misperceived as "quotas." For example, if caseworkers, on the average, make two thousand placements a year, or about eight a working day, that data should not be interpreted as a necessary "quota" for sufficient productivity. That is, it is unreasonable to expect every caseworker to make two thousand placements a year or eight a day. Rather, the average should be a basis for analyzing reasonable deviations, and then determining a minimum acceptable level of output. After all, a caseworker's job involves a mix of different outputs. Obviously the placement of none or only a dozen clients a year is unreasonably low. Should a reasonable minimum be 100? 200? 500? That is a managerial decision, but a decision that can only be made with a full appreciation of management principles and other productivity catalysts.

A major obstacle to productivity analysis, a deficiency that can probably be remedied easily, is that some managers do not have basic statistical skills. But an even more substantial problem may be that many public administrators have not the least idea of incremental benefit/cost analysis. Yet without that type of analysis it is virtually impossible to evaluate capital investments or objectively assess whether a private contractor should be asked to perform a certain public function.

Those administrators with more extensive training in management principles are more likely to recognize which measures are relatively meaningful and how various indexes can be used to enhance productivity. Those same managers are less likely to misuse indexes, allow their misuse by others or ignore the influence of external factors beyond the organization's control. Their training may also facilitate their ability to convince subordinates that they have a comprehensive, systematic grasp of productivity management; although they choose to direct attention to only one or two factors at a time, they are as aware of qualitative as of quantitative considerations, as cognizant of effectiveness measures as of internal measures, and as steeped in behavioral management findings as in classical principles. Thus, an unrecognized but major constraint on productivity is the often unchallenged presumption that management skills are merely a function of common sense, intuition or on-the-job experience. That presumption is actually detrimental to enhanced productivity if it at all constrains or prohibits systematic management training.

PART ONE

WHY CONCERN OURSELVES WITH PUBLIC PRODUCTIVITY

DAN CORDTZ

1 CITY HALL
DISCOVERS PRODUCTIVITY

For generations, the biggest bargains in American government were those essential and desirable public services that make life pleasant—or at least possible—for city dwellers: police and fire protection, garbage and trash collection, operation of libraries, museums, parks, and recreational facilities, and maintenance of the public streets. By some standards, they're still a bargain. The average resident of a U.S. city of 50,000 or more inhabitants, for example, pays a mere $30.25 a year to be guarded against the immediate threat of crime. It costs him $392.41 a year to maintain the military establishment that shields him from more distant perils.

Nowadays, however, it would be hard to convince most city dwellers that they are still getting a good buy for their taxes. Though urban services haven't improved—in fact they often give the impression of deteriorating—their costs have risen steeply. In the decade of the sixties, general municipal expenditures rose by 135 percent. Last year alone they went up by more than 13 percent. And a study by TEMPO, General Electric's Center for Advanced Studies, predicts that they will increase by another 47 percent in the first five years

Research associate, Aimée Morner
Reprinted from the October 1, 1971, *Fortune* Magazine by special permission; copyright 1971 Time, Inc.

of this decade. A rising population guarantees that the demand for existing and new services will continue to grow. Inflation and rapidly rising wages for city employees suggest that the cost of providing those services will grow even faster. These increasing costs are on a collision course with a widespread mood of citizen rebellion against higher local taxes. Even though local levies amount to only a fraction of the federal income tax, voters are quicker to vent their anger on nearby officeholders than on a distant Congress or Administration. Federal income-tax rates have been high for decades and are largely accepted with resignation, whereas local taxes have only lately gone up sharply. Moreover, many federal programs directly benefit one group or another in society, and a substantial number of voters can thus persuade themselves that they personally are getting something back. Local government services have long been taken for granted and are generally noticed only in their absence or as they decline in quality. A survey reported in a recent issue of *Nation's Cities* confirms that most urban residents don't believe they are getting their tax dollar's worth.

Productive Desperation

Even when urban officials are not dissuaded from boosting taxes by the fear of constituent retaliation, they have difficulty finding money to pay the mounting bills. The property tax, which yields 70 percent of municipalities' total taxes, has reached almost confiscatory levels in some distressed cities. In Newark, the annual tax bill on a $30,000 house is now $2,700, enough to pay for the house in eleven years. Other levies, in the overwhelming majority of cities, may be imposed only with the approval of state legislatures, whose members frequently are inclined to deny to the cities any potential sources of revenue that the state itself might wish to tap.

Nor are there grounds for much expectation that the

federal government will bail out the hard-pressed municipalities. Federal revenue sharing, in the form that the cities want it, has been temporarily shelved by the President and faces great congressional resistance anyway. And there is almost no chance that conventional grants from Washington or the state capitals, which now provide about one fourth of city-government revenues, can keep pace with the inexorable rise in demand.

It would be hard to paint a darker picture. Yet amid the gloom there is a faint but important glimmer of hope. For a growing number of public officials, facing up squarely to the disparity between needs and available resources, are showing interest in the question: Is it possible, by better management and the application of modern technology, to slow down the runaway costs of urban services? That question has rarely been addressed in the past. If the cities enjoyed the federal government's easy access to their citizens' pocketbooks, it probably wouldn't get much attention now. In the long run, therefore, the great urban financial squeeze may produce important benefits in the form of more efficient, more effective local government.

So recently have people begun to think about controlling urban costs that systematic study is barely under way, and much of it is still in the stage of problem definition. The obstacles are staggering, and few researchers have any illusions about panaceas. But they are confident that significant discoveries are possible and well worth the investment of time, money, and intellectual energy. A variety of federal agencies, led by the Department of Housing and Urban Development, are offering encouragement and modest financial support. The most promising projects are being directed by the professional staffs of the International City Management Association and the National League of Cities-U.S. Conference of Mayors.

At the local level, for obvious reasons, effective interest is much more limited. Harassed municipal officials, preoccupied with immediate crises, have little time for seeking better ways of doing things. Few have the analytical aptitude to study the problem usefully, or the financial resources to hire professional help. Here and there, though, cities are auditing some of their operations and trying to devise rough measures of cost effectiveness.

New York Tries Brainpower

Only the biggest cities can afford the money required for this effort. New York City, although in dire financial straits, is devoting nearly $20 million of its $10.2-billion current budget to studying its own performance. It has assembled what an admiring urban-research expert calls "the greatest aggregation of analytical talent ever put together in a city government." The city has also joined with the Rand Corporation in a joint venture, the New York City-Rand Institute, to make a more independent appraisal of its operations.

New Yorkers, watching their services deteriorate while their taxes soar, can be pardoned for wondering if all this proves that city-government operations are unresponsive to the application of brainpower. But such a conclusion may be premature and unfair. New York City represents urban problems at their zenith, and its government's ability to deal with them is hampered by an almost unparalleled set of political complications. Conceivably what is learned about efficient performance of specific functions in New York City could more readily be put to use elsewhere. In any case, if New York City is clearly making the biggest effort, it is not alone. Cities as diverse as Los Angeles, Dallas, Tacoma, and Kansas City, Missouri, are also undertaking similar self-examinations.

The potential for savings cannot be gauged without a brief look at where cities now spend their funds. In fiscal 1970, outlays of all municipalities totaled $34.2 billion—$27.7

billion of that for general expenditures. These were distributed as follows:

Table 1-1. How Cities Allocate Funds

Function	Amount (millions)	Percentage of total
Education	$4,548	16.4
Police protection	2,994	10.8
Highways	2,499	9.0
Public welfare	2,215	8.0
Fire protection	1,762	6.4
Hospitals	1,464	5.3
Sewerage	1,458	5.3
Parks and recreation	1,306	4.7
Housing and urban renewal	1,216	4.4
Sanitation other than sewerage	1,095	3.9
All others including general administration and control	7,187	25.9

Education is by far the largest of the specific items, but more than 37 percent of that figure was spent by New York City alone—it is one of the few cities with responsibility for school operation. Similarly, New York City accounted for more than $1.6 billion of the public-welfare total and for $628 million of the hospital expenditures. Those three items, in other words, are not typically of great significance in municipal budgets. Consequently, those seeking ways to improve local government are directing most of their attention at the performance of four services that make up 26 percent of the average city's general expenditures: police and fire protection, garbage and trash collection, and the maintenance and operation of parks and recreational facilities.

For all their differences, these four functions have in

common one key characteristic: they are extremely labor-intensive. Approximately 70 percent of their total cost goes for personnel, including not only wages but such fringe benefits as generous pensions and sick leave and short work weeks. The number of workers engaged in providing these services, moreover, is increasing much more rapidly than the population as a whole. The Department of Labor recently predicted that state and local government employment will be by far the fastest-growing segment of the U.S. labor market during the 1970s. The department foresees a 52 percent increase in such employment, while the nation's total work force is rising only 23 percent.

Not only will there be more workers per capita, but each worker will be making much more money. Local government wages in the past decade have been soaring at a rate far outstripping those of workers in the private sector of the economy. Since the early 1960s, when President Kennedy advocated substantial raises for federal workers on the ground that they had been left behind private industry, muncipal employees—partially benefiting from the federal example but increasingly as a result of their own unions' efforts—have wrested large annual pay hikes from local governments. In 1970 the average city worker was paid $8,172, compared with $7,462 for the average employee in private industry.

A recent eleven-city survey by the Bureau of Labor Statistics shows that public employees sometimes even do better than their privately employed counterparts in specific job categories, ranging from messengers and typists to switchboard and computer operators. In New York City, public maintenance workers—carpenters, electricians, automotive mechanics, painters, and plumbers—are paid 51 percent more than the private-industry average. Clearly the old notion that job security—not pay—is the primary attraction of local government employment is now open to question.

The labor unions that obtained these big pay hikes, moreover, are gaining strength. The rolls of organized municipal employees have now passed the two-million mark and are continuing to grow. According to Professor Jack Stieber of Michigan State University's School of Labor and Industrial Relations, more than one third of all state and local government employees now belong to labor unions or union-like associations (compared with less than 20 percent of workers in the private sector). In cities of more than 10,000 population, says Stieber, three out of five government employees belong to unions or associations. The largest single union, the American Federation of State, County and Municipal Employees, now has some 441,000 members and in less than one decade has moved from nineteenth to seventh place among affiliates of the AFL-CIO. Professor Stieber predicts that it "is destined to become one of the largest and possibly *the* largest union" in the country.

Union militancy is also on the rise. In the first quarter of this year, according to the Bureau of Labor Statistics, 50 strikes were called against local governments in the eastern half of the United States. That was an increase from 24 in the same period of 1970. Strikes by sanitation workers led the list with 17; 10 walkouts by either policemen or firemen were also recorded.

These strikes have been cause for frustration among public officials, who had earlier assumed that they could prevent them simply by outlawing them. No one has yet come up with an effective response to the problem, but one consolation is that as strikes become more familiar they may become less terrifying. They may even generate a serious voter backlash. "More and more cities are willing to take a strike," asserts Al Leggat, labor-relations adviser to St. Petersburg, Florida, and formerly head of labor relations for Detroit. "Resistance is setting in." Where strikes have been called, citizens have seldom rallied to the workers. New Yorkers in particular displayed their displeasure and their unwillingness to be intimidated when policemen struck last January and when other city workers walked out in June—a fact that was not lost on leaders of the unions involved.

If the ire of taxpayers is not enough by itself to cool off the hotter heads among government workers, the hard facts of urban fiscal life have been persuasive for some union leaders. In Detroit, more than 500 city employees have been dropped from the payroll and 2,179 budgeted positions are not filled. Cleveland has fired 1,725 workers, and many others have been put on shorter work weeks (with less pay). A recent survey run jointly by the International City Management Association and the National League of Cities-U.S. Conference of Mayors revealed that 70 percent of the nation's largest cities have had to reduce some services—with either absolute cuts in employment or reductions in new job opportunities as the inevitable consequence. So serious has the threat become that several locals of the American Federation of State, County and Municipal Employees have shifted their primary bargaining objective from gains in pay or fringe benefits to bolstering job security.

Learning How to Bargain

The ability of local governments to drive home these unpleasant truths to their employees is being enhanced by new efforts to upgrade the professionalism of officials charged with negotiating contracts. The League of Cities-Conference of Mayors (and the National Association of Counties) early last year launched a Labor-Management Relations Service under the direction of Sam Zagoria, a politically experienced former member of the National Labor Relations Board. Zagoria, with the aid of a small staff and a grant from the Ford Foundation, publishes an educational newsletter and a series of pamphlets and is sponsoring regional workshops to help train local officials in the mysteries of collective bargaining. He will also edit the report of an American Assembly conference, to be held later this month [October 1971], on collective bargaining in government. "Local government people have been accustomed to setting wages and working conditions unilaterally," Zagoria explains, "and this new concept of public unions and collective bargaining caught most of them unprepared. Our task has been to educate them about what's happening and to help them to build up expertise and experience so they can hold up their end of the relationship. Mistakes can be painful and costly, but then you can't reasonably expect unions to negotiate for both sides of the table."

One of the principal concepts that city officials need to adopt from business is the essential link between productivity and wages. That concept, it's true, is often honored in the breach when industrial negotiators line up across the bargaining table. But in government there has seldom been much awareness of a connection between output and input. This has been true not only of the employees but of their supervisors and elected superiors as well. The attitude has generally been that public services must be performed, workers must be employed in numbers that do not increase the individual work load, and taxpayers must pay whatever it costs to do the job.

What Is a Policeman's Output?

Increasing productivity is at the heart of any drive to slow down, however slightly, the rising cost of urban services. But before officials can even approach this task, they confront the knotty problem of measuring—or even defining—the output of government workers. How does one gauge the efforts of a policeman, or the results of that effort? The uniform crime statistics collected by the Federal Bureau of Investigation, police officials contend, are only crude indicators of police-department effectiveness. Policemen in many cities are required to keep a log of their daily activities, which shows how much time they spent on various incidents. But their work load is largely out of their control; they must react to situations that arise. There is clearly no way to determine how much crime they *prevent*—and this is the main objective of the patrolling that is one of their principal duties.

Complications arise even in garbage collection, which seems at first glance to pose a straightforward measurement problem (tons collected per man-day). For the test of the effectiveness of garbage and trash collection is not how much is picked up and hauled away. It is how much unsightly litter is left behind when the trucks and sweepers have finished their routes. Recognizing this fact, the Urban Institute, a private research group largely supported by federal funds, is now conducting an experiment in Washington, D.C., to devise an objective indicator of how good garbage and trash collection is. A research team took dozens of photographs of streets in various neighborhoods, rating their cleanliness on a four-point scale. Later, residents were surveyed by phone for their opinions of the degree of litter. There was a surprising agreement among citizens and researchers as to what constituted good, bad, and indifferent conditions. Several cities have already expressed interest in the results, and New York City is now carrying out a similar test.

Notwithstanding the difficulties, many city officials are convinced that they can improve productivity by the same two methods relied upon by private companies: new technology and better management. The first probably fascinates them more, if only because they share the traditional American faith in progress through gadgetry. The most promising effort is the Technology Application Program. TAP had its inception in a survey of 79 cities that turned up almost 500 suggested problems to which space-age technology might usefully be applied. After duplications were eliminated, the number was eventually winnowed to 15 high-priority problems. Closely advised by committees of municipal officials, NASA scientists are now at work on six projects and will shortly ask for bids from private manufacturers to turn out experimental hardware.

Four of the projects are aimed at cutting costs and improving the effectiveness of fire departments. They involve the design of independent life-support systems for men working in smoke-filled buildings, of better protective clothing for men exposed to flame and heat, of short-range communication systems to link individual firemen and their superiors, and of a water-pressure regulator for hose nozzles. The last is a more important development than it may appear. Pressure is now generally controlled by equipment on the fire truck, and its regulation requires the full-time attention of one man for each truck. If the water flow can be regulated by the man at the end of the hose, it will not only provide quicker response to changing conditions but will free another man to fight the blaze. TAP officials estimate that the system could save New York City alone $15 million a year. The protective gear, beyond its humanitarian value, will also have important cost implications. The high rate of death and injury to firemen is a significant compensation item in many municipal budgets.

TAP's other projects involve the design of an efficient locator of underground pipes and conduits and a more durable material for pavement striping. No figures are available on anticipated savings, but their value was reflected in the high ranking that city governments in the TAP survey accorded them in their list of problems. There is probably no more irritating sight in city streets than public-works crews digging and refilling holes in inefficient quest of a faulty water, gas, or power line. And this is an activity with an enormous manual labor content. Similarly, painting and repainting pavement stripes occupies the attention of a heavy proportion of street-department employees.

The Do-It-Yourself Trend

A number of other efforts to put technology to work are under way in individual cities. The New York City-Rand Institute has developed a "slippery water" that vastly improves the efficiency of existing fire-fighting equipment. Addition of a long-chain polymer to the water reduces its turbulent viscosity by about 70 percent, which increases the flow at a given pressure by the same amount and more than doubles the reach of the stream. Firemen can thus use much smaller, lighter hoses that enable them to climb more quickly to remote locations. Alternatively, they can pour much greater volumes of water into a fire with conventional hoses.

Perhaps the most promising field for productivity gains through technology is trash and garbage collection. Widespread adoption of the compacting garbage truck has already enhanced efficiency in most localities. (Sanitation is one of the few urban functions in which per capita employment has declined over the past decade.) But the mere introduction of closable plastic bags can further boost the collector's productivity. He need not carry heavy metal cans back and forth all day, and there is much less spillage to be cleaned up.

When a householder takes the time and trouble to put his garbage in a plastic bag, of course, he is taking over part of the job once done by the sanitation worker. The same thing is true if he carries his containers out to the curb, crushes his trash in an electric compacter, or grinds up his garbage in a sink disposal unit. This is a continuing trend, and may turn out to be a part of the solution to the problem of keeping up with the fantastic accumulation of waste in a society devoted to packaging almost everything it buys. But there is no question that collecting and disposing of refuse will continue to be a formidable and growing job.

There is still a lot of room for improved mechanization of the collection task, which accounts for about 80 percent of the cost of sanitation services. An example of the dramatic gains that even limited resources can produce is the experience of Scottsdale, Arizona, in developing a fully mechanized garbage-collection system. With a hard-won $100,000 grant from the Department of Health, Education, and Welfare and a matching amount of city funds, Scottsdale designed a system of standardized plastic containers—some of which will hold all of the trash normally generated by four families between collections. The city also designed a truck with a crane-like arm that picks up the containers and empties them into the truck bed. The machine is operated by one man, who sits in an air-conditioned cab—listening to stereo tapes, if he wishes. He can fill the truck in as little as one hour; previously it took three men half a day to do the same job. Savings are estimated at $210,000 annually when the system is fully operable. Monthly costs have already been cut from $1.80 per family to $1.07. The trucks and shared containers obviously cannot be used in every city, and Scottsdale, a relatively rich community of 67,000, finds it easier than most to replace its old equipment. But the system should be applicable in many localities.

Wichita Falls, Texas, is experimenting with an attempt to cut down on the time wasted by crews while collection trucks make the long run to the incinerators or dumps. As garbage is collected, it is put into baby trailers, which are pulled around in trains. As each trailer is filled, it is left behind and its contents are later transferred to a huge mother truck, which then makes the trip to the disposal site accompanied only by its driver. Not only does the system enable the men to keep working steadily, but it reduced the number of workers from 132 to 110.

Other projects, not feasible at present but with great potential, are due for testing in at least three locations. A giant apartment complex planned for New York City will substitute a vacuum collection system for the traditional incinerators. Trash will be piped to central locations and compacted, drastically reducing the collection process. A conveyer belt for garbage trucks, which extends to the curb and eliminates the need for carrying heavy cans, is in the blueprint stage in Los Angeles. And a slurry system, in which garbage and trash will be pulverized and pumped in a watery solution through pipes, has been developed by the Stanford Research Institute and may be given a trial in Menlo Park, California.

Getting Down to Calories

At the interface between technology and better management stands the computer. Its potential is as great for more efficient government as it has been for more profitable business operations. But governments at the local level are many years behind business in realizing that potential. Far too many still use computers for little more than record keeping. Even this can be an important personnel and money saver. But the possibilities of using computers as analytical tools for decision making have gone almost untapped.

A number of municipalities, however, are demonstrating some of the ways in which computers can be put to work. One of the most interesting is a project at Los Angeles' Bureau of Sanitation. The bureau first fed into its computer (which it shares with the police and fire departments) data on routes: stops, starts, distance, time elapsed, and tonnage collected. This enabled the bureau to schedule the most efficient use of 500 trucks to pick up refuse from 200,000 homes per day. It next analyzed the activities of its crews and the time and effort required. This involved some sophisticated measurements of the energy expended by crewmen. Officials learned, among other things, that a man uses four calories a minute just to hang onto the truck, and that walking back and forth from the truck to garbage containers is one of the main consumers of energy. (This finding was the inspiration for the conveyer-belt system that Los Angeles hopes to install experimentally if it can get the money.)

The Sanitation Bureau now uses its computer to analyze each day's activities of each crew: the amount of refuse collected, time spent, mileage covered, manpower, and absences. By 6 A.M. each day, 30 foremen know precisely how well their crews performed the day before. The information is sometimes used to "counsel" individual workers or crews, according to Jack M. Betts, assistant director of the bureau, or to make needed adjustments in routes. Finally, Los Angeles uses its computer to make a forecast, once every four weeks, of the future generation of trash and garbage. Seasonal variations in demand require the addition of temporary employees (as many as 15 percent of the regular force in summer months), and the forecast minimizes overhiring. The result of all this is that Los Angeles has cut the man-hours required to collect a ton of refuse from 2.68 in 1958 to 1.67 today.

Los Angeles and Kansas City, Missouri, are using computers to establish their own historical patterns of crime—by time and location—and to deploy cars and policemen so as to counter the probable threat in the optimum way. Half in earnest, Robert B. Gaunt, assistant police chief in Los Angeles, remarks that "traditionally, officers have just stuck pins in maps over their shoulders to decide where to patrol." If it can obtain a supporting grant, Los Angeles would like to test an even more ambitious computer system that would correlate its crime patterns with the *modus operandi* of potential suspects, whose addresses, auto license numbers, and known associates would also be filed in the computer.

Calling All Cars

Computers might also be used to keep track of the whereabouts of all police vehicles, minute by minute, and of their availability to respond to calls. Under a $240,000 federal grant, Los Angeles has designed such a system, and many other cities are interested. Computers also have obvious potential in assigning fire-fighting equipment and locating fire stations at the sites where they will do the most good.

Even without computers, there is room in almost every city government for important gains in efficiency through more imaginative management. San Francisco's parks and recreation department, simply by scheduling regular meetings between representatives of the recreation and park-maintenance staffs, has minimized the "us and them" attitude that formerly led to such counterproductive activities as watering golf courses and baseball fields at times when they were most in demand. New York City's police department appointed a planning sergeant for each precinct to plot the incidence of crime, and brought about almost 10 times as many arrests in some precincts. One sergeant actually predicted a crime and had policemen in the immediate area when it took place. Dallas has greatly expanded its use of lower-paid "para-police" civilians, has revised its charter to permit easier merit promotions within the civil-service system, and now reimburses all tuition costs for city employees who take college courses.

One man who is firmly convinced that much of the latent imagination of city employees is going to waste is William V. Donaldson, who has been city manager of Tacoma since April, and formerly had the same post in Scottsdale. It was his encouragement of municipal employees to spend some of their working day thinking about better ways to do their jobs that led to Scottsdale's mechanized garbage trucks. By making transfers much easier and retraining readily available, he also encouraged many employees to move into jobs that excited their interest much more than their old duties.

"I have seen city workers who do the most creative things in their off-duty hours—designing jewelry, building racing cars, and a lot of other things," Donaldson says. "Then on the job they often turn into automatons. It's management's job to motivate them, to encourage them to put that creativity to work on their regular tasks." How do you do it within the framework of a system that rewards success only in minor ways and severely punishes failure if it can be blamed on unorthodox methods? Donaldson is frank to admit that he has no pat answers. "But it seems to me that the ability to use creativity is an important incentive by itself," he suggests, "and maybe the reward is more and more freedom in the works."

Featherbedding by State Mandate

Imagination and innovation are surely worth cultivating, but more immediate gains can probably be made simply through better work organization and supervision. Across the country, there is a lot of plain old featherbedding in city government. Much of this is merely patronage carried over from an earlier time when city employment was a reward for the ruling party's faithful vote hustlers, and it is largely confined to big cities that still possess strong political machines. But there are other forms of featherbedding that are more serious and harder to deal with.

Many cities are constrained by state laws from assigning or transferring personnel freely, or from redefining their duties or work loads. In New York City, for example, legal obstacles make it difficult to concentrate firemen in places and at hours that match the obvious incidence of fires. Changes in firemen's working hours require approval of two sessions of the state legislature plus passage of a city referendum. In order to have enough men available at peak fire-hazard periods, the city must also put on additional men at slack periods to keep the manpower balanced. Another state law provides that the same number of policemen must be on duty at all hours of the day, even though crime soars at certain predictable times. To overcome the problem, the police department in 1969 added a fourth shift to overlap two of the normal three. Officials label such managerial restrictions "state-mandated featherbedding."

The obstacles to raising worker productivity have prompted some urban officials and academicians to look closely at the other side of the urban-services cost equation, to ask what can be done to slow down rising demand. One idea that is thoroughly feasible for a limited number of services is simply to turn the job over to private companies. Garbage collection is unquestionably the best candidate, and a growing number of cities are getting out of the business. The example of San Francisco, which has never been in it, illustrates why. The city's garbage is collected by two private companies at an average cost of $18 a ton. Yet the workers, half of whom own stock in the firms, can earn as much as $16,000 a year including dividends. It is small wonder that their morale is high and that San Franciscans are generally delighted with their service and its cost.

Can Private Enterprise Do It Better?

By contrast, New York City's sanitation men—resentfully aware of the low esteem in which they are held by citizens and fellow government workers alike—are among the most militant of the city's workers. And, some contend, among the least efficient. A controversial and still unpublished study by the staff of the city administrator showed that sanitation-department collection costs are $49 a ton. Private carting companies, which serve restaurants, hotels, and many other private businesses, do the same job for $17.50 a ton. Since 1968 the city has bought more than 1,200 new trucks. Each was expected to raise the productivity of its crew by 20 percent over the old models. In fact, there has been no improvement at all. City-owned trucks are in the shop for repairs 35 percent of the time; the average for private carting firms is about 5 percent. It is not surprising that New York City officials are seriously considering handing over still more of the task of collecting the city's refuse to private companies.

Not in every city, obviously, would the benefits of private collection be as dramatic. But the profit incentive, closer supervision, managerial flexibility, and the ability to deal more effectively with the work force are advantages that probably weigh heavily almost anywhere. Perhaps more important, when a city abandons a service like garbage collection, the householder must assume the full cost of the service directly. City savings seldom are handed back to him in the form of a lower tax rate. The money is simply available for other purposes.

Another way that cities could reduce demand for some of their services would be to charge users directly. This is common practice with publicly owned water, power, and transit companies, of course. But Dr. Selma Mushkin, director of Georgetown University's Public Services Laboratory, contends that there is almost no limit to the imaginative application of user fees. In a forthcoming book, *Public Prices for Public Products*, Dr. Mushkin and her associates argue that it would even be feasible to charge for some of the functions performed by the police. The most obvious example is the control of traffic and crowds at stadiums or other places of entertainment. But prices could also be established for patroling in business or residential areas, and for such services as the finding of missing persons or lost property. Clearly, few cities are likely to start selling police protection, but as the financial squeeze tightens many of them may impose user fees on less sensitive services such as parks and recreation.

It is much too early to make any firm assessment of how much will come out of the newly awakened interest of municipal officials in more efficient management and improved productivity. The overwhelming majority of such officials are still preoccupied with finding new sources of funds, not lowering costs. But the pressures and realities are such that more and more local leaders will have to begin rethinking their functions, priorities, and methods of operation. As Donaldson of Tacoma explains it: "If we keep on trying to do things the way we have, there is just never going to be enough money around to make our cities work."

2 PRODUCTIVITY
NOT ONLY INDUSTRY'S PROBLEM

When people say that the U.S. can no longer "afford" this or that—going to the moon or feeding needy school children or cleaning up pollution—they are not talking about money. Money can be created with ease. What they are talking about, really, is that there are more demands on what the nation produces than there is production. One result: inflation. Another: unsatisfied needs in housing, transportation, education and the like.

Hence the emphasis today on productivity, on the need to get more production from a given amount of labor and of capital. Higher productivity would speed up economic growth, of course, and leave more money for attaining social goals. It would also help counter inflation. It would lessen the drain on the U.S. balance of payments—by making U.S. goods more competitive.

At a recent session of the powerful and influential Business Council, the most talked-about speech was on—you guessed it—productivity. The speaker: Patrick E. Haggerty, the thoughtful and articulate chairman of Texas Instruments. Impressed with waves that Haggerty's talk created, *Forbes* sought him out for his views. Haggerty does not pretend to

Reprinted by permission of *Forbes* Magazine. Published February 1, 1971.

know the answers. He raises some provocative questions, however.

The first thing Haggerty emphasized was this: It's a mistake to think of productivity only in terms of manufacturing industry; productivity in services is even more of a vital issue.

"So often when I get into a discussion of productivity, people think I'm talking only about the real goods part of the economy. That's not true. I don't even think that's where our principal problem is anymore.

"There is a great deal of concern, some of it justified, about the wage pressures brought by organized labor on industry. But the wage increases in industry, however inflationary, are closer to being in line with productivity gains than are wage increases in other sectors of society. For example, in education, in city and state government, it is highly dubious that we have had any increase in productivity. It would be pretty hard to look at New York City and conclude that productivity has improved."

Haggerty, like many businessmen, is appalled by the low productivity in education and the rising costs and the declining effectiveness, reflected often in bored students, less often in rioting students and always in a burden on parents and taxpayers.

Quality and Costs in Education

"In education it is very clear that the entire emphasis has been on improving quality without any attention to cost. I don't want to be negative about improving the quality of education. But you have to simultaneously worry about how much it's costing. In industry, you know, we have an enormous consciousness of quality, but it is accompanied by an equal consciousness of how much it costs. You are constantly in a dialog with those who are paying for the quality—your customers—relating the improvement in quality to how much they're willing to pay for it.

"I think the voters are instinctively or intuitively beginning to react to the fact that there has rarely been much visible improvement in education despite costs having increased three, four or five times. There has been little relating of costs per student hour, costs per teaching hour, to the improvement in quality. Educators are not even conscious of the fact that they have just as big a burden of increasing productivity as does the rest of society. It is just as important to struggle with the costs of education as with the content. If administrators tried to achieve improvements in the costs per teaching hour for the same quality education, perhaps you could cut costs by half or a fourth. Those savings could be used where you have to have individual instruction and things like that.

"I mean, I tell college presidents, 'Look, you train all the industrial engineers that we use in industry, but you don't use any of them. How come? How is it that what you teach is applicable only to us and not to your own institutions?' "

Productivity-Consciousness in Government

Patrick Haggerty, 56, is an electrical engineer who has spent his life in business. Since 1945 his business has been Texas Instruments, where he became chairman and chief executive in 1958. TI is a leader in electronics, one of the most competitive businesses in this country. But with whom does education or government services compete? We suggested that this might have something to do with the lack of productivity-consciousness in government. Haggerty agreed, pointing out that most leaders in government—politicians—are lawyers by training.

"Productivity is foreign to lawyers, but service is not since law is a service function."

Haggerty went on to emphasize the importance of making

government people more productivity-minded. Education is not his only target: he regards all public services as at fault.

"The recent General Motors settlement was high, but the pressure for those wage increases was generated by the enormous increases in costs in the service sector. In the last four or five years, in spite of pay increases, the take-home pay of the autoworker has been pretty flat. But he has also been paying increased taxes. These were supposed to bring him better education, transportation, etc. In short, an improvement in his standard of living. But because of the lack of improved productivity, they did not. So the man's standard of living has not improved."

One reason it has not improved, Haggerty feels, is that, unlike business, which has return on investment as a standard, government services have no such standards.

"Productivity is not something that has come into the consciousness of government people at all. They don't realize that increasing productivity may take capital investment, with all that implies for a return on our money. It is an extraordinarily complicated subject, and we just do not have adequate measurement tools for the public services. For example, I wouldn't begin to draw the conclusion that the subways must be self-supporting. But I suspect that the productivity of the subsidy could be measured if we came closer to recognizing what we have to pay for. If we don't have mass transit, traffic congestion will be worse and that is a cost and pollution of the atmosphere is a cost.

"The difficulty is that things have got so very complex with no real consciousness of what's been happening to us in costs of service. It begins to overwhelm you. And I think a large part of the celebrated flight to the suburbs is just that: individuals reacting to all the things that make the city unlivable. It's not just race, as is often said."

Social Goals

On that score, Forbes asked, isn't the criticism valid that we've got our priorities wrong and we're spending too much on defense and not enough on urban life?

"I think we can spend a little less on defense now, but it looks difficult to say we're going to be able to spend appreciably less on defense. On the other hand, if we can increase total resources and we don't spend any more relatively on defense, we will begin to have sizable resources to devote to other things."

Haggerty went on to say that as things now stand, social goals that can be achieved through private industry have a better chance of success.

"I do think that intelligent and major efforts to tackle problems like pollution will be successful. But I think automobile exhaust pollution—apparently the biggest culprit in air pollution—will be solved before other kinds of pollution. It is simply that in the automobile companies we have large institutions that are capable of coming up with cures. They are used to setting tangible goals and achieving them, and because they are driven by economics in their everyday business, they don't do things in unrealistic ways. Now law is forcing them to do it, sure, but because they are competent, I'll bet the auto pollution problem will be one of our smaller ones by the mid-Seventies.

"But when you move into other areas like cleaning up the lakes, we don't have institutions. The cities and states are weak. They don't have large technical staffs, and they are not used to setting tangible standards. Economics does not run them. They know the problem, so they want to legislate. That won't do it.

"Now their lack of understanding isn't because of any lack of good will, but because there aren't institutional mechanisms. You haven't got the research and development organizations, and in water pollution you don't have a General Motors to put $50 million down for the Wankel engine."

In passing, Haggerty took a swipe at those—on the left and the right—who think the answer to pollution is the acceptance of a lower standard of material living.

"I think we have to recognize that some of the forces in this society that go for smallness, for zero economic growth, militate against the generation of institutions that have a competence to tackle the problems that are generated by this society."

From there, Haggerty proposed a first step toward making government more productivity-conscious.

"You have in the Congress a priority-setting institution. That is why I think it important that the President should convert his economic report into a report on the standard of living, all of the elements that go into standard of living. Then we would have a basis for measurement and for choice. You can't get a better standard of living by stopping economic growth. On the other hand, if all the growth goes into material things—the only things we can measure at present—then you aren't increasing the standard of living either.

"Such a report would cover education, decreases in crime, improvements in health. And you'd arrive at measures. After all, the gross national product is a statistic that dates to just before World War II. We take it for granted. The measuring of unemployment is very recent, and we take that for granted. I think these measurement tools arose because we needed them in the 1930s when the need was more fundamental.

"Now we have come to a point where we do need measures of these other things that are better than what we've had. They may not be as tangible as economic measures, but don't forget it wasn't so long ago that the economic measures weren't tangible either. I think there could be progress toward defining what we mean by standard of living."

We couldn't visualize the form such a Presidential message would take. . . .

"All right, let's say studies were made about costs per class-hour in an experimental area. These showed that it used to cost $200 a year for a certain number of student hours. And with television networks or data processing, the President might report, we're now accomplishing the same education for $150. You can't make progress until you can measure."

Going from there to another major set of problems— unemployment and poverty—Haggerty said:

"We don't lack for places to use people. We lack for definitions of problems, organization of institutions, training of people and application of resources in a way we can afford. If one recognizes the necessity of increasing total resources, then you can improve the productivity of a total society, and the system is much more elastic than it is now."

In the expression of his views, Haggerty certainly left out some important considerations: That productivity in all fields has suffered from the decline of the Work Ethic, that education cannot be made more efficient unless someone can agree on what education should accomplish, that "studies" and "reports" by the Administration—like many other such projects—may just end up in the bottom drawer of somebody's desk.

For all this, however, much of what he says makes great sense: Taxes, like any other outlay, are part of the cost of living and the cost of doing business; they total more than $300 billion or one third of the gross national product. Shouldn't we look for ways to measure their effectiveness and to make their use more efficient?

JOHN V. LINDSAY

3 ADDRESS AT
NATIONAL PRODUCTIVITY
CONFERENCE

Productivity in New York City is not a technical term. It is not simply a concept. And it is more than just a system.

Productivity is a new approach to the art and the science of modern government, which must meet the rising expectations of the citizens who finance it. Services are being demanded of all governments as never before. The taxpayers expect tangible, measurable results from the public sector to which they contribute, just as they do of the private companies from which they buy.

New York is the first major public jurisdiction to develop and implement a comprehensive way to plan, achieve, and account for the delivery of those services. We call it a Comprehensive Productivity Program, and it is working—both by its own measure and by the measure of the number of people who want to know why it has taken all levels of government so long to adopt the principle of productivity.

The answer is simple. The orientation of a traditional government structure toward productivity goals requires a complicated and comprehensive process of planning and persuading, and sometimes outright battling. Establishing such a program has been compared to opening a huge door that has blocked the efficient and accountable delivery of

Reprinted by permision of John V. Lindsay. Address delivered March 1973.

services for many decades. But it is a door with many, many locks, and all the keys must turn together.

The reorganization of more than 70 city agencies into a manageable, accountable structure of administrations had to come first.

After long and bitter battles, we were successfully able to streamline a Byzantine bureaucracy into 10 major administrations with group-related programs, provide a point of coordination between them, and establish manageable lines of authority. Other governments, including the federal, are just beginning to take this critical step. Some states have modeled their own reorganization on New York City's pioneering effort, and we have been glad to help all who have asked.

Our new structure made possible a systematic review of all city functions, and the beginnings of the kind of analysis of projects and programs that private industry has relied upon for years.

We began to build a data base. Some critical information was scattered throughout the city—stored at random in cardboard cartons, forgotten files, and in the brains of veteran employees. But most of the information we needed had to be generated—it simply had never existed.

Making use of this gradually accumulating data required the specialized skills of economists, project managers, analysts, and the kind of middle management people who had rarely considered working for a municipal government.

In 1962 the first industrial engineer in all of New York City's government was hired. Only a handful were at work for the city four years later when this Administration began. Now there are 350. Similarly, the city found it could attract men and women with master's degrees in business administration, and almost 400 of them were hired.

The roster of analytic specialists in all city agencies has expanded to the point where *Fortune* magazine called it "The most impressive array of analytic talent at work in any government in the country."

Our first application of project management began with construction. In 1966-67, it took an average of 12 years to build a hospital, 80 percent of which was preconstruction time. The pipeline was so clogged that out of a billion dollars' worth of potential construction, only 200 million could be called "in the works." Last year, through application of the most sophisticated project management strategies, we hit a billion dollars in municipal construction. Most important, we were able to take full advantage of federal moneys available in the last several years, and even to capture some that other cities were not ready to use.

Then, as we learned from the management of "one-shot" projects, we applied our knowledge and skills to "softer" programs such as the rapid hiring of 5,000 new policemen and the reorganization of welfare services.

More and more programs were designed to improve the delivery of services. For example, one of the reasons for inadequate sanitation collection was that at any given time 38 percent of our trucks were down for repairs. At first, we believed this was solely the result of a fleet that operates around the clock under extreme conditions and that had averaged eight to nine years of use.

But as we began to analyze every detail of the repair process, we found that trucks were sitting in garages because the right parts were not being delivered, that major repairs were being undertaken in poorly equipped local garages, and that the best mechanics were not being assigned to the toughest jobs.

And so we not only replaced the trucks, reducing their average age to less than three years with an unprecented capital purchase program, we also reformed the entire repair process and the "down rate" went from 38 percent to 9 percent.

When we announced our massive program to build large-sized neighborhood swimming pools, it was predicted they would take years to complete. Yet we finished 60 of them in one year.

Incredible as it may seem, the city for years had Parks Department lawn crews standing idle while they waited for lawnmowers to be delivered to their work sites, and Highway Department crews unable to fill potholes because there were no exacting schedules for asphalt deliveries. Project management tackled both of these absurdities and dozens like them. We aimed to eliminate every variable obstacle to greater return on the taxpayer's dollar that might be attributable to inefficient or ill-informed management.

A New Approach to Budgeting

We were able to couple this new approach to managing city projects with a completely new approach to budget administration and budget planning.

New York City had always existed on a line budget system, which showed only an accountant's understanding of dollars and cents and did not translate into meaningful cost analysis of programs. Too often, there was no way to tell what a health inspector did with his day, or even what he ought to do. We had to know how much time on the average should be required to complete a particular type of inspection before we could begin to set reasonable goals.

And in 1965, the whole science of program performance budgeting was still in its earliest formative stages in the federal government and had not yet been applied in state and local contexts.

When one considers the thousands of city functions, the hundreds of thousands of workers, and the millions of pieces of paper that are mandated by the needs of New York City, one is hard put to imagine how it could have possibly functioned before the systematic application of productivity principles. And it is abundantly clear how necessary and effective this approach to management of public funds is when New York City is compared to other municipalities and to the state. Management information systems now produce more data on New York City operations than in any other state or local administration.

Even data by itself can be useful. Sometimes just the fact of quantifying a problem will increase the pressure to solve it. Many times the data in one field can lead to insights into another—such as the correlation of false alarms with social unrest, or the relation between crime and narcotics.

All of these advances—reorganization, computerization, project management, and budget reform—often too dull and drab to excite public attention, make up the basic infrastructure without which a systematic productivity program would be impossible.

The current phase of the New York City Productivity Program began in December, 1970, when the Mayor's Labor Policy Committee announced guidelines for the upcoming contract negotiations with the uniformed services. The guidelines included the unprecedented statement that the city would consider no salary increases that were not justified by cost-of-living increases—which are beyond city control—and, for the first time anywhere in government, measurable increases in productivity.

This was a personal decision that required standing firm through 18 months of long and very hard negotiations. During those 18 months, I also made the decision to extend this principle to all other contracts under negotiation—most notably negotiations with our social service workers. As a result of a hard fight, it is now an established fact that the City of New York will not sign a labor contract without clearly defined productivity advances built into it.

This is probably the most important single factor in a successful productivity program where the vast majority of workers—both rank and file and superior officers—are unionized.

The Fire Department negotiations present an example where productivity could not have been put in the contract without years of careful analytic work preceding negotiations. In 1971, for example, of the 280,000 alarms received by our Fire Department, 38 percent of them were false. Of all the remaining "real" alarms, only 17 percent were for structural fires; all the rest were for rubbish fires, smoky oil burners, and other miscellaneous emergencies. Despite the small number of actual structural fires, the department had responded to all alarms with three engines and two trucks. Thus, too often men and equipment were wasted responding to false alarms, while real fires were not being responded to quickly enough.

The challenge to management was to develop a profile of response for a force of 14,000 men that would fit the pattern of emergencies in diverse city areas. We discovered, for example, that in the Bronx 55 percent of all alarms occur in 25 percent of the area. And that during certain hours in Brooklyn, firemen could receive as many as 30 alarms, while at other hours, they might predictably receive only 15 alarms. For the first time in its 300-year history, New York had the information regarding work schedules, new methods, equipment and deployment that was needed to enter intelligently into contract negotiations. The result was a contract providing for variable responses according to time and place, which means greater security at less cost.

And this kind of progress on the labor front was matched by new management efforts in a growing number of original projects. The City's Human Resources Administration undertook the separation of income maintenance functions that can be performed by clerks from social service functions that require professionals. We are saving millions of dollars in time and payments.

The City's Health and Hospitals Corporation has completely overhauled its processing of third-party hospital billings, which are essential to its financial stability. The success achieved in these projects prepared us to expand the productivity program to cover all city agencies.

Similar programs were begun in other agencies, so that by the time our comprehensive productivity plan was drawn up there were more than 150 individual projects already completed or underway.

But while our program of individual projects and labor and budget reform progressed, New York City was encountering an extremely painful series of fiscal developments.

Launching the Comprehensive Productivity Program

Each year the natural upward forces of mandated costs tended to raise expenses by as much as 15 percent. Strict budgeting kept those expenses to between 8 and 9 percent, but our revenue was only increasing by some 5 percent. This budget gap meant that we were forced to place a freeze on the size of the work force—because, by law, New York City cannot have a deficit. At the same time we were experiencing a huge increase in workload demands.

The agony of the 1972-73 budget approval process made it clear that a Comprehensive Productivity Program had to be launched this fiscal year. Services could not be allowed to suffer, despite the shrinking labor force imposed by budget realities.

On June 11, I directed all senior managers to develop productivity goals that could be announced and monitored during the year at four points, two of which have already been reached. The two reports are a public record of our successes and failures. They clearly show that our June 11 directive has produced the most penetrating across-the-board analysis of city programs ever undertaken by this city.

The Comprehensive Productivity Program attempts to increase the quantity and quality of public service provided per dollar invested in four basic ways:

• Where output is easily measurable, such as the number of tons of refuse collected per sanitation truck shift, it aims to reduce unit costs and improve the responsiveness of city operations.

• Where output is very hard to measure, such as in providing police or fire protection, it aims to improve the deployment of resources so as to maximize the probability that our resources will be available at the time and place they are needed most.

• It aims to improve the organization and processing procedures of government, particularly through imaginative use of computers.

• It aims to develop new technological devices and approaches, such as the development of plasticized rapid water for fire-fighting, to make the best possible use of every increasingly expensive city employee.

This is the first Comprehensive Productivity Program mounted in any major public jurisdiction in the United States. It also provides the first set of objective measures of administrative accomplishment ever made available for public scrutiny and comment by any major government.

Certain favorable national developments have helped us, especially the trend toward equalization of salaries between the public and private sectors symbolized by the Federal Pay Reform Act of 1962 and the many federal social programs that are now being terminated in Washington.

But without the direct link between pay and productivity that we had established, rising salaries may not have meant better service for the public. And without an overall plan to keep the procedural pipelines open, we would not have been able to capture the enormous number of federal dollars that have helped this city move forward in spite of national trends that have left others fighting for survival.

Most important, these productivity improvements were not accompanied by explosions of personnel and salaries out of proportion to other American cities, in spite of much political rhetoric and some incorrect current opinions.

In fact, from 1966 to 1972, of the 10 major cities, New York was ninth in labor cost rises for common municipal functions, and eighth in percentage of employees added for those functions. Those are the U.S. Department of Commerce figures, and they totally contradict popular misconceptions about the municipal payroll of New York City.

The mid-year productivity Progress Report shows that city agencies met or exceeded 77 percent of their productivity targets for the period, and that more than 85 percent of city services were operating with measurably greater efficiency than during the year before.

Of course, this report also contains some disappointments. Some of them reflect damaging action or inaction by federal and state authorities, but most are in agencies that still need strengthening at the middle-management levels.

And we must give equal attention and energy to training and job enrichment, which can make enormous contributions to overall productivity. Productivity is in large part dependent on the attitudes of workers, which are, in turn, heavily influenced by the training they receive and their confidence in opportunities for promotion.

But the basic message of all our figures is that productivity analysis and performance are just as feasible and important in government as in private business. The inquiries we have received from all over the country indicate that many states and cities want to join in this pioneering attempt to give the taxpayer clear, quantitative information on what he should expect from his government and how well it is delivering on its promises.

The day of the know-nothing, opportunist critic is past. From here on, any commentators—federal, state, or local—on the quality of New York City's public service must speak in the hard, specific terms that our reforms have made possible.

Above all, it is clear that government productivity is here to stay—not as empty political rhetoric, but as an indispensable tool of management and public understanding.

We in New York take great pride in the unprecedented talent and dedication of the members of this government who helped to make our approach to public service a lasting political and practical reality.

PATRICK J. LUCEY

4 WISCONSIN'S PRODUCTIVITY POLICY

As an elected public official and the chief executive of a state, a governor must be concerned with both the quality of services the state provides and the cost of those services. If he is a good politician, he knows that in order to be re-elected, he must walk a narrow line between the demands of those who want government to do more and those who want to pay less for whatever it is that government does. If he is a good administrator, he may be able to widen that line—by improving the efficiency and productivity of government. In a time of increasing fiscal constraints on state government (and political constraints on raising taxes), achievement of his programmatic goals may depend on just such administrative success.

When I assumed office as Governor of Wisconsin in 1971, state government was completing a period of unprecedented growth. From 1960 to 1970, total state expenses more than tripled. State general purpose revenue expenditures for education at all levels grew from $108 million to $510

Reprinted by permission from the November/December, 1972, issue of the *Public Administration Review*, journal of the American Society for Public Administration, by permission of the American Society for Public Administration and the author.

million during the decade; outlays for correctional institutions jumped 339 percent; state support of local government through shared taxes increased by 240 percent. To some extent these escalating costs were a reflection of inflationary pressures and the salary and wage improvement brought by increasingly assertive public employee associations. Mainly, however, they represented a major expansion in services provided by the state. During the 1960s, AFDC caseloads in Wisconsin doubled, public college enrollments tripled, and vocational rehabilitation cases went up 800 percent. In response to these and other pressures, the state work force grew from 38,000 to 73,000 in 10 years. In addition, new demands by the public, in fields such as pollution control, meant expenditures of millions of dollars in program areas that had not previously existed.

Changes of this magnitude could not be funded without a corresponding escalation in state tax levels. Personal income tax rates were raised on four separate occasions during the decade. A sales tax was instituted, coverage expanded, and the rate increased, as were state gas taxes, and—at a number of different times—state cigarette taxes. Property taxes, levied by local governments and highly regressive in their impact, nearly matched the level of state tax growth. They doubled over this period, approaching $1 billion by 1970.

The growth that Wisconsin's government experienced during the 1960s was not unique. Throughout the decade, state and local payrolls expanded at a far greater rate than the federal government. One legacy of that growth is the nationwide "taxpayers' revolt" of the 1970s, which has already toppled a number of mayors and governors. Citizens in high tax states such as Wisconsin are demanding relief, particularly from the regressive burden of the property tax. They argue that rising taxes have not been accompanied by a much-improved level of services and, in some cases, have led to greater inefficiency and "boondoggling." The public official who ignores these demands and charges—even if they are exaggerated—does so at his peril. The problem, of course, is how to bring about meaningful tax relief and assure the public that it is getting full value for its tax dollars without sacrificing essential public services. A comprehensive approach to this problem requires many steps, including program cuts and the discovery of non-tax sources of revenue.[1] In the long run, however, I believe the only real solution will be a successful public productivity policy.

Although related to the problem of lowering taxes and costs, the issue of public productivity should be distinguished from these concerns. Government officials like to put the name "productivity improvements" on their programs because, in principle, no one can be opposed to more efficient government. When they speak of improved productivity, what they most likely mean are cuts in services, or budget ceilings on agencies, which will have the effect of holding down taxes and costs, but which have nothing to do with increasing the level of public employee or agency output per dollar expended. Politically, it is easier to say that productivity will be improved than that the services will be curtailed; actually doing something to increase productivity, however, is another question entirely.

The major reason that it is so difficult to achieve productivity gains in the public sector may be seen by comparing the governmental situation with that of industry. The private sector has pioneered in the use of technological and managerial innovations such as computers and the PPBS budget. These advances came in part because of the pressures of the marketplace. In a competitive economy, prices must be kept down. Rising labor and materials costs will mean lower profits unless ways can be found to improve output per man-hour. In the public sector, there are no profit margins and there are few competitors. The "product" being "sold" is usually service, and the quality of that service is frequently more important than its quantity. It is often difficult to measure productivity, much less know what an improvement in productivity represents.

Productivity Conferences

Before setting productivity goals for state agencies, therefore, it was first necessary to define the meaning of productivity in the public sector, and to rigorously examine the approaches available for taking productivity improvement beyond the state of pious public pronouncements. With the active encouragement and involvement of state officials, a national conference on "Productivity in the Public Sector" gathered at Wingspread, the Johnson Foundation's conference center, near Racine, Wisconsin, in mid-May of this year.[2] Out of this conference came numerous specific suggestions, but more importantly, a broader awareness of the issues involved. Some agency officials were exposed for the first time to such commonplace subjects in business as performance measurement and accountability, productivity incentives, and behavioral motivators. Other agency executives, who had been all too eager to view government as a business and productivity improvement as a science (which reached its peak under Frederick Winslow Taylor), received a much-needed corrective. They were reminded that justice and equity are more important goals for government than "efficiency for efficiency's sake," and that sometimes the achievement of social goals (e.g., hiring the educationally disadvantaged) may be measurably "inefficient" in the short run—although immeasurably efficient over the long haul.

Wisconsin Productivity Plan

Getting agencies to think about productivity was an essential first step to a state productivity policy. Next, working with the Department of Administration (our budget bureau), we decided upon a target figure for productivity improvement— 2½ percent per year—a figure that is less than the average yearly productivity gain in the private sector. A memo, reproduced here, was sent to all agencies of state government asking them to outline ways in which they would meet this figure for the first year of the 1973-75 biennial budget, and suggesting avenues of approach which they should explore. By setting a target figure and putting agencies on record as to how they would meet it, we made certain that they would do more than "think" about productivity. By giving them sufficient lead time and an active involvement in the planning process, we strengthened the possibility that they would become seriously committed to the goal itself.

It is too early to evaluate with any degree of thoroughness the effectiveness of this approach. On the basis of the memos received from agencies so far, however, a few trends are evident. First, many departments are still not sure what improved productivity really means. Their response has been to "lop off" 2½ percent from the level of staff salaries, or to cut positions from the payroll, or to eliminate low priority programs. While each of these actions may cut expenses, it does nothing to increase productivity. There is reason to believe that, in some cases at least, departments have adopted this approach for political reasons. Cuts of this type usually result in a great deal of pressure for their restoration from employee associations, interest groups, and citizens' lobbies. These actions are also a way of turning an inherently positive concept—improved productivity—into something with deservedly negative connotations—the speed-up. For this reason, it is essential that employee groups be involved in productivity plans from the earliest stage of negotiations, and that their advice be listened to; and that clientele groups, and members of the public in general, be kept well-informed of the probable impact of proposed efficiency measures.

A second trend is that "technical" agencies appear to be finding the productivity target far easier to achieve than high-"service" agencies. Among the former are the Department of Revenue, the Department of Administration, and the Department of Agriculture. Their work output per man-hour will be increased in the coming year by the application of technology (e.g., new data-processing equipment) and by improved organizational methods (e.g., the sharing of computer programs between agencies, rather than their independent development in each). Estimates of productivity improvements run as high as $1.2 million for the Department of Administration and $1/3 million for the Department of Agriculture. Steps to be taken range from the purchase of three automated presses at the cost of $10,000—in order to save $127,000—to a reduction in the distribution of the Cooperative Insect Survey Report to those readers who are actively interested in the statewide control of forest and agricultural crop pests (estimated savings: $700).

The high-service agencies, such as the Department of Health and Social Services or the Department of Transportation, are labor-intensive and have many local or district functions. Obvious productivity strategies, such as the consolidation of local offices, may result in a significant diminution of services, or great inconvenience to the public. Other strategies, involving new behaviorial incentives for workers in the field, increased worker participation in management, or innovative concepts such as work teams, require far more time to implement because they depend on changed human attitudes, and cannot be imposed from the top down. For the shorter term, perhaps the best that can be hoped for in these labor-intensive fields is the elimination of regulations and procedures which *impede* productivity. An example of this was a rule we discovered requiring that female probation workers counsel only women. By allowing these counselors to deal with probationers of both sexes, we not only equalized work loads, but also cut down the number of employees necessary to perform this function.

The area where our productivity program appears to be producing the least success is the state university system. Last year, in an attempt to improve the quality and reduce the cost of public higher education in the state, I promoted a merger of all state colleges and universities into one system. In this way I hoped not only to save the almost $1 million spent annually coordinating the two public university systems in Wisconsin, but to avoid the costly log-rolling that had been necessary in the past to balance appropriations for both systems. Mindful of projections indicating that college enrollments have peaked and will decline for the next decade, 1972 did not appear to be a bad time for efficiency improvements in the newly combined state university system. This judgment was reinforced by a report on "The More Effective Use of Resources" from the Carnegie Commission on Higher Education, which argued that, for example, the consolidation of graduate programs in certain fields would result in an *improvement* in the quality of education offered, as well as financial savings. Unfortunately, with 73 percent of the university budget going for instructor salaries, any cuts are painful, and subject to public criticism by one of the most articulate interest groups imaginable. In a state that has traditionally supported higher education at a level second to none, the politics of educational productivity sometimes have little to do with the reality of the situation.

A university official recently argued (shortly before submitting a budget request that included a record $100 million increase): "We have a quality system. I for one am unwilling to preside over its decline." Although it is never easy to deal with this form of argument, I am confident that eventually we will be able to educate the educators to the fact that improving productivity (through consolidation of programs, expanded use of technology in the areas where it is applicable, and more efficient utilization of existing resources such as classroom space) will mean greater, rather than less, quality in the university system.

Local Government Aid

The Wisconsin productivity program was initiated with a full recognition of the existing obstacles to substantial productivity improvement. We feel that the program, once it is on its way, will create its own momentum, and that eventually agencies will compete with each other to demonstrate innovative approaches to greater efficiency as they have always competed with each other for a larger share of state appropriations. One limit on potential savings is the fact that most of the state's budget does not go for state administrative operations, but for aid to local governments. A recent study prepared for the National Commission on Productivity, *Improving Productivity and Productivity Measurement in Local Governments*, highlighted the problem here: "There is widespread feeling that local government productivity in the United States is dropping."[3] This feeling has been reinforced by reports that, for example, municipal garbagemen in New York City accomplish half as much per day as their privately employed counterparts, or widely publicized stories of policemen "cooping" on late-evening shifts. As Governor of Wisconsin, I intend to use the full influence of my office to promote responsible and efficient practices on the part of local units of government. The state can have a substantial effect on local productivity through its tax policies, financial aid incentives, program requirements, and the planning and administration of program functions. The state may also be able to develop model procedures and standardized administrative approaches that all municipalities can copy.

There remain a number of institutional barriers to a

Wisconsin productivity policy that will not be easy to overcome. The rigidity of civil service and merit laws substantially limits the flexibility of public administrators. In many cases, organizational restructuring is not possible because of the statutory constraints. Meaningful public accountability is stifled when, as is true here, the governor cannot appoint the operating heads of many agencies. Finally, many department executives are restricted by laws that dictate not only what programs they conduct but also how these programs must be administered and organized.

A defeatist attitude has never been characteristic of Wisconsin government, however. We are confident that our productivity program will work, and like so many earlier Wisconsin innovations, become a model for the nation. We are also confident that this program will not degenerate into mere cost-cutting, or a single-minded pursuit of efficiency. Improving productivity should not lead to the insulation of government functions from the people, or the mechanization of services where more of a human touch is necessary. It should mean neither the sacrifice of service quality nor the sacrifice of important social goals that are not subject to easy cost-benefit analysis. I see a productivity program as a humanizing force in government, providing job enlargement for those trapped in tedious positions, offering new challenges to both administrators and workers, facilitating participative management, taking greater account of the individual capabilities of employees and, most importantly, giving the public higher quality service at a lower price.

WISCONSIN'S PRODUCTIVITY
IMPROVEMENT POLICY

Governor's Policy Statement:

As a matter of policy, all state agencies will be required to improve their management efficiency in the 1973-75 budget years, maintaining essential public services but cutting service delivery costs by at least 2.5 percent annually.

Specific Instructions:

1. Each state agency must submit a preliminary productivity improvement report to the Bureau of Planning and Budget by June 15, 1972. The report should identify the proposed areas of improvements in methods, the timing of those improvements and the estimated savings associated with them.

2. Productivity improvements must be reflected in the budgets for all general fund, program revenue and segregated fund state operations, excluding debt service and those costs which will be identified as aids to individuals and organizations and local assistance. To the extent possible, federally funded programs should be handled in a manner to maximize state fund savings.

3. The continuing level budget request for the 1973-74 fiscal year should be reduced by 2.5 percent of the 1972-73 base for state operations. In the second fiscal year, 1974-75, the continuing level budget should be reduced by 5.0 percent of the 1972-73 base, reflecting an additional 2.5 percent increase in productivity above the first year's level.

4. Agencies with several appropriations or programs may apply different amounts of savings to different programs or appropriations but must meet a grand total equal to 2½ percent the first year and 5 percent the second year for all programs or appropriations. Agencies are expected to propose the most significant productivity improvements throughout the department, and that may well not occur uniformly among programs and organizational units.

5. Limited shifting between years within the biennial total may be approved (for example, a first-year reduction of 3 percent and second-year reduction of 4½ percent).

6. Agencies may propose limited offsets to the productivity savings for investments in the purchase of equipment, systems studies or other investments that are directly tied to improved productivity.

7. The dollar amount of these productivity improvements should be shown as a net cost reduction in the Methods Improvement columns of the B-2 forms. These cost reductions should be shown as a separate decision item in the continuing level for each affected program. Budget narratives should describe the productivity improvements to be made.

8. Agencies are expected to propose means of controlling costs or increasing productivity in all other categories of appropriations: local assistance, sum sufficients and aids to individuals. Agencies are to accompany their budget request with a separate report on cost controls in these other areas.

9. Agencies are not permitted to propose elimination of programs or make major reductions in services as a part of this productivity

improvement policy. This policy is intended to improve the efficiency of governmental services, without reducing essential public services.

To further assist you in this effort, a checklist of improvement criteria is available in a separate pamphlet entitled, "Governor's Productivity Improvement Program." You may wish to contact the Chief of the Management Development Section for assistance in studying and selecting potential productivity improvements.

JAMES D. HODGSON

5 PRODUCTIVITY IS KEY ELEMENT IN GOVERNMENT AND BUSINESS

Sooner or later, productivity discussions inevitably get around to the fearsome question of government productivity. That hour has arrived. I know it is an hour some may await with relish—it's a good chance to get in all those licks at government. It's also an hour others may await with despair. It's pretty much uncharted land out there. Who knows what monsters lie in wait?

But let us take our courage in our hand and move in. Actually, the way may not be so dark as we think.

It is no secret now that government is big business. It is far and away our biggest business, and at the state and local level our fastest growing business. It employes almost 13 million men and women—one of every six American workers. Government employment has shot up by 50 percent in the last 10 years—a growth rate about twice that of the private sector. Most of this increase has been in state and local governments, which now employ over 10 million people.

That's a quick "people profile" of government. Now let's look at costs. Again you will not be surprised to hear that

Reprinted with permission of the author from the *Defense Management Journal*, October, 1972.

costs have grown even faster. Ten years ago the annual cost of all government—Federal, state, and local—was $108 billion. Today it has more than doubled to $233 billion. The percentage of the nation's gross national product devoted to government is now a staggering 22 percent.

Growth in Government

I suppose I ought to pause here to make a couple of comments. There is, of course, the too obvious one—government costs us a great deal of money. But we have done it to ourselves. The recent phenomenal growth in government was not imposed on us. We voted—or our elected representatives did—for all those public services supplied by all those governmental jurisdictions. Like the man in the TV commercial, we sometimes can't believe "we ate the whole thing."

Certainly we have had public problems. And with them came demands for public services. Still, we do pay an awful lot for these services. And many of us apparently are beginning to think we're paying too much. Taxpayers are increasingly standing up and shouting, "No." They are increasingly voting down bond issues for schools and parks and sewage treatment plants and other public services. They are fighting property tax and other increases. And, when you put the question—and even when you don't—a great many of them will tell you they are "fed up" with government.

The message is clear. A lot of people don't think they're getting their money's worth out of government, and they're not very happy about it.

So here you have a problem—a gigantic government business, a much needed business, slated to grow bigger, and already costing more than people want to pay for it. So what do you do? Well, one of the things you simply must do is start thinking about how to improve its productivity. And this means finding ways to make more effective use of manpower, equipment and facilities. We have more than a normal reason for doing this. We must do it if we are to continue to maintain and improve vital public services. We must do it if we are to realize our national dream of a better life. And we must do it to avoid public outrage and restore the confidence of our citizens in their government.

Develop Productivity Yardsticks

But is there anything that offers promise of achieving a faster rate of productivity gain in government? I think so. Let me outline a five-pronged approach to this problem.

First, we must develop "productivity yardsticks."

These yardsticks are objective measures of performance. We need these yardsticks in government because government managers lack the systematic feedback that the private market automatically gains through the profit and loss statement.

Right now, in state and local governments, we don't have them. There is, however, better news on the federal scene. We have been pulling together the work of more than a decade on ways to measure productivity change covering federal programs, and the result is the first government-wide index of real output per man-hour based on data obtained directly from the federal agencies themselves. We have developed adequate quantitative output data covering approximately 55 percent of federal employment. Some 600 measures of output include such indicators as the number of patents processed, insurance checks disbursed, claims adjudicated, coins minted and many others.

Preliminary results of this productivity measurement effort come somewhat as a pleasant surprise. The results show a significant improvement in output per man-hour in the federal government over the past four years. Productivity in FY 1971 was about 8 percent higher than in FY 1967. The rate of gain averaged about 2 percent a year. Not a spectacular increase, of course, but you must remember that for this period it compares with a rate of 1.5 percent for the private non-farm sector. What is most important is that we now have a new and useful yardstick to help us improve our performance. It's a real breakthrough.

Technological Advances

But let's move on to our second need. And this one in the realm of technology I would like to call the "slippery water syndrome."

Let me explain. In New York City someone has developed a way to get greater water flow per minute through a fire hose. How? By using "slippery water"—water made slippery by adding a chemical which reduces friction in the hose. This means fire hoses that are smaller, lighter, and easier to handle can be used to improve fire fighting capability and reduce costs.

This is only one example of government's use of new technology. Private industry is very skillful in this; government must be equally skillful. President Nixon has proposed a new technological opportunities program that targets increased expenditures for civilian research and development on urgent problems involving government in such areas as education, transportation, pollution and health. We in the federal government are determined to devote an increasing proportion of our research capability to finding technological breakthroughs to enhance the efficiency of government. On the local level, a consortium of national organizations of local officials—the International City Management Association, the League of Cities, Conference of Mayors, and others—is undertaking a technology application program. This program will try to identify new technical breakthroughs in the $30 billion local government market and then spread this new knowledge across the country. It ought to pay big dividends in improving state and local governments.

The Three R's

Let's turn to a third need—overhaul of government operations. We must dismantle the government red tape machine. And how do we do this? By reorganization, revenue sharing and reprivatization. Quite a mouthful of longtailed, Latinized words! But let me explain.

• First we need action on the President's historic proposal to the Congress to restructure the basic organization of the domestic side of the federal government around four major purposes—natural resources, human resources, community development and economic affairs.

• Second we need the President's revenue-sharing concept to relieve some of the financial burden on state and local governments. Here again we must upset the status quo if we are to achieve better government.

In some cases, what is now done by government can be better done by the private industry sector. One of my own pet ideas involves the building up of private sector competence to perform useful social programs. The "big government" philosophy was pretty well entrenched when government started to undertake major social projects so today most of them are done by government people. There are a lot of spurious reasons for this but no good reason. Someday as a nation we'll reach sufficient maturity where the word "profit" used in connection with a social program won't be received with invidious rhetoric. We must develop means to "reprivatize" certain public activities at the local level, too. For example, a study in New York City has shown the cost of trash removal per ton by private firms was more than 50 percent below the city's cost.

Productivity Bargaining

Now I've arrived at number four in Professor Hodgson's

prescription for productivity gains in government. This is one I have a special interest in because it falls in my own sphere of collective bargaining. It is productivity bargaining.

We are seeing productivity bargaining beginning to take hold in the private sector in such industries as railroads, longshore and construction. In a narrow definition, it is a matter of bargaining away restrictive and unproductive work practices in exchange for other benefits to employees. In the broader sense that I prefer, it involves effort to improve productivity by any means. The steel industry has taken the lead here.

We need to introduce the same concept into management-labor relations in the public sector. Public unionism has become the fastest growing sector of organized labor in the past decade. In 1970, about 2.3 million government employees were members of unions, twice the number for 1960. Another 1.7 million were members of employee associations.

This remarkable growth in the power of organized labor in the public sector should be accompanied by a sense of responsibility. Joint productivity improvement effort forces the parties to focus on this obligation. The National Commission on Productivity is working in this area.

Develop "Esprit de Corps"

Let me get to the final approach to increasing government productivity. It's one that applies equally to the private sector. To build productivity we must build people—people who regard their work as challenging, respected, rewarding and worthwhile. In the final analysis, productivity in government, as in other labor intensive services, depends on the success of managers in providing conditions for high motivation. Too few organizations—government or private—succeed in fostering an "esprit de corps," but those that do are known and respected throughout our society for quality and excellence of performance.

How do we generate a spirit of working together for the common good? It may be more difficult in government than in private industry because, among other things, of the lack of competitive pressures. But because motivation is elusive, it's difficult in both sectors.

Nevertheless, difficulty is no reason for default. The behavioral sciences are at least producing some intriguing concepts for us to work with, and we must set about to test them.

So now, as we stand back and look at these approaches, the government productivity countryside doesn't seem so bleak as we might think. Up to now government productivity improvement has been something like the Loch Ness monster. There have been occasional sightings but no proof. Now at least we have hauled the monster out of the water, and he looks better than we thought.

But, of course, the whole program of improving productivity in the American economy remains a gigantic and perplexing one. And like most problems, eventually it gets down to people.

Educate the Worker

I would like to contribute a thought or two on productivity and the American worker—really only one thought.

Take our Economic Stabilization Program as an example. The American worker bought it and, I believe, still buys it. The message has pretty well got through to him now that its object—controlling inflation—is very much in his own interest. He knows how soaring prices can erode his paycheck. If he tends to forget, his wife reminds him in colorful language every time she comes back from the supermarket.

So he goes along with the objective, and he will also go along with the program as long as he thinks he's in the same boat with everybody else.

But let's apply all this to another area—productivity. Here,

I think, we can say that any national productivity improvement program must meet the same criteria before the American worker will buy it. And here we run into some problems. The American worker has just as big a stake in improving productivity as he does in controlling inflation. It is almost axiomatic that the only way he can raise his real wages is by increasing productivity. Studies going back over the years reveal an undeniable correspondence between real wage gains and productivity gains.

However, he does not understand this the way he understands inflation. It's not his fault. Productivity is a bloodless, abstract concept with which most Americans have trouble. And this suggests a lesson to those of us who are interested in helping him understand. We've got to put more sex and soul into the concept. We've got to show him how more productivity will indeed translate into more purchasing power in his own pocket. We've got to show him how more productivity will help to give him the better life, the better environment, the social benefits we all seek.

Share Equitably in Gains

And, to pick up our other two requirements, we have to make sure that he, in fact, *does* share equitably in our nation's productivity gains. We can help enlist his support in achieving those gains if we invite him to help out in setting up and participating in the mechanism. The steel industry I mentioned earlier has a fascinating joint labor-management program under way right now to do exactly that.

I have noted the American worker is a pretty canny fellow. He will work hard for the things that will help him, but he's quick at figuring out what will help and what won't. Right now, he's not very sure about productivity. One of the great challenges we have ahead is to make him sure. To do this we must demonstrate completely and without any possible doubt that productivity gains are in his best interest, and that it's in his best interest, as well as the best interest of all of us, to work as hard as we can for them. It may be the top order of business for us during the rest of the decade and probably beyond.

HERBERT STEIN

6 THE MEANING OF PRODUCTIVITY

The rate at which productivity grows is central to two of the major issues facing the country. One is the issue of inflation. The other is the speed at which the society's demands on the economy are rising—not only for the traditional purpose of private consumption and investment but also for improving the environment, health, domestic security, and general quality of life.

Recognizing the key role of productivity increase in meeting the Nation's goals, and the potential contribution of all sectors of the community, the President on June 17, 1970, announced his intention to establish a National Commission on Productivity. The commission when established included six members each from business, labor, and the public at large, and five members from the federal government.

Subgroups of the commission have been established to deal with specific problems. While its work still lies largely ahead of it, some points raised in early discussions by the commission, with participation by the President, deserve public attention at this time.

Reprinted by permission of the author from U.S. Department of Labor/Bureau of Labor Statistics, Bulletin 1714, *The Meaning and Measurement of Productivity*, September, 1971.

The Meaning and Measurement of Productivity

The most commonly used definition of productivity is real output per hour of work. Productivity in this sense is a rough measure of the effectiveness with which we use our most important productive resource—labor. It has important social implications because it takes account not only of the chief source from which individual and social desires are met—that is, the total output of the economy—but also of a major source of getting that output, namely work. We should surely think that an increase in output achieved by raising the output per hour of work does us more good than an increase in output achieved by working more hours. The definition of productivity as real output per hour of work has economic significance also. If all terms are consistently defined, if labor compensation per hour rises at the same percentage rate as productivity, then unit labor costs will be stable; and if the shares of compensation in the national income remain unchanged, then prices on the average will be stable. In fact, the price level generally moves very closely with the ratio of compensation per hour to productivity per hour except for cyclical or other short-term interruptions. Finally, estimates of productivity defined in this simple way are available to permit interesting and analytical comparisons of different times and countries, whereas more sophisticated measures are not.

The most commonly used measure of productivity relates the total output of goods and services in the private economy, that is, private Gross National Product (GNP) to the man-hours of all persons engaged in the production of those goods and services. This measure is expressed in the usual GNP constant dollar terms. Other measures, at the firm or industry level, may be constructed in a similar conceptual framework but more often are derived by using some physical concept of output unique to that firm or industry such as tons of steel or kilowatt-hours of electricity.

The most common definition and measure of productivity

is sometimes called inadequate or even irrelevant on the ground that it reflects only the "quantity" and not the "quality" of economic performance. It is true that like all measurements, the measurement of productivity relates to a quantity, but it is untrue that the quantity measured is unrelated to the qualities that human beings value. The value of gross national product is a product of the quantities which people buy and the prices which people are willing to pay for them. The quantities people buy, and the amounts they are willing to pay for them, reflect the qualitative values that people find in the different products. Thus, GNP and its components reflect a value or "quality" choice among consumers, subject to limits imposed by income levels and the available supply of goods and services.

There are, of course, consequences of economic activity that are not reflected in existing measures of output per hour and the country has become increasingly conscious of some of these in recent years. On the output side these are generally consequences of activity that does not pass through a market. The outstanding case is the deterioration or improvement of the environment. The deterioration of the environment is not counted as a cost or a deduction from the product, and an improvement of the environment is not counted as an addition to the product. Thus, as far as this factor alone is concerned, our ordinary figures may have overstated the growth of productivity in the past and may in the future understate the growth if more and more resources are used to improve the environment. However, this is only one among many omissions in the measurement of output and productivity. Going further, it is obvious that productivity statistics do not measure justice, security, happiness, beauty, or the lack of them, and we cannot be sure in what direction our available measurements may be biased. But this obvious fact does not belie the importance of the statistic as an indication of the ability of society as a whole to achieve its goals.

There are other limitations of the statistical measures of

productivity that are a consequence of our inability, thus far at least, to perfect our methods of national accounting. In construction, for example, we do not yet know how to measure properly the output of complex and diverse structures such as homes, hotels or hospitals. Nor do we yet know how to assign a correct market value to products that are not sold, such as those of education and many government activities.

For many analytical and policy purposes the simple figure of output per hour is inadequate. We would like to know why total output and output per hour are larger in one country, industry or time than another and for this purpose we need additional measures. We need to measure output per unit of all resources, including at least capital as well as labor. And we need to recognize that different kinds of labor, distinguished by skill, in a sense, are different amounts of labor per hour and have different productivities. When we measure output per unit of capital and labor combined and adjusted for quality we have another measure of the efficiency of resource use. When we break down this measure into its various components we then have a family of measures that permits better estimation of the contribution of different factors to the growth of output and provides insights into the effects of different policies in the future.

Measurements of productivity have been improved substantially in sophistication, variety, and accuracy in the past 20 years. They are still inadequate to answer all the questions that might be asked of them. Further improvement and dissemination of the statistics will contribute to better understanding of our economic problems and to better policy. The commission hopes to contribute to this.

Why Productivity Is Important Now

By any available measurement the level of productivity in America has risen persistently over the decades, except for brief cyclical interruptions, and for many years has been the highest in the world. One might think in these circumstances that productivity growth would be a matter of no great concern. Nevertheless, the discussions of the commission have confirmed the premise which underlay its establishment—namely the great importance of the productivity question today.

The claims upon the economy, expressed through the political process or in the market, are very large, even relative to the great capacity of the American economy. The size of these claims results at least in part from past rapid economic growth, which has led to rapidly rising expectations among workers and consumers. We shall come closer to meeting these claims if we can increase the rate of growth of productivity.

During the past four years the rates of growth in productivity and GNP slowed down. At the same time the real income gains that workers have come to expect with rising wages also deteriorated. A return to a more normal productivity growth rate can help to restore the rate of gain in average real income.

This striving for higher productivity must not be viewed as a whip-cracking exhortation to "work harder" in order to raise some arbitrary abstract measure of economic performance. Increasing productivity is a way of increasing the ability of people to do what they want to do. It can provide the wherewithal for achieving a higher standard of living for families now living at the low end of the income scale. It can provide for a choice of leisure—not idleness—in the form of more holidays and vacations and entrance to an earlier retirement from the world of work, and it can provide the resources for improving the physical quality of the environment.

We may be entering a period in which sustaining the rate of growth of productivity will be more difficult. For several decades the shift of workers out of agriculture, where productivity was below the average, contributed substantially to the increase of productivity. The number of workers left in agriculture is so small that this can no longer be significant. On the other hand, there will now be an increase in the proportion of the labor force employed in those industries, loosely called "service industries," where productivity and its rate of growth have been low relative to the national average.

Productivity, in recent years, has been increasing more rapidly in Japan and in several Western European countries than in the United States. The reduction of the gap between our productivity and theirs is not a matter of concern; it is to our advantage that their productivity should be high. Neither does it necessarily indicate any superior effectiveness of their economic policies. The fact that they are behind us in productivity by itself helps them to grow more rapidly because it means that they have opportunities to exploit—such as advanced production techniques—which we are already using. In some cases where they have embarked on new product ventures they have built plants embracing the most modern technology. But technology and methods may not be the whole story, and the experience of others requires us to consider carefully whether there are steps that could be taken here to speed up the increase of productivity.

The higher rates of productivity growth in other countries were accompanied by increases in hourly compensation which, in the past 5 years, tended to exceed those in the United States. The relationship of trends between output per man-hour and compensation per man-hour, however, was closer in those countries than in the United States so their unit labor costs did not go up as much in those years.

In comparing the trends of productivity and earnings among countries, we must draw a distinction between real income and unit costs. Certainly we must applaud the rising productivity and standard of living of workers in the rest of the world. But the gap between changes in money earnings and changes in productivity which determines unit labor cost trends, is an important element in the difference between a stable or improving or deteriorating position in international trade.

Within the United States, no less than among countries, to recognize the distinction between costs and income is useful. The last three years were witness to the highest three-year increase in average compensation per man-hour (of all persons working in the private economy) since the early 1950s. And yet, when these figures are adjusted for the rise in consumer prices, the resultant real compensation per man-hour showed the smallest three-year rise over the same period. There was a deterioration in the rate at which higher real income was being achieved.

The important point here is not so much that compensation rose rapidly but rather that there was a large gap between productivity and compensation gains with a resultant large increase in unit labor costs. It is a part of the syndrome of inflation in which prices and wage rates each rise—and each, at different points of time, tries to catch up with the other. One way to break into the syndrome is to increase the rate at which productivity grows so that wages can rise without increasing unit costs and the pressure on prices is abated.

Increasing productivity may thus be regarded as the keystone to an improved standard of life and environment for all of society. It is with this broad view in mind that the National Commission on Productivity has set its task of finding ways to continue or accelerate the historical rates of productivity gains in the United States.

PART TWO

MEASURING PRODUCTIVITY

7 PUTTING PRODUCTIVITY MEASURES IN PERSPECTIVE

As a result of research and extensive discussions with agencies, the joint productivity team concluded that there is a need to clearly state what productivity measures *are* and what they *are not*.

Productivity measures are:

• Primarily after-the-fact "scorekeeping" techniques, covering repetitive operations. They show *not* what *should have* happened but what actually happened.

• Techniques to make managers explain past trends in resources expended per unit of final output.

• Devices for predicting and then gauging future trends in unit costs resulting from planned changes in organization, systems, capital equipment, and facilities.

• Research tools for examining basic causes of productivity changes in functional areas common to several agencies.

• Means of reporting productivity change to the Congress and the public.

Reprinted from *Measuring and Enhancing Productivity in the Federal Government, Summary Report*, Joint Federal Productivity Project, 1973.

Productivity measures are not:

• Substitutes for any other measurement technique used by managers, budget analysts, and other evaluators. They supplement or round out other measures.

• Measures of effectiveness or public benefit. They may indicate this; but in most cases they must be correlated with other kinds of performance data (descriptive or quantitative) to truly reveal end-product benefits.

• Suitable tools for measuring current performance versus "should take" standards.

• Measures of activities having no consistent output.

• Complete measures of federal activities, since the team's best coverage thus far is 60 percent of federal man-years and its best estimate of ultimate coverage is 65 to 70 percent.

HARRY P. HATRY

8 ISSUES IN PRODUCTIVITY MEASUREMENT FOR LOCAL GOVERNMENT

Productivity recently has become the object of rejuvenated interest. National concern over rising prices without apparent rises in output has been a major cause. This inflation pinch has been felt severely in the local government sector of the economy where expenditures have been increasing at a rapid pace. Pressures to make the local government dollars go as far as possible—through increased productivity—appear likely to continue over the next few years at least.

The attempt to keep costs down and to improve efficiency has always been a task of local government management. The revival of concern over productivity simply reflects the heightened challenges to local governments today to meet the demands for services within very tight cost-revenue constraints.

Why should local governments worry not only about productivity, but also about productivity measurement? Productivity measurement itself involves added cost. Ultimately, productivity measurement has to be justified as

Reprinted by permission from the November/December, 1972, issue of the *Public Administration Review*, Journal of the American Society for Public Administration, by permission of the American Society for Public Administration and the author.

helping to lead to improved productivity. Following are some specific uses of local government productivity measurement, first, for that carried out by local officials, and next, for that carried out by federal or state officials.

Productivity measurement generated locally can help to:

• Identify problem areas and priorities for improvement efforts. The measures will afford a perspective on the current level of productivity and how it is changing over time for various services.

• Determine progress toward targets or goals. Individual programs aimed at increasing productivity need to be evaluated. Local officials may be tempted to "fiat" annual increases in productivity, such as five percent per year, but this would be meaningless without means to measure actual accomplishment.

• Establish and implement employee incentive plans. Measurable productivity changes can be considered as items for bargaining between labor and management.

Comparative productivity measures of local governments can help federal and state officials to:

• Identify overall nationwide (or state) trends as a basis for setting priorities for resource allocations. Funds, research, and technical assistance can then be assigned more specific targets for improving local productivity.

• Give national attention to productivity improvement opportunities. For example, productivity measurement can be included in evaluations of demonstration or experimental projects; then local officials generally can be alerted to successful new approaches (and to failures that may be avoided). Also, high performers can be identified and others encouraged to emulate them.

In summary, productivity measurement can help governments to identify priority areas needing attention and the degree to which specific actions have helped. Unless governments continually monitor productivity, they will lack feedback to determine whether their courses of action have been successful and whether they should be continued in the future or modified.

Productivity measurement will be particularly useful if the following three types of comparisons are made:

• Comparisons over time, to provide information on trends and progress, if any. Lacking external standards, a government's own past history can be used.

• Comparisons with other jurisdictions, particularly those with similar characteristics, to provide some baseline against which a government can measure its own performance.

• Comparisons among operational units within a jurisdiction, such as among solid waste collection crews, police precincts, or social service offices, so the more productive units can be recognized (and their methods duplicated) while the less productive units can be given the necessary attention to improve their performance.

What Is Productivity Measurement?

Productivity measurement essentially means relating the amount of inputs of a service or product to the amount of outputs. Traditionally this has been expressed as a ratio such as number of units produced per man-hour. National productivity measurements for the private sector have been made for many years. This is not as easily accomplished for the local government sector because its "products" primarily fall into the classification of services; hard-to-measure quality of service then becomes an essential ingredient of output along with physical output measurements such as "number of cases processed" or "tons of solid waste collected." Even in the private sector productivity measurement efforts have failed to measure services adequately.

Thus, a principal difficulty in productivity measurement for local government services is in defining and measuring output, a familiar problem to public administrators. Some government services such as utilities do have physical outputs, but here, too, quality is an important aspect. For example, treating so many million gallons of water or sewage is important, but the quality of the treated water or effluent is an equally important dimension.

Solid waste collection offers a more typical and subtle example. Suppose that tons of solid waste collected is used as the measure of output. Then merely shifting from backdoor to curbside collection can increase *workload* productivity (tons collected per man-hour) significantly. However, the quality of the service to the public will have been diminished; that is, part of the collection activity—transporting the gargabe from door to curb—has been shifted to the customer. Furthermore, obtaining the tons of garbage collected fails to indicate whether the streets are clean. A city could show an increase in total tonnage collected (or in the tonnage collected per man-hour) while the streets were actually getting dirtier.

Perverse measurement is another serious problem. Governments need to avoid leading employees to take actions that make the measurements "look good," but which may be against the public interest. For example, the "number of arrests per policeman" seems like one highly plausible measure of police productivity. Using this measure by itself in productivity incentive plans, however, would generate considerable temptation to increase the number of arrests at the expense of arrest quality. Another example: overemphasis on waste tonnage collected might tempt collectors to look for heavy objects, to douse waste with water, etc. Clearly, local officials want to avoid such perversities and need to seek productivity measurement procedures that reduce their likelihood.

Thus, simplistic notions of productivity measurement should be treated with great caution. Rather, it seems advisable to consider a multiple set of measurements for each service. These should include workload measures, quality measurements, and other local condition factors that could affect the interpretation of the findings. Table 8-1 provides an illustrative set of such measures for a number of local government services.

Current State of Measurement

The current state of productivity measurement for local government is poor—both at the individual local government level and at the national level. Little has been done. A surprising number of local governments apparently do not even systematically keep workload measurement data on many of their services. Fewer seem to examine systematically and regularly their unit cost data, e.g., cost per unit of workload. The inverse of unit cost data, workload per unit of cost, is a productivity measure. Seldom are these reported for local government services.

Measurement of service effectiveness to include quality aspects of services—how they serve the citizens of the jurisdiction—is quite rare in many, if not most, local services. Only in very recent years have local governments (and state and federal as well) begun to take steps to correct this deficiency. Many governments are now beginning to develop "performance measurement" systems. Without the consideration of quality in service effectiveness, productivity measurement is too likely to be deficient if not actually perverse.

In addition, there is currently little effort by the federal government to measure productivity of local government services—either to provide comparative city-by-city data or nationwide aggregates.

Measuring the Amount of Input

Thus far, this discussion has focused on measurement of

Table 8-1. Illustrative Set of Workload Measures, Quality Factors, and Local Condition Factors That Should Be Considered in Productivity Measurement[a]

Selected service functions[b]	Illustrative "workload" measures[c]	Illustrative quality factors (i.e., measures of citizen impact) that should be considered in interpreting productivity	Illustrative local condition factors that should be considered in interpreting productivity[d]
Solid waste collection	Tons of solid waste collected	Visual appearance of streets "Curb" or "backdoor" collection Fire/health hazard conditions from solid waste accumulation Service delays	Frequency of collection Private vs. public collection Local weather conditions Composition of the solid waste (including the residential-commercial-industrial mix; type of waste, etc.)
Liquid waste treatment (sewage)	Gallons of sewage treated	Quality level of effluent, e.g., "BOD" removed and remaining after treatment Water quality level resulting where dumped	Initial quality of waterway into which the sewage effluent is released Community liquid waste generation characteristics
Law enforcement (police)	No. of surveillance hours No. of calls No. of crimes investigated	Reduction in crime and victimization rates Crime clearance rates, preferably including court disposition Response times Citizen feeling of security	Percent of low-income families in population Public attitude toward certain crimes
Law enforcement (courts)	No. of cases resolved	No. of convictions/no. of plea-bargain reduced sentences Correctness of disposition Delay time until resolution	Number and types of cases
Health and hospital	No. of patient-days	Reduced number and severity of illnesses Conditions of patients after treatment Duration of treatment and "pleasantness" of care Accessibility of low-income groups to care	Availability and price of health care Basic community health conditions
Water treatment	Gallons of water treated	Water quality indices such as for hardness and taste Amount of impurities removed	Basic quality of water supply source

Selected service functions[b]	Illustrative "workload" measures[c]	Illustrative quality factors (i.e., measures of citizen impact) that should be considered in interpreting productivity	Illustrative local condition factors that should be considered in interpreting productivity [d]
Recreation	Acres of recreational activities Attendance figures	Participation rates Accessibility to recreational opportunities Variety of opportunities available Crowdedness indices Citizens' perceptions of adequacy of recreational opportunities	Amount of recreation provided by the private sector No. of individuals without access to automobiles; and the available public transit system Topographical and climate characteristics Time available to citizens for recreation activities
Street-maintenance	Square yards of repairs made	Smoothness/"bumpiness" of streets Safety Travel time Community disruption: amount and duration Dust and noise during repairs	Density of traffic Density of population along roadway Location of residences, homes, shopping areas, recreational opportunities, etc.
Fire control	Fire calls Number of inspections	Fire damage Injuries and lives lost	Local weather conditions Type of construction Density of population
Primary and secondary education	Pupil-days Number of pupils	Achievement test scores and grade levels Continuation/drop-out rates	Socioeconomic characteristics of pupils and neighborhood Basic intelligence of pupils Number of pupils

[a]More extensive lists of workload measures and quality factors (often called measures of effectiveness or evaluation criteria) can be found in references #1, 6, 9, 10, 16, 17 and 26 of the Bibliography in "Improving Productivity and Productivity Measurement in Local Governments."

[b]Numerous sub-functions each with its own sub-measures could also be identified. However, care should be taken to avoid going into excessive, unuseful detail.

[c]Dividing these by total dollar cost or by total man-days yields workload-based productivity measures.

[d]Such local conditions as population size and local price levels are relevant to all service functions.

Source: *Improving Productivity and Productivity Measurement in Local Governments*, by Harry P. Hatry and Donald M. Fisk, The National Commission on Productivity, 1971, p. xvi-xvii.

output, but input measurement is also an integral part of productivity measurement.

Three general options are available: first, a measure of manpower such as man-hours or man-years of effort; second, cost in constant dollars, i.e., dollars evaluated in terms of some base year price; and third, cost in current dollars without deflating for price level changes.

Man-hours is the classical productivity measurement. It has the virtue of focusing on the output of specific employees, and to this extent is certainly useful. However, it has some major limitations. It does not reflect potential tradeoffs with other input factors such as capital items. For example, a city might choose to purchase a more automated piece of equipment, such as a new waste collection vehicle with a mechanical arm to pick up garbage cans. The additional capital investment is likely to reduce collection man power, but raise vehicle maintenance costs. Thus, productivity in terms of output per unit of collection manpower would show an increase, but productivity in terms of dollars, constant or current, might show a substantially different picture.

The example just cited illustrates another caution. If a government hires personnel for maintenance activities, such additional manpower, it can be argued, should also be considered in evaluating the changed productivity. In addition, if the government decides to contract out for the maintenance work rather than hire its own personnel, its productivity, if measured solely on a per man-hour basis, will appear improved.

Another example: what are the productivity considerations when a local government employs computers for preparing the payroll and for tax and utility billing? The number of clerical personnel is typically reduced. Yet additional higher paid personnel for the computer and various other computer-related expenses may be required. In net, the computer-related costs may have absorbed much, if not all, of the dollar savings. Actually, the primary payoff may be an increased quality of output, both in terms of accuracy (fewer payroll mistakes to raise the ire of employees) and quicker payroll and billing, as well as the ability to do more things and provide more information with the computer.

Thus, government productivity in the big-picture sense is not just a function of manpower but of the other cost elements as well. It seems necessary for governments also to express productivity in terms of dollars.

The third option listed above, output per *current* dollar, is not normally labeled a productivity measurement. Economists would press for the use of cost deflators to provide *constant* dollars. This has the virtue (or drawback, depending on one's outlook) of removing the effects of price changes. Local officials are, however, also concerned with actual current costs, including any price rises.

Thus, local governments probably will want to use all three forms of input measures to obtain a better perspective on productivity.

Input measurement can also prove inadequate or misleading unless it includes *all relevant man-hours or dollars.* Employee fringe benefits, related maintenance costs, facility costs, and the like should all be taken into account. The handling of indirect and shared joint costs is a dilemma which affects this problem as well as many other cost analysis issues.

In making productivity measurement decisions, a government needs to address the question: the productivity of whom or what? For example, for some purposes a government would likely be interested in the productivity of specific collection crews. For other purposes, local officials would probably also need a more complete picture of the entire waste collection department. If the local government develops an agreement to share productivity gains with employees (and this may become a reality for at least some local governments), the government would want to estimate the actual net gains after consideration of such expenses as improved equipment and increased maintenance costs. This

would permit the productivity resulting from these investments to be allocated equitably.

As will be discussed in the next section, when a city's
performance is to be compared against others, an additional
problem arises—that of commonality of reporting practices.
For example, some governments may typically include
employee fringe benefits as part of employment costs; others
may normally keep them separate.

Inter-City Comparisons

Dependable, meaningful data on other, similar governments
can help to provide targets or standards for a jurisdiction. In
the United States, comparative productivity data on local
government services for individual cities or counties is not
generally available. There is information available on expenditures and manpower for various services such as that
collected by the U.S. Bureau of the Census and by the
International City Management Association. However, on the
output side there is little meaningful comparative information.

Possibly only in the police crime control area is there at
least partial output information. There the federal government has undertaken to obtain crime and arrest data using
common definitions. Adherence to the reporting requests is
dependent on voluntary compliance by individual local
governments. The resulting data has come under considerable
attack for its insufficiencies and for lack of common data
collection practices in at least some cities.

A major effort to obtain commonality is needed for
adequate comparative productivity analysis. Federal agencies
might provide a basis for comparison by undertaking periodic
tabulations of service data in a sampling of local governments, rather than attempting to cover all governments each
year.

Assuming commonality of data, a further question is: what

jurisdictions are sufficiently similar to provide fair comparisons? Hundreds of characteristics differentiate the various cities and counties, with each jurisdiction as unique as is each human being. Yet categories can narrow the band of significant differences for certain purposes. The little data that is currently collected on local governments, such as fiscal data, is generally grouped by population category. Demographic, socioeconomic, organizational, and miscellaneous characteristics abound—climate; central city vs. suburban vs. rural area; form of government (e.g., manager-council vs. elected executive); racial composition; household income; class mix; and so forth.

There is surprisingly little theory or research on how such characteristics should be expected to affect efficiency, effectiveness, or productivity of specific local services. For example, convincing analyses of the economies or diseconomies of scale for local government services are sparse indeed.

Each particular public service needs to be examined in light of its own characteristics. For example, in solid waste collection, housing density, as a proxy for how close together pickup points are, would instinctively seem to be an important productivity factor. Yet the little available analysis presents conflicting evidence.

What seems clear, however, from existing data sources is that major city-to-city productivity differences often do exist. This is true even after allowing for variations in selected service and community variables. An examination of solid waste collection data from a special 1971 survey indicated that for once-a-week curbside or alley pickup the tons collected per man varied from 940 to 1,900. Tons collected per $1,000 expended varied from 41 to 90. Based on 1970 police data, the number of clearances of reported crimes per police employee ranged from 1 to 7 among cities of approximately 100,000 population.

While a portion of such wide ranges may result from different data collection practices, real productivity differences appear to exist after adjusting for these practices. What is not known is how much of the remaining differences is due to inherent local characteristics not found elsewhere and how much due to better practices by some of the jurisdictions.

Much closer examination is needed to determine why certain jurisdictions appear to be doing better. Once this is accomplished, the insights gained may be used to help improve the poorer-performing jurisdictions.

Examples

To illustrate some of the major issues in productivity measurement, two examples are presented in the following sections: one on solid waste collection and the other on police crime control. The first is a relatively easy local service for productivity measurement; the second is considerably more difficult.

Solid Waste Collection

Inspection of data indicates that solid waste collection may be too complex to measure as such. It needs to be broken down further to distinguish residential-commercial trash and garbage collection from street cleaning activities. The former also can usefully be divided so that residential and commercial collection are measured separately. Otherwise different or changing proportions of these activities can result in apparent productivity changes that are in reality due to the particular mix of activities.

Two basic output measures for workload productivity of waste collection seem appropriate: total tons collected and number of units (e.g., households) served. However, level-of-service factors also need to be considered: pickup location and frequency of collection are examples. Considerably more difficult to measure are the quality factors, cleanliness of streets and citizen satisfaction with collection services. Few cities currently collect data on either of these quality aspects, although they are clearly significant. Procedures have been developed that enable local governments to make such measurements—through systematic visual inspection rating systems for street cleanliness, and through citizen surveys for indications of satisfaction.

If the level (or quality)-of-service aspects change substantially from one year to the next, these may cause major changes in workload productivity. Thus, if a city changes to curb from backdoor pickup, one would expect a significant increase in tons collected per man-hour. This change is not an improvement in productivity as defined in the broad sense. When evaluating one city's performance against those of other cities, these factors should again be considered. Cities might be grouped by selected quality and level-of-service characteristics, or more complicated adjustments may be made to provide a basis for comparability.

Table 8.2 illustrates the type of data and computations that could be made.

Police Crime Control

Measuring police productivity presents many conceptual difficulties. There appear to be two major purposes of police crime control: deterring crime and, given that it has not been deterred, apprehending criminals. There is currently no effective way to measure how many crimes have been deterred by governmental actions, such as by increasing the size of the police force.

Apprehension productivity is more tangible. The "number of arrests per policeman or per dollar" is an obvious productivity measurement. As already noted, this measure could lead to perversities if used alone. It does not consider the issue of the quality of the arrest. A partial way to account for quality of arrest for felonies is to examine the percentage of arrests that "survive" preliminary hearings in the court of limited jurisdiction (normally the first court into which a felony is placed). In addition, percentage of arrests that lead to convictions can also be used as an indicator of the full productivity of arrests. Note, however, that both these factors, the second more so than the first, involve the performance of other parts of the criminal justice system in addition to the police.

Other productivity information can be obtained by examining clearance rates (that is, the percentage of reported crimes that lead to an arrest) perhaps divided by dollars (or employees) per capita.

Note that such measurements as "number of calls answered per man-year" seem of limited usefulness as measures of productivity, although they may be of interest to city management for other purposes.

A critical input measurement difficulty is trying to separate manpower costs for traffic control from those for crime control. The same personnel may have both functions. On the output side, problems include apparent inaccuracies in reported crime rates and vague or conflicting definitions of certain crime categories. There is also the problem of which crimes to consider in measuring crime and clearance rates. For example, the FBI uses such classifications as "Part I and Part II" crimes, "Index" crimes, "property crimes," and "crimes of violence."

Summary

Productivity measurements are important devices for letting a local government know its current status. They reveal, after action is taken, how successful it has been. Measurements can help to identify new procedures or approaches that are worth pursuing, and those that are not. Used in dealings with employees, they can provide a basis for incentive plans and the sharing of benefits of increased productivity.

Unfortunately, the state of the art of productivity measurement for local government services is disappointing. The temptation is and will be great to stick with the more readily available and traditional workload type of measurements. But used alone these measurements can lead to perversities and misallocations of effort. The collecting and at least arraying of various quality considerations should also be undertaken and used in interpreting workload productivity calculations. Single, readily available, physical measurements, tempting as they may be, should be viewed with a jaundiced eye. Inevitably, for a government to obtain a reasonable perspective of its productivity for any service, it will need multiple measurements.

Table 8-2.   **Illustrative Productivity Measurement Presentation (Solid waste collection example)**

Data	1970	1971	Change
1. Tons of solid waste collected	90,000	100,000	10,000
2. Average street cleanliness rating[a]	2.9	2.6	−0.3
3. Per cent of survey population expressing satisfaction with collection[b]	85%	80%	−5
4. Cost (current)	$1,200,000	$1,500,000	+$300,000
5. Costs (1970 dollars)	$1,200,000	$1,300,000	+$100,000
Productivity Measures			
6. Workload per dollar (unadjusted dollars)	75 tons per thousand $	67 tons per thousand $	−11%
7. Workload productivity (1970 dollars)	75 tons per thousand $	77 tons per thousand $	+3%
8. Output index: $\frac{(1)\mathrm{x}(2)\mathrm{x}(3)}{(4)}$ (unadjusted dollars)	0.185	0.139	−25%
9. Productivity index $\frac{(1)\mathrm{x}(2)\mathrm{x}(3)}{(5)}$ (1970 dollars)	0.185	0.160	−14%

[a]Such rating procedures are currently in use in the District of Columbia. The rating in line 2 is presumed to be based on a scale of "1" to "4," with "4" being the cleanest.

[b]The figures in line 7 indicate some improvement in efficiency, but line 6 suggests that cost increases such as wages have more than exceeded the efficiency gains. Productivity has gone down even further on the basis of decreases in the street cleanliness ratings and decreased citizen satisfaction. However, such indices have to be studied carefully and interpreted according to local circumstances to be fairly understood.

Source: *Improving Productivity and Productivity Measurement in Local Governments,* by Harry P. Hatry and Donald M. Fisk, The National Commission on Productivity, 1971, p. 19.

Effort by the federal government seems vital if adequate comparative data on local government productivity in the United States is to be provided. A set of common definitions and, to the extent possible, common data collection practices need to be provided for each public service to encourage at least reasonable comparability of data—both of the input figures (man-years and dollars) and of outputs.

Many new productivity improvement approaches need to be tried out in local governments if productivity is to be improved. These include a number of approaches used in the past by industry such as value engineering, time and motion studies, employee incentive plans (possibly for supervisory as well as supervised employees), various cost reduction programs, and new technological and procedural changes.

Whether funded by federal, state, or local governments, these attempted innovations need proper evaluation of their net effects on productivity. The governments undertaking the tests need this information. In addition, widespread and rapid dissemination of the results, at least of those innovations with most potential, is highly desirable. However, without adequate measurement, so-called evaluations are likely to be little more than public relations stories by the sponsors and of minimal practical use.

The current lack of effective means to seek out potential innovations, to give them thorough and objective evaluation, and to effectively disseminate the findings is restraining local governments from helping themselves and from reducing waste of resources. Adequate productivity measurement tools would do much to fill part of this gap.

Bibliography

This article is based primarily on research undertaken by the Urban Institute for the National Commission on Productivity and the U.S. Department of Housing and Urban Development on various aspects of measuring the effectiveness of local government services and on measuring local government productivity.

For some recent attempts to identify local government service quality measurements, see the following publications:

1. The Urban Institute and the International City Management Association, *Improving Productivity Measurement and Evaluation for Local Governments* (Washington, D.C.: The National Commission on Productivity, 1972).
2. Harry P. Hatry and Donald M. Fisk, *Improving Productivity and Productivity Measurement in Local Governments* (Washington, D.C.: The National Commission on Productivity, 1971).
3. Louis H. Blair and Alfred I. Schwartz, *How Clean Is Our City: Measuring the Effectiveness of Solid Waste Collection Operation* (Washington, D.C.: The Urban Institute, 1972).
4. Harry P. Hatry and Diana R. Dunn, *Measuring the Effectiveness of Local Government Services: Recreation* (Washington, D.C.: The Urban Institute, 1971).
5. Richard E. Winnie and Harry P. Hatry, *Measuring the Effectiveness of Local Government Services: Local Transportation* (Washington, D.C.: The Urban Institute, 1972).
6. Kenneth Webb and Harry P. Hatry, *Obtaining Citizen Feedback: The Application of Citizen Surveys to Local Governments* (Washington, D.C.: The Urban Institute, 1972).

9   WORK MEASUREMENT SYSTEMS

Work measurement systems can contribute to effective management decision-making by providing information on how much time is actually spent in performing certain tasks as compared to a standard. With this information, managers can decide such things as how many men will be needed to perform predicted future workloads and whether work performed has been accomplished efficiently. To be useful, such systems must be soundly conceived and accurately maintained and the results must be effectively used. In performing its work, the joint team made a number of inquiries into such systems to obtain some insight into whether the work measurement systems in use by governmental organizations are functioning as intended and whether effective use is made of the results. These approaches involved analysis of measurement systems in selected agencies, questionnaires administered to about 100 members of federal executive boards, and management interviews of approximately 250 managers at various levels in the field establishments of five agencies.

Some of the data we obtained at one installation we visited illustrates how such data can be used. At that installation daily reports are produced on such functions as loading items

Reprinted from *Measuring and Enhancing Productivity in the Federal Sector*, U.S. Government Printing Office, 1972.

to be shipped on railway cars. Actual time spent is compared to the standards established for the steps involved, such as loading containers on pallets, to determine the degree of efficiency achieved in performing the work.

This data is summarized into broader categories as it goes up the line. For instance, it is summarized by branch and reported weekly to the division level. At the division level it is summarized monthly and reported to the directorate level. An example follows:

Actual man-hours for the month	2,551
Standard hours for work accomplished	2,025
Percentage of efficiency (line 2 ÷ line 1)	79%
Actual man-months required for work accomplished	15.1
Man-months required for work at standard	12.0

The agency's director gets information on problems within any of the agency's functional areas in a monthly formal briefing. These briefings involve comprehensive performance appraisals that examine the status of each major program in terms of relative indicators of progress. The briefings include assessment of the performance of individual installations as well as organization-wide accomplishments. While certain items are reviewed regularly, the content of each briefing varies to be fully responsive to the changes in operational environment and to the current needs of management. Data are presented on (1) current trends in workload and performance efficiency, (2) status in meeting key program objectives, (3) qualitative indicators of mission performance, and (4) status of progress in special interest areas.

Figures 9-1, 9-2 and 9-3 are examples of the type of information utilized in the briefings.

Figure 9-1 displays 13 months' information. The solid line depicts the actual workload while the dotted line is a 3-month moving average that smooths out the peaks and valleys and provides a better basis for trend analysis or forecasting.

Figure 9-1   Depot Operation Function:
              Production

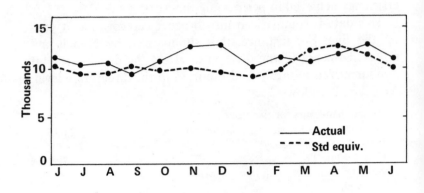

Figure 9-2   Depot Operation Function:
              Productive Personnel Equivalents

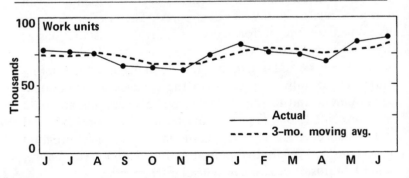

Figure 9-2 shows productive personnel equivalents used to accomplish the workload displayed on the preceding chart. If an activity is 100 percent efficient, the dotted line, which represents standard equivalents, would be identical to the solid line, which represents actual equivalents. If the solid line is above the dotted line, efficiency is less than 100 percent. Conversely, when the dotted line is above the solid line, efficiency is more than 100 percent.

Figure 9-3   Depot Operation Function:
Measurement of Efficiency

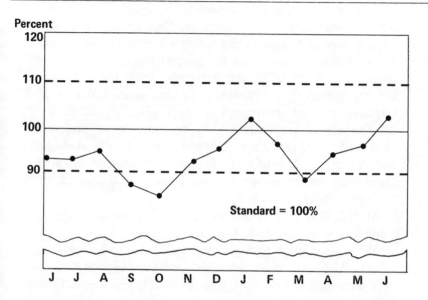

Figure 9-3 is an example of how the overall efficiency of a major function is reported to top management. Ranges (acceptable tolerances shown by the dotted lines) provide a basis for evaluation of the function's performance and, as warranted, action—usually on the management-by-exception basis.

The figures and supporting data form a basis for decision-making in terms of planning for manpower needs; scheduling work; and identifying, investigating, and correcting problems that are preventing achievement of the agency's performance goals.

Results of Our Studies

Comparison of Two Systems

Our inquiry indicated that there is considerable variation in the accuracy and use of the output of the work measurement systems included in our inquiry. The range of these variations is perhaps best illustrated by comparison of the results of our work at two organizations at which we looked into the work measurement systems in considerable detail. Both of these organizations have similar missions. They are responsible for buying, stocking, and issuing supplies and materials. To work efficiently, they must have the necessary stocks and transmit them quickly to using organizations. With the purpose of accomplishing these functions in the most efficient and effective manner, both organizations establish standards to do the work, accumulate data on time spent and work produced, compare the work produced with the standards, and prepare a series of work measurement reports. However, there were significant differences between the organizations as to the validity and utility of the data.

At the first installation we found that by and large the standards were accurate. Moreover, management was consistently seeking ways to make the standards more reliable and useful. Also, our tests disclosed that management control over data reported on work actually performed was sufficient to ensure reasonable accuracy. As a result, the output of the system had the confidence of and was used by various levels of management which included management at the work centers, division level, directorate level and the installation head.

At the second installation, the situation was almost directly the opposite. The work measurement system at the second organization was separate and distinct, with an insignificant degree of integration into the overall management system. Moreover, the accuracy of the data in the system was doubted by management at all levels. Lack of confidence in the accuracy of the system appeared to result primarily from two causes.

• First, the standards were not kept current. Because of changing work conditions, standards need to be reexamined frequently to see that they are still appropriate to the tasks being performed. At the time of our review 57 percent of the standards had not been reexamined within the last two years. Moreover, in many cases there was a lack of documentation to support the standards, and where documentation did exist we found a number of errors.

• Second, the data on actual work performed was not verified by independent check. Our tests disclosed several instances in which there were errors in this data.

As might be expected, the difference in confidence in the accuracy of the data made a significant difference in the extent to which the system was used. At the first installation the system was an integral part of the management system and was used by management at all levels on such things as

• translating workloads into manpower needs
• preparing schedules for performing workloads
• planning future needs for manpower and other resources
• determining efficiency of performance attained in carrying out specific functions.

At the second installation, limited use was made of the work measurement data and most subordinates thought its primary use was as a basis for reductions-in-force. Of 116 managers at various levels that we asked about the system, 80 (69 percent) felt it was not worthwhile.

We also learned that the training course for managers in the use of the system had been reduced from 20 hours to 2 hours and that those below the management level received no formal training at all. The paucity of training in the use of the system appeared to us to be a substantial factor in the failure to use it.

We do not know if either of the above systems is typical of government work measurements systems. However, they do illustrate the considerable differences that can occur, depending upon whether the system is kept reasonably accurate, the people who use it are adequately trained and the output from the system is made a part of the information which management uses in decision-making.

Results of Additional Inquiries

The briefings and questionnaires we obtained from other agencies indicate that there is substantial room for improvement in the data produced by governmental work measurement systems and the use of that data. Some of the information we obtained from the briefings and questionnaires follows:

• Briefings obtained at nine other organizations disclosed instances in which work measurement systems did not exist or covered only part of what was possible.

• Members of the federal executive boards were asked to identify the reasons why managers are not making greater use of measurement data in the management process. Of 47 who commented, 28 percent noted that there were problems in obtaining valid data and 26 percent cited the lack of knowledge, training, skill, and interest.

• Members of the boards were asked to provide suggestions for making measurement data more effective. Of 54 who responded, 17 percent suggested additional and more complete training and 15 percent suggested that more feedback data was needed.

• Managers at five agencies were asked to comment on areas needing better technical advice and assistance. There were 159 responses. The area cited most often (31 percent) was the need for improvement in the use of work standards and measurement of productivity.

We also found that managers at different levels need different data. For example, the first line manager is usually interested in data in sufficient detail to effectively evaluate and supervise groups of workers. He is interested in data such as the output per employee. On the other hand, the middle manager usually does not need or want this much detail. He is interested in summary data such as the total number of units produced for the day. The top level manager wants his data even more succinct. He wants to know only such things as whether shipments are getting out on time and is concerned with the number of units produced this year to date compared to last year to date in order to examine long term trends.

Conclusions

Effective planning for manpower needs and effective scheduling of work are important means of improving productivity because they tend to make the best use of manpower and avoid lost time and wasted effort. Work measurement systems are prime tools for management in achieving effective planning and work scheduling, and therefore the use of such systems should be encouraged. To obtain effective use of work measurement systems, both management and their subordinates must have confidence in the systems. Securing such confidence requires an accurate, up-to-date system and sufficient training of personnel to permit them to understand how it works and know how to use the results. Management needs to ascertain that the data produced by existing systems is reliable enough to be accepted.

Extending work measurement techniques to susceptible functions not now covered and improving the reliability of the data for those systems whose veracity is challenged would in our judgment make a worthwhile contribution to the productivity of the federal government.

10 TECHNIQUES IN ESTABLISHING STANDARDS FOR WORK MEASUREMENT

There are various techniques and procedures used for establishing standards to measure work performance. These techniques can be categorized as follows:

- Time study.
- Work sampling.
- Predetermined time systems.
- Standard data.
- Technical estimates.
- Historical (statistical) standards.
- Staffing patterns.

There may be many variations to any of the above techniques. Therefore, when considering a particular technique for purposes of evaluation, it may be necessary for an expert to determine if a variation is acceptable. Each of the above techniques is discussed in the following paragraphs.

Time Study

Time study is a technique in which direct observations are

Reprinted from *Guidelines for Evaluating Work Measurement Systems in the Federal Government*, Joint Federal Productivity Project, July, 1972.

made of work performance. A stopwatch or some other timing device, such as motion picture analysis or a time study machine, is used to time the work. When a time study is used, the job method must be completely described, the cycle or elemental times must be obtained, the performance of the operator must be compared with the concept of normal, and allowances must be made for personal and unavoidable delays.

The standard developed using time study techniques is generally considered a valid and reliable standard. The job content and the standard time are specifically defined, and because the method, quality, working conditions, and operator performance are standardized, it is possible to identify deviations from standard and to assign a cause for the deviation.

Work Sampling

Work sampling involves recording a series of randomly spaced observations of personnel performing specific tasks and then synthesizing the data obtained into a standard time. The application of this technique is very flexible and, depending on how the study is conducted, may or may not yield an engineered standard.

When work sampling is used, the job must be broken into categories of work and nonwork, and these categories must be described. At random intervals, the activity must be observed and the observations must be classified into the proper categories. The number of observations taken must be sufficient to insure that the sample is reliable. The performance of the operator must be compared with the concept of normal, and allowances must be made for personal and unavoidable delays. It is also essential that a production count be obtained while the job is being observed and while the total time of the study is being recorded.

Where there is a clear distinction between working time

and idle time, work sampling standards will give substantially the same results as time study standards. When using work sampling, the observer must be alert for changes in operators' methods because even a slight change can result in an invalid standard.

Predetermined Time Systems

Predetermined time systems (PTS) is an entire series of specific techniques that are based on a detailed breakout of fundamental hand and body motions to which time values have been assigned. Therefore, by analyzing the motion patterns of a job in terms of the body and hand movements, the time for performance can be synthesized from the predetermined times.

When using PTS to set a standard, the method of performing the job must first be described in terms of elements. The elements must then be broken down into basic motions pertinent to the particular predetermined time system being used. Time values are then assigned for the motions identified, and allowances are made for personal and unavoidable delays.

The standard set using PTS may be as valid and reliable as a standard based on time study. However, the use of the PTS requires that the person applying it be completely familiar with the system and the job under study. This requirement could prove quite costly in that it requires considerable time to analyze in detail the basic human motion patterns necessary to establish the standards.

Standard Data

Standard data employs the same basic principles as PTS. The standard time to do a job is described in elemental times and then is synthesized into a total standard time for the job.

When using standard data, the method of performing the job must be broken down into its elements. Time values are then selected for each element (from tables, curves, charts, or formulas), and allowances are made for personal and unavoidable delays. With the above information the standard can be established. When standard data do not exist for all elements of a job, time study, work sampling, or some other technique must be employed to establish times for these elements.

Technical Estimates

Technical estimates yield nonengineered standards. The standards developed by using technical estimates are established without a timing device or sampling technique. Technical estimates should be used only by a person technically qualified in the area under study. They should be based on a procedure that breaks the estimate into a series of small individual estimates, which are then summarized to obtain the standard time.

This technique relies considerably on the personal judgment of the person making the estimate. This estimate may vary greatly from the actual time to do the job. Therefore, it is difficult to accurately assign causes to deviations from these standards.

Historical (Statistical) Estimates

Standard times to do a job can be developed by using a statistical or mathematical analysis of historical data where labor expenditures can be correlated with a measure of output. When using historical (statistical) estimates to establish a standard, a relationship between units and man-hours must be developed and must be statistically validated.

A major drawback to the use of this technique is that it is based on the assumption that what has happened in the past is a good practice and that what will happen in the future will not change the relationship between units and man-hours. Therefore, it is difficult to identify a significant deviation from the standard and even more difficult to assign a cause for the deviation.

Staffing Patterns

The use of a staffing pattern does not result in a standard in the sense that other techniques do because no work unit is involved. Staffing patterns are merely manning ratios—expressions of manpower of spaces required to support a certain activity. Staffing patterns may be developed by using any of the previously mentioned techniques, as well as simulation, queuing theory, directed requirements, or historical data.

The use of this technique relies significantly on the background of the person making the estimate. Therefore it is difficult to assign a cause for a deviation from the estimate. You cannot determine whether the deviation was a result of poor performance, poor working conditions, or an incorrect original estimate.

11 IMPROVING PRODUCTIVITY MEASUREMENTS IN LOCAL GOVERNMENT

The Challenge of Productivity Diversity

Reasons for Productivity Measurement

To study the operations of one city alone at one point in time provides little basis for saying whether citizens are getting their money's worth. But when, as in this study, it appears that some cities are performing twice or six times or ten times as well as others of comparable size, a clearer picture emerges. This diversity, with some localities excelling and others showing up relatively poorly, indicates the potential of looking more closely at local government productivity. Almost staggering service improvements and cost savings nationwide could result from bringing all localities closer to the level of the top performers. Once

Reprinted from *Improving Productivity Measurements and Evaluation in Local Governments*, June 1972. Prepared for the National Commission on Productivity by the Urban Institute and the International City Managers Association.

sufficient attention is given to improved productivity, it also may develop that even the present high performers are achieving far less than what reasonably can be attained with modern management methods.

Diversity also may provide vital clues within single jurisdictions. As data are assembled over time, indications of falling productivity may serve as a warning that a particular local government service is slipping and in need of attention. Analysis of data by neighborhoods or clientele groups can be undertaken to detect whether certain citizens are experiencing serious inadequacies or inequities in service compared to others in the community.

At the outset, it should be established what is meant by "local government productivity." A Bureau of the Budget study provides this general definition: "Productivity estimates compare the amount of resources used with the volume of products or services produced."[1] One further refinement is important, namely that the "volume of products or services produced" is interpreted in the broad sense to include the ideas of effectiveness and quality, not merely efficiency and quantity. In other words, the biggest effort at the least cost is not necessarily best if it leaves citizen "customers" less well off or dissatisifed.

The major reason for attempting to measure productivity has already been implied: to encourage the kinds of comparisons and public scrutiny that lead to better value for citizens from their local governments. Productivity measurements also have additional uses:

• To provide an index of progress—or lack of progress—to individual local governments.
• To develop standards of performance, based on aggregate data for similar communities.
• To dramatize diversity and thus generate effort to determine the reasons for success and whether these reasons can be applied more widely to treat the causes of poor showing.
• To serve as a basis for performance incentives that can be

used by government management and labor in wage and working condition establishment.

- To guide the federal government in allocating resources to raise the level of performance throughout the nation.

Nature of Study

This exploratory study, undertaken from October, 1971, through May, 1972, and involving approximately one and a half man-years of effort, barely skims the surface of a complex subject. But it suggests the kinds of improvements in productivity and productivity measurement that can be anticipated through further work in the short and long run.

The study comprised three basic tasks: (1) ways to improve the measurement of productivity in solid waste collection, (2) ways to improve the measurement of productivity in police-crime control, and (3) development of procedures for searching for and the evaluation of innovative approaches to improved productivity (using these same services—solid waste collection and policing—as test areas). This report has four parts—Part I, summarizing the findings and recommendations, and Parts II, III, and IV, describing each of the basic tasks in more detail.

It was decided to focus on two local services, with somewhat less depth of analysis than might have been achieved by concentrating on a single field, in order to arrive at more generalized conclusions about local public service productivity.

Encouragingly, many cities and counties throughout the United States are breaking away from traditional approaches in the attempt to improve productivity. Three innovations in solid waste collection and three in policing are examined in enough detail (Part IV) to suggest that further analysis should yield still more valuable results. The emphasis in the exploratory work is not so much on the case studies themselves as on the procedures for locating and evaluating innovations.

Measurement Difficulties

Among the many problems in measuring local government productivity, three of the most serious need to be emphasized. One is the difficulty of knowing precisely what is to be measured. Another is that a measurement itself can have perverse effects. And a third is the simplicity versus complexity issue.[2]

Knowing what is to be measured is relatively simple if the end result (as in much of the private sector) is a physical product. Local governments, however, chiefly offer services. Even when a physical product is involved, as in a swimming pool or water supply system, the quality aspects tend to loom large.

Little progress in measuring productivity can be expected unless one first grapples with the attempt to define numerous quality aspects of the intended services, troublesome as this may be.

The possible perverse impact of measurement instruments can be explained by illustration. If policemen (individually or by department) are rated according to the number of arrests per employee, this may lead to excessive pressures to make arrests, even in instances where justice and order are better served by avoiding arrests. Or if housing programs are evaluated largely by the number of new units constructed, this may encourage the neglect of older units.

A too simple measurement system that locks on to a sole indicator of productivity may provide a distorted and possibly unfair picture. A measurement system that attempts to cover all facets of a service may become so complex that it cannot be comprehended by officials or others. The aim should be to seek a middle ground between these extremes.

Summary of Four-Part Study

The following sections present a series of general recommendations that emerge from the study.

While this study focuses on productivity measurement through the use of data collection and analysis, this should not be conceived as an end in itself. Rather, the underlying emphasis is on *use* of the statistics and measurements to *improve* productivity.

II. Measuring Solid Waste Collection Productivity

Findings

Part II identifies improved procedures for estimating the productivity of solid waste collection at the local level and makes suggestions as to how such productivity might be assessed nationally. The principal findings of this investigation are as follows:

• Numerous solid waste collection statistics are currently collected by local governments that operate their own collection systems. Using these statistics, many jurisdictions prepare workload measures such as cost per ton, cost per residence, and cost per curb mile cleaned. These measurements usually provide some idea of the level of productivity and how it is changing.

• Local statistics generally fail to take into account the level of service and quality provided to the citizens. These factors can dramatically affect the cost and hence true productivity of local government operations. Productivity measurement should take these factors into consideration. Fortunately, there are only a few basic service variables that seem to affect productivity significantly—location of pickup and frequency of collection seem to be most important. (For example, by simply changing from a backyard to curbside residential pickup location, a jurisdiction can often increase its "productivity" by one third. But by such action it has also decreased the level of service to its residents.)

• Basic workload statistics can be categorized or rapidly adjusted to take into account the major service variables.

• Procedures are becoming available for the systematic measurement of quality factors, but no fully satisfactory procedure yet exists for translating them into productivity computations. (Systematic inspection procedures recently have been developed for evaluating various levels of cleanliness. Other measurable quality factors include missed collections, damage to private property, and citizen perceptions of service adequacy, using citizen survey techniques.)

• No ongoing survey currently collects national data annually on solid waste collection. (Attempts to fill this void have included three surveys over the past decade, some producing data of questionable validity. One survey sought to amass statistics for approximately 6,600 jurisdictions. Such data as does exist may be used to demonstrate interjurisdictional productivity comparisons.) •

• Data definitions and collection procedures differ among municipalities with widest variations among smaller jurisdictions. (APWA [American Public Works Association] and OSWMP [The Office of Solid Waste Management Programs] have made initial efforts to develop standardized data collection procedures.)

• Present knowledge of how community differences affect solid waste collection productivity is skimpy. (Topography, climate, income and density are examples of factors possibly affecting productivity. However, existing research gives conflicting or ambiguous evidence on their importance.)

• City-to-city differences in solid waste collection productivity of 300 to 500 percent have been uncovered (even after controlling for certain service variables and community factors).

Example 1: For twice-a-week residential curbside or alley pickup, the tons collected per man in 1971 varied (in our study sample) from a low of 334 tons in one city to a high of 1,645 tons in another. Even a city of approximately the same size and only 30 miles from the low city collected 908 tons per man. For these same two cities, the tons collected per $1,000 of expenditure were 35 and 88 respectively. Collection in the high productivity city, moreover, is handicapped by narrower alleys and streets. The low productivity city, however, appears plagued by high absenteeism, poor management, and a militant union.

Example 2: For once-a-week curbside or alley pickup the tons collected per man varied from 941 to 1,905; tons collected per $1,000 expended varied from 41 to 90.

Example 3: Disparities also are great in street-cleaning operations. The figures for sample cities varied from 55 to 434 tons per man per year. Tons per $1,000 expended varied from 6 to 47.

However, it cannot be assumed that all of these differences are due solely to productivity differences. Differences may also be due to such factors as data errors, differences in data definitions, service quality, or service and community factors not controlled for.

Recommendations

(1) The National Commission on Productivity should encourage the development of a national system to measure the productivity of local government solid waste collection activities. The Office of Solid Waste Management Programs of the Environmental Protection Agency seems the most logical organization to direct the effort.

The system should be directed at providing local governments (particularly those with low productivity) encouragement for, and guidance on possible means of, improving their own productivity.

(2) Local governments to be included in this national system should report through a simple, voluntary survey, providing both workload statistics and important service and quality variables such as suggested in Part II. Local governments surveyed might include those over 50,000 or possibly over 25,000 population.

Many statistics required are readily available in most, if not all, local governments with populations of about 50,000.

Once established, the annual survey effort should cost about $100,000. The actual survey could be done internally or contracted out. The survey form should be no longer than three pages and should require on an average no more than an hour for the municipalities to complete. A sampling of jurisdictions, rather than a complete enumeration, may be desirable to keep costs down. Despite the temptation to collect more and more data, there is much to be said for keeping it simple. It is not obvious that a system costing a million dollars would produce significantly better answers.

(3) Productivity teams should be created to investigate localities with apparent high productivity in order to determine the reasons for successful performance, especially those that may be transferable to other jurisdictions.

Teams may be drawn from government and private personnel in the fields of solid waste engineering, budget analysis, economics, operations research, and systems analysis. A visiting team might include two persons. On-site observation and data collection might require one to three weeks, with a total time including analysis and reporting of three man-months. Four such investigations per year would cost approximately $50,000, or less if only government employees were utilized. Team findings should be disseminated rapidly and effectively to communities throughout the country. (Because of the speculative nature of the team proposal, the concept should be re-evaluated after several visits and a year of operation.)

(4) The data derived from the national survey should be used to isolate and analyze crucial factors affecting productivity.

When combined with other readily available data on climate, topography, socioeconomic characteristics and so forth, the regular data (as collected under Recommendations 1, 2, and 3) will permit such analysis. As time series are accumulated, these analyses will be strengthened. Continuing analysis would require an estimated annual budget of

$100,000 including salaries and computer time. Results of such studies should be valuable to local solid waste managers, manufacturers of collection equipment, city program planners, and the Environmental Protection Agency, particularly in its development of demonstration projects.

(5) An annual report should be prepared to summarize findings for the use of national and local decision makers.

One year after the national system is established and staffed is not too early to provide useful, if less than perfect, results. The report should include overall averages, averages for different types and levels of service (particularly pickup location and frequency of collection), averages by regions, and averages by city size, as well as the findings of the analyses proposed in Recommendations 3 and 4. (The FBI's annual crime reporting system and the Bureau of the Census' annual survey of governmental finances are examples of part of what is envisaged.) The report should indicate any limitations or interpretation problems associated with the assembled data.

(6) Standardization and validation of data should be high priorities of the national system.

The current APWA and OSWMP efforts to achieve standardizing measurements are an excellent starting point for arriving at meaningful interjurisdictional comparisons. To assure accurate and reliable data collection, survey personnel should make on-site examinations or audits of sample localities. Special incentives may be required to encourage localities to upgrade their data gathering techniques.

(7) Individual local governments should for their own internal use collect, calculate, array, and evaluate productivity measurements.

This is important so that local officials and citizens can examine productivity trends and respond properly to observed changes.

(8) The possibility should be explored of using local government productivity measurement procedures such as

described in this report, to assist in the development of solid waste collection performance incentives agreeable to local government management and labor.

There has not been the opportunity in this project to explore directly this particular application of productivity measurements. The importance of this problem clearly indicates the need for such an effort.

III. Measuring Police Crime Control Productivity

This part of the study deals with improving procedures for estimating local government productivity in police crime control.

Findings

(1) Currently there is considerable work on the collection and analysis of crime statistics and police outputs.

Little of this work is directly addressed to police productivity, yet much of it is related and relevant. Weaknesses in much of the basic data have been discussed extensively. These have led some to reject any analysis of the data as self-defeating. This position appears overly pessimistic, however. Major trends that show up in the data, even for most individual governments, seem more likely to be useful than misleading, especially if the known data limitations are kept in mind.

(2) Local governments display striking variations in performance on a number of current productivity indicators. This suggests that important lessons can be learned from examination of the apparently high and low productivity localities.

Example 1: Major ("index") crimes per police employee among medium and large cities averaged 22 in 1970 but ranged from 4 to 32. For smaller cities, the range was from 3 to 54.

Example 2: Number of clearances (arrests for specific crimes committed) per police employee average 4 but a ten-fold difference occurs between the highest and lowest. In cities of about 100,000 population, the clearances per police employee range from 1 to 7. In cities of about 250,000 population, the clearances per police employee range from 1 to 8.

Example 3: Police expenditures can vary by over a factor of three for cities of similar crime rate and size. One city with 3,700 index crimes per 100,000 spends less than $10 per capita for police, while another with an equivalent crime rate spends $42.

(3) Measuring police productivity is a complex task involving many conceptual difficulties. Partial, if not distorted, perspectives of police crime control productivity result from reliance on single or incomplete combinations of indicators.

(4) The major (perhaps unsolvable) problem is to identify the relation between policing and prevention or deterrence of crime.

The difficulty is the inability to estimate the number of crimes that do *not* occur because of police activity. At best, what currently is done is to measure observed non-deterrence. Even here current data is incomplete because of extensive non-reporting by victims on many types of crime. The amount of reporting may change, thus leading to potential misinterpretation of the crime data. LEAA (Law Enforcement Assistance Administration) is currently encouraging victimization surveys as one means of providing better estimates of total crime.

(5) Apprehension productivity seems to be the most readily measurable aspect of crime control. Data on arrests or clearances per man-year or per dollar expended can be readily derived from existing data. Yet these are far from perfected, and used alone as a measure of productivity could lead to perverse effects.

The number of arrests or clearances does not attest to their ultimate disposition or quality. Also, the arrest and clearance data on the one hand and manpower and expenditure estimates on the other hand are difficult to link precisely.

(6) Some new directions in measuring police performance are coming into use.

Non-traditional productivity-related measurements, such as citizen feeling of security and citizen perception of quality of treatment by police, have been attempted in a few instances through citizen surveys. Victimization surveys, noted in Finding 4, are a further example.

(7) Some correlation was found between socioeconomic and population characteristics and police productivity measurements, but not as much as one might expect. The correlations that were found explained very little of the total variation in productivity measurements that were observed. This may be due to data problems, measurement technique limitations, or the existence of more complex or other relationships than those examined.

Correlations were found between crime rate and total population size and between crime rate and the percent non-white. Correlations were not found between crime rate and youths of ages 15 to 24 or percent households with income under $5,000. Clearance rates correlated with population and poor households for cities of 100,000 to 250,000 population, but not for larger cities. Clearances per police employee correlated mildly with various socioeconomic variables, but differently for different population groupings of cities. (See Part III.)

(8) An apparently significant relation was found between clearances per police employee and reported crimes per police employee.

The greater the number of reported crimes per police employee, the larger the number of clearances per employee.

(9) For crime control purposes, some of the police manpower and expenditure data are ambiguous and misleading.

Statistics usually include activities other than crime control, particularly for traffic control, that make it more difficult to analyze particular cities or to compare jurisdictions. Handling of capital costs is also a problem.

Recommendations

(1) A limited national police crime control productivity measurement and analysis effort should be undertaken on a trial basis.

Initially, existing data collected from police departments across the country would be utilized. Such new data series as arrests per police employee can be readily prepared from these data. A start should be made toward procuring additional data for the type of measurements suggested in Part III. These include measurements of quality aspects of police services such as disposition of arrests and clearances, citizen feelings of security, and citizen perception of treatment by police. Periodic surveys of citizens on a national basis, perhaps as part of annual victimization surveys, should be strongly considered for collecting systematic annual information on certain of these measurements. The cost for operating this effort is estimated at $100,000 per year.

(2) A police productivity analysis team should be formed to monitor the national effort, to improve police crime control productivity measurement, and to encourage their effective use. Provision should be made for the teams to receive continuing guidance from police, local government officials and criminologists. Missions of the team and of the national effort would include the following:

• Providing information on specific jurisdictions and on jurisdiction averages so local governments can compare themselves with others.
• Providing improved perspectives on crime control progress in the nation as a whole including possible ways to increase productivity.

- Identifying communities that are doing particularly well in police productivity, with identification of the probable factors leading to success.
- Developing better understanding of the relationship between crime and police activities (to the extent the research in last item permits).
- Spelling out data limitations to avoid misrepresentation of crime data, especially on national trends and comparisons of localities.
- Improving the data base by standardizing definitions and recommending compatible data collection procedures.
- Continuing research of the kind described but only begun in this study.

(3)   A major component of this effort should be analysis of the information collected. The analysis effort should begin to seek reasons for high or low productivity and to identify ways to improve it.

Local governments that appear to be relatively highly productive (based on the data collected) should be identified and examined (including on-site visits) by the productivity analysis team to identify the reasons and to identify programs that may be transferable to other governments.

(4)   To obtain as reasonable a perspective on police crime control productivity as possible, a number of productivity indicators should be considered simultaneously. These should include quality indicators.

Some of these have been mentioned in Recommendation 1. In addition, for apprehension productivity, the use of indicators that reflect ultimate disposition and, at least partially, the quality of arrests, is recommended. We suggest for initial consideration: "arrests leading to convictions" or "arrests that are not dropped by a court of limited jurisdiction." Both count only arrests reviewed and validated by court tests. Comparisons still would need to be tempered by awareness of differing court practices throughout the country (many reasons for dropping charges are not due to poor police work), but the resulting statistics should reduce the perverse incentive to make false arrests to make a department look good in a statistical yearbook.

(5) Comparisons should be made among cities grouped by population size and socioeconomic characteristics (such as racial composition and poverty).

This will permit fairer comparisons and ones more likely to reflect police-related factors. The correlations we observed of police productivity with certain population and socioeconomic variables were small but indicated the need for some such groupings. More research is clearly needed on the relationship of other urban characteristics to police productivity and crime.

(6) Because of the inevitable problems with comparability of data among local governments, periodic audits of local data collection procedures should be undertaken. For practical reasons these probably would have to be limited to a sample of governments each year. As with the data collection itself, this audit would be on a voluntary basis.

(7) Local governments and other criminal justice agencies should undertake their own productivity studies, collecting and analyzing data according to the most up-to-date procedures available.

The greatest benefit of police productivity analysis in the long run will be to the local governments. The focus on national data can provide useful benchmarks for comparison purposes and help dramatize the importance of the local work. In addition, local governments should examine their own trends, compare productivity of various geographical units such as precincts or beats within their own jurisdiction and perhaps compare different types of units within the police department. Some examples of the types of productivity analyses local governments should undertake are presented in Part III.

(8) Because of the existing inability to measure the causal connection between police performance (whether of individuals, teams, or all police department employees) and crime control, we cannot recommend usage of police employee

performance incentives based on such causality. However, it may be acceptable to consider incentives based on changes in productivity indicators, such as are identified in this study, without requiring that improvements be definitely *attributed to* police performance. It was beyond the scope of this study to identify possible incentive procedures based on productivity measurements, but we recommend that work in this area be undertaken in the future.

(9) Productivity analysis should be applied to the entire criminal justice system, not to police alone.

It is difficult to extract the roles of the police from those of other parts of the criminal justice system such as the courts, correction institutions and other aspects (e.g., drug treatment and street lighting programs) of the system.

12   ENCOURAGING EFFECTIVENESS MEASUREMENT

The purpose of this project was to determine the extent to which federal agencies measure the impact or effect of their programs and to encourage more valid and useful means of measuring effectiveness.

It was found in Phase I of this project that most efforts to evaluate programs or organizations have been concerned with measuring productivity in terms of input-output relationships. The outputs are usually expressed in units of goods or services immediately produced, such as number of claims processed, number of persons trained, etc. These measures assume that the activity is doing what it should be doing and provide no means for evaluating the contribution or success of the activity relative to its cost. Therefore, this project was added in Phase II to emphasize the importance of developing effective measures in conjunction with productivity measures.

Most of the existing measurement systems deal with aspects of organizational efficiency, which are determined by comparing actual performance (unit costs, for example) with

Reprinted from *Measuring and Enhancing Productivity in the Federal Government*, Summary Report, Joint Federal Productivity Project, 1973.

some standard. The major problem in progressing from efficiency to effectiveness measurement is that the latter involves establishment of complex external and internal cause-effect relationships with the external tending to be the more difficult to determine. For example, the mission of the National Highway Safety Bureau, DOT, is "to reduce the mounting number of deaths and injuries resulting from traffic accidents on the nation's highways." Establishing a direct relationship between the outputs of the bureau's three programs and the incidence of traffic deaths and injuries appears feasible, but not easy.

Effectiveness measurement provides the means of determining whether the agency is proceeding toward the objectives and of establishing a relationship between management actions and mission accomplishment. Both efficiency and effectiveness measurements are thus essential tools of managers in assessing true productivity, the former determining the cost of producing the agency's outputs and the latter the value of the agency's outputs to the recipient of its goods and services.

Measures of effectiveness will provide information on:

• Whether programs are accomplishing their intended objectives.
• Ways to improve the operation of the program.
• Which programs should be abolished and which new programs should be undertaken.
• How well programs are operating for which no final output can be readily defined.

In developing recommendations for encouraging the utilization of effectiveness measurement, we have attempted to profit from the experiences of Programming Planning and Budgeting (PPBS). In summary, the implementation of a government-wide PPB system in the mid-1960s had the following deficiencies:

- Rigidly forced from the top down, on a government-wide basis, it was adopted rather than adapted.
- Not well understood, supported, or used by top management.
- Perceptions of PPB's purposes not clear at all levels (OMB, agency heads, managers).
- Little impact on resource allocation decisions, and not related to any system of rewards or penalties.
- Not integrated with the decision-making process within a department or agency.

Unfortunately, PPBS was often viewed as a single, well-defined system based on sophisticated techniques of analysis and intended to produce an optimal plan of government activity.

Since the introduction of PPBS, there have been several attempts to develop effectiveness measurement for program evaluation and analysis. For example, in President Nixon's May, 1970, memorandum to agency heads, he asked for program evaluation involving three steps:

- First, a critical examination of the objectives of the program.
- Second, an analysis of the effectiveness of the program. Does the program adequately serve its target population? Does the program achieve its objectives in an economical manner?
- Third, consideration of alternative approaches to achieving the objectives that would produce the same or greater benefits at the same or lesser costs.

While several program areas were identified for termination, reduction, or reform as a result of the President's memorandum, there was no significant quantification of objectives or measures of effectiveness.

In September, 1970, OMB developed a system for assessing results of federal domestic programs. The approach, called the Performance Management System (PMS), has been installed in selected programs. With OMB staff working with agency personnel in developing definitions of objectives and performance measures, the Narcotics Control Program was the first system to become operational.

In developing our recommendations and action plan we are advocating no particular approach or technique for effectiveness measurement but simply building a foundation for the continued development of effectiveness measurement.

An initial step in developing recommendations was to assess what techniques and systems agencies had devised for evaluating effectiveness. As a result, a workshop on effectiveness measurement was held in November, 1971, with representatives from 17 departments and agencies in attendance.

The purpose was threefold:

• To learn what agencies are doing in the field of effectiveness measurement.
• To provide for an interchange of ideas on the subject.
• To initiate plans for encouraging effectiveness measurement throughout the federal government.

The workshop lessons can be summarized as follows: First, there is evidence of strong and increasing interest among federal managers in determining the effectiveness of their programs. This interest is being given an impetus by OMB, CSC, and GAO, who are devoting more of their efforts toward helping agencies measure their effectiveness in accomplishing assigned objectives.

Second, the benefits of effectiveness measurement are many. In no other way can a manager objectively assess the extent to which his programs are meeting the needs of the public.

Third, there are a number of ways to approach the task of effectiveness measurement. The systems discussed at the workshop vary in scope and detail. This is as it should be, because agency needs differ. What is important, however, is that they have in common the quantification of objectives and some provision for holding managers accountable for results.

The proceedings of the workshop were published as a separate staff paper and copies were distributed to all departments and agencies.

Two effectiveness measurement systems discussed at the workshop serve to illustrate the varying approaches and levels of sophistication that can be taken in developing a system for measuring effectiveness.

HEW Operational Planning System

The Department of Health, Education and Welfare has developed a management-by-objectives system in order to assess performance against objectives. The approach, called the Operational Planning System (OPS), provides a mechanism in HEW for management by objectives and towards results. HEW defines objectives as concise statements of what the HEW dollar is buying for the concrete, measurable achievements stated in terms of impact on a problem or progress towards a long-term goal.

Basically, the system communicates the Secretary's program priorities to all operating managers. In response to these priorities, managers submit operating objectives and an operating plan which shows all the critical milestones necessary to achieving the objectives for the fiscal year to the Secretary. These objectives are drawn from the budget and state, in measurable results-oriented terms, what will be done during the fiscal year to carry out the Secretary's priorities at the field level. The Secretary reviews all of the objectives and selects those which he personally will monitor during the year. The keystone to this system is the bimonthly management conference between the Secretary and program heads.

The Secretary uses them to review progress to date on each objective. The program head details problems and successes in meeting those objectives and corrective action is identified where required. This provides accountability by clearly identifying the individual who is responsible for the achievement of that objective.

It is, of course, difficult in HEW to quantify effectiveness measures for all their programs. They have looked at each program carefully to see whether it makes sense to try to define its effectiveness in measureable terms or to simply rely on an output measure. They have had some success in developing effectiveness measures and will continue to work in this direction.

FAA Goal Planning System

Another approach is the system being developed by the Federal Aviation Administration. Their system, while it is also built around management by objectives, differs from the HEW system in that FAA has expressed all goals and objectives in the form of impact on the public—a goals-oriented approach to decision-making. The goals approach requires:

- Clear articulation of the public benefits to be achieved for each major program.
- Determination of appropriate indication of goals achievement.
- Translation of goals into specific activities.
- Goals-oriented resource allocation.
- Establishment of a reporting system.
- Evaluation in terms of goal achievement.

For the goal or objective to be meaningful, it must:

- Be relevant to higher objectives or goals.
- Lead to identification of activities.

- Permit measurement of achievement.
- Be expressed, communicated and understood.

A specific example will help to clarify FAA's approach.

The FAA approach traditionally started with the general ideas of safety and efficiency in air transportation. But this provides no real direction or frame of reference to assess the relative impact of any proposed or ongoing programs. Therefore, the next step is to change the broad goal to something more tangible. As a result of the application of this type of procedure, the goal "Improve Safety" can be supported with a group of objectives expressed in terms of specified reductions in the probability of an accident. Activities to be undertaken can then be identified and related to these objectives by their impact on reducing the probability of aviation accidents.

This system is not operational as yet, but goals and objectives have been developed and comprehensive training has been provided to most managers on the management-by-objectives approach.

In addition to the Workshop Proceedings, a compendium of articles on Effectiveness Auditing has been published in cooperation with the Northern Virginia Chapter of the Federal Government Accountants Association. (The compendium is a separate publication.)

An important aspect of effectiveness measurement is the auditing of program results to see whether the programs accomplished prescribed objectives and goals and did so with due regard to efficiency and economy; such audits provide management with unbiased information on how well they are achieving the results they set out to accomplish and whether they have used their funds wisely. The compendium of articles provides a reference work that can be used to gain insight into effectiveness auditing, its conceptual basis and its usefulness.

Based on discussions at the workshop and follow-up discussions with the agencies having some form of effectiveness measurement system; interviews with groups who have looked into this area such as the Committee for Economic Development, the Urban Institute, and Senator Roth's staff; and discussions with staff from the General Accounting Office and the Office of Management and Budget, a series of recommendations have been developed which, we hope, will encourage the development and use of effectiveness measurement.

RICHARD E. WINNIE AND HARRY P. HATRY

13 MEASURING EFFECTIVENESS OF LOCAL GOVERNMENT SERVICES: TRANSPORTATION

Local officials cannot meet their transportation responsibilities adequately unless they know how well they are serving community needs. Unfortunately, there are major gaps in the data that would answer this question in a fair and comprehensive manner. This is an attempt to help local governments overcome this deficiency.

An effectiveness measurement system is proposed. It emphasizes the quality of local transportation from the standpoint of the citizen-consumer.

The system begins with the formulation of major objectives of a local transportation system: ease of access to the places people want to go, convenience, travel time (reasonable speed), comfort, safety, economy, maintenance of a habitable environment and satisfaction among citizens with the overall adequacy of the system.

One or more measures for each of these objectives is specified. For example, under "time," the travel time between major destinations and the duration of congestion

Reprinted by permission of The Urban Institute, from the monograph by the same title, 1972.

would be calculated. Local officials are encouraged to review the objectives and measures carefully, modifying them when appropriate because of local needs and circumstances.

The suggested measures are intended to apply to all modes of transportation, not, for instance, to automobiles or bus service alone. But if a community becomes particularly concerned about a single type of transportation, the measures can be focused separately on that one mode.

The measurement system aims to assess the general quality of transportation within local jurisdictions. Equally important, it aims to throw light on transportation for distinct segments of the community—different neighborhoods, the rich and the poor, the young and the old, those with autos, and those who rely on public transportation.

A major part of this report describes procedures whereby data may be collected for each of the effectiveness measures. The recommended data-gathering techniques include field measurements, the use of mapping to analyze public transit in relation to population distribution and citizen surveys. Annual collection of data and preparation of measurements are urged.

Annual costs of carrying out the proposed measurement system are estimated at about $37,500 for cities of 150,000 and about $93,000 for cities of 750,000. This would be in addition to current costs of statistical operations. The outlay of funds for implementing the system can be reduced, substantially in some cases, by using present municipal staff, applying for federal funding, sharing costs and operations with other local agencies (such as regional transportation planning bodies) and cooperating with local transit firms.

The measurement system is not recommended for its own sake. No matter how well it is devised and carried out, no matter how well it is financed and staffed, and no matter how sophisticated the analysis of data, the value of the system ultimately rests on its utilization by local officials. By comparing the measurements over time and among different segments of the community, officials may identify problem areas, trends, and progress (or lack of progress). The measurement system may not tell what should be done but will point to the areas that require further detailed investigations. The system is expected to help officials reach improved decisions on the level of local spending for transportation, on the way those funds are expended, on the kinds of regulations needed, and on the overall policies pursued.

The techinques set forth apply generally to municipalities, urban counties, and metropolitan transportation agencies whose jurisdictions have 50,000 or more people. The measurement system has not yet been field-tested. However, it is hoped that these tentative findings will be useful to local governments that are attempting to devise better measurements and will also help stimulate interest in improved measurement practices.

Introduction and Scope

Transportation has many facets. The emphasis here is on *local* transportation—intra-city or intra-county—and on the movement of *people* rather than of goods.

Current transportation measures generally fail to reflect the effectiveness of transportation systems from the citizens' perspective. This information gap impairs the ability of officials to judge present conditions or to arrive at sound decisions on transportation changes.

Because of the local emphasis, the modes of transportation of most interest in this work are automobiles, buses, taxis, rapid rail, and, to a limited extent, walking. The concern is with the way people get back and forth from local destinations, between their homes and their places of employment, recreation, and shopping.

In devising the data collection procedures, the aim was to produce methods that are practical and economic for local governments. In some cases, the need for new data seems imperative. Whenever possible, the measurement system calls for the use of data that are already available.

Few issues create more civic tension than disparities in public service—with some citizens receiving a high quality of service while others are relatively neglected. Officials typically have not had many ways to get a clear perspective of the service levels provided to different subgroups in their communities. This work seeks to correct this in the field of transportation by giving considerable attention to the quality and variety of service available to different population segments within a jurisdiction. Major residential neighborhoods are to be measured separately. Special attention is given to the elderly, young and others who do not have access to automobile transportation and who therefore must rely heavily on public transit.

Major uses of the proposed measurement system include the following:

• To indicate the effectiveness of transportation services currently available to the jurisdiction as a whole and to specific socio-economic and geographic segments.
• To provide baseline data. As the data are collected annually over time, the community's progress toward improving transportation services can be measured.
• To help identify existing transportation problems.
• To help analyze and evaluate proposed and experimental programs.

The measurement system is not set forth as a remedy for local transportation difficulties. It is designed to pinpoint what the conditions are, but it will not necessarily explain why these conditions exist or what programs should be undertaken to deal with them. Major transportation solutions often require detailed analysis and evaluation. The construction of a new highway system, for instance, affects a complex set of issues and proper planning would entail in-depth studies of anticipated impacts on the community's economy, land use pattern, and residential movements as well as on traffic conditions.

The report encourages the use of not just one measure, but rather a set of a dozen effectiveness measures. Each focuses on an important segment of service quality. Yet no single measure alone suffices for a comprehensive picture of local transportation service. Decision-makers often tend to concentrate on the beneficial aspects of a proposal without explicitly weighing potential negative side effects. For example, introducing bus service in a residential neighborhood may improve service to persons along the route but, at the same time, cause noise and fumes that disturb other residents. Improving service according to one or a few measures can result in poorer performance on other measures. If, as frequently happens, one aspect of service must be sacrificed at the expense of another, this should not be a matter of accident but should result from a deliberate policy decision related to local priorities. Thus, while all measures may not pertain directly to every decision, each should be considered, at least briefly, to identify the various ways citizens may be affected by changes in transportation services.

As noted earlier, the data collection procedures have not yet been field-tested and are neither detailed nor definitive for operating purposes. However, the general approach has proved useful for other local services such as recreation and solid waste collection. The authors hope that their tentative conclusions will assist local government and regional planning bodies as they attempt to improve their assessments of transportation service.

Current Measurement Practices

Of all public services in urban areas, transportation has

received the most attention from professionals and academics. Government at all levels, transportation firms, and public interest organizations develop and disseminate a wide variety of transportation data and analytical techniques. As a basis for this report, we reviewed the transportation measurement techniques currently utilized by local governments or proposed in transportation literature.

The statistics usually available to local governments include descriptive information on the transportation system, such as miles of roadway, number of vehicles, seating capacities of public transit modes, yards of road surface constructed, number of street signs installed, man-years of maintenance effort, and traffic volume on various routes.

Local government traffic departments also regularly measure traffic volume on local and arterial streets. In its simplest form, traffic volume is counted for a period of time, such as 24 hours. More detailed cordon counts are also sometimes conducted to measure the number, type, and occupancy of vehicles entering or leaving a city. Public transit agencies monitor passenger volumes on transit lines, especially when a change of schedule or route is contemplated.

Usually local governments and transit agencies regularly collect information on transportation-related accidents, injuries, and fatalities. Official schedules and routes of public transit generally are available from transit firms. Some firms also monitor factors which affect user comfort, such as cleanliness and noise of vehicles, but seldom do the governments monitor such information.

Some cities measure the speed of traffic flow on major arterials during peak travel periods. These data may be displayed on maps that show the distance it is possible to travel from a central point in various lengths of time. Travel time measurements may also be made for non-central trips, but this is not a common practice among cities.

Most measurements of travel time, traffic volume, and congestion are conducted in connection with specific proposed changes, for example, to compare congestion before and after the addition of a left-turn lane. Infrequent collection of such data does not enable them to be used for systematic comparisons over time.

Some metropolitan areas have access to increasingly comprehensive information on travel patterns as well as traveler behavior and mode preferences. Postcard or at-home surveys are conducted occasionally, but seldom on a regular basis, to ascertain attitudes of citizens toward available or proposed transportation services. Public transit surveys are apparently conducted infrequently, again, usually in connection with specific proposed changes.

To assess such factors as road surface condition, traffic control problems, and transit vehicle comfort, local governments generally rely on volunteered citizen complaints. A few state agencies occasionally measure road surface quality with mechanical devices, but local governments have not yet instituted this type of measurement.

The major deficiencies in current data collection practices for assessing the quality of local transportation services are:

• Data are not collected on some important effects of the transportation system on the community and on various neighborhoods and citizen subgroups. Among these neglected effects are accessibility, rider comfort, convenience, air and noise pollution, and general satisfaction as perceived by citizens.

• Many data, such as those indicating travel times, are not collected regularly or systematically to permit comparisons of facets of a transportation system over time.

• Citizen complaint information alone may give misleading signals. Reliance on this information is inadequate for program planning because it is not necessarily representative of community sentiment. People differ widely in their tendency to complain; some refrain because they do not know how to file complaints or because they believe their complaints would be ignored. Even to the extent complaint data could be useful, the information is seldom aggregated or systematically arrayed to indicate trends.

The effectiveness measures and data collection procedures in this report are intended to supplement—not replace—traditional traffic data or sophisticated transportation surveys and models. These are quite valuable. The additional recommended data are intended to correct the deficiencies just described, by providing information that reflects the impact of transportation systems on citizens. Such customer-oriented data should prove useful to those charged with local government transportation policies and programs.

Transportation Objectives and Suggested Effectiveness Measures

Setting Local Objectives

Intra-urban travel is rarely an end in itself. Rather, it facilitates satisfaction of other needs and objectives of individuals in the community. The general objective of local or community transportation services may be expressed as follows: *To provide access to desired destinations such as employment, shopping, and community services or facilities in a safe, quick, comfortable, and convenient manner for all population groups of the community without causing major harmful side effects.*

This overall objective can be further clarified in various formulations. One possible list of transportation objectives can be divided into six components:

(1) *Accessibility and convenience:* To provide residents of the community with reasonable access to an adequate choice of important destinations such as employment, personal services, and recreation.

(2) *Time:* To minimize or at least keep within reasonable limits the travel time between home and such destinations as for employment, personal services, and community facilities; and between community, commercial and government centers.

(3) *Comfort:* To make travel comfortable for the drivers and passengers.

(4) *Safety:* To minimize loss of life, injuries and damage to property resulting from travel within the jurisdiction.

(5) *Cost:* To minimize the financial cost to citizens of intra-city travel.

(6) *Environmental effects:* To avoid disrupting social and economic life or creating a less attractive living environment for city residents due to unintended harmful effects of transportation, such as noise and air pollution.

In most situations it will be difficult to achieve all objectives simultaneously. Thus their relative importance to an area is dependent upon the characteristics of a particular community—current performance of the local transportation system, citizen preferences, climate, etc.—and the judgments of local decision-makers.

Major Effectiveness Measures

The list below presents those measures that assess progress toward the objectives listed above. Each objective has one or more associated effectiveness measures. Each measure tests a different and potentially significant characteristic of the transportation system. As already noted, at any given point in time, or depending on unique community characteristics, all the measures listed are not likely to be of equal importance. For any given transportation decision, usually only a few measures are pertinent. However, all measures should be scanned briefly for possible relevance to the decision. Measures obviously relevant to a particular decision then should be examined in detail.

SUGGESTED MEASURES OF EFFECTIVENESS[a]

Accessibility and convenience

1. Percent of residents not within X minutes of public transit service or more than one hour from key destinations
2. Citizen perception of travel convenience

Travel time

3. Time required to travel between major origin and destination points
4. Congestion—duration and severity of delay

Comfort

5. Index of road surface quality ("bumpiness")
6. Citizen perception of travel comfort

Safety

7. Rate of transportation-related accidents: injuries, deaths, and property damage
8. Number of crime incidents related to transportation

Minimum cost to users

9. Cost per trip

Maintenance of environmental quality

10. Noise levels along transportation corridors and number of persons possibly affected
11. Air pollution attributable to transportation sources and number of persons possibly affected

General public satisfaction

12. Citizen perception of overall adequacy of transportation services

a. Major changes to a community's transportation system (creating rapid rail transit or substantial new road construction) would require consideration of additional measures such as the likely impact on the economic well-being and housing quality of the community.

At times, attempts to improve performance according to one measure may result in adverse changes by other measures. For example, an improvement that decreases the number of traffic injuries might result in increased travel times. Clearly, policy makers need to consider trade-offs among objectives when considering proposed changes, and then make use of the appropriate effectiveness measures.

Table 13-1 illustrates how data for measures of effectiveness might be summarized each year to form one type of status report for policy officials and local government managers. This summary highlights the comparisons between the quality of transportation service being received by different population segments and indicates changes over time. It presents measurement data for one clientele classification, namely neighborhood. Note that some of the measures (as in the case of Measure 4, "Congestion duration," which pertains to travel links) would not be classified by neighborhood.

Presenting an array of effectiveness data can highlight problem areas. For instance, by revealing a significant worsening of performance according to a particular measure from the previous year or a significant decline in performance for some neighborhoods relative to others, such a summary may indicate the need for greater government attention or reconsideration of existing policies. (Before remedial action is taken, of course, further analysis may be necessary to identify causes of the problem, to determine possible correctives, and to estimate the costs and effects of alternative solutions.)

As stated earlier, there is no automatic formula for identifying which measure or measures of effectiveness should be emphasized in a locality at a given time. This is ultimately a matter of judgment. The measures and procedures in this report cannot replace that judgment and should not be considered in that light. However, they can provide decision-makers with a better basis for arriving at their judgments. This may happen, in the first place, during

Table 13-1. Illustrative Summary of Annual Data on Selected Measures of Effectiveness

Measures of effectiveness	Category	I	II	III	IV	V	VI	VII	VIII	IX	Total 1971	Total 1970
1. Percent of residents not within 5 minutes of public transit service	Accessibility & convenience	27	32	38	7	23	78	18	45	19	26	29
2. Citizen perception of convenience (percent satisfied)	Accessibility & convenience	64	68	53	88	72	23	78	59	83	73	68
3. Average time required to travel between key origins and destinations (minutes) a) Public transit	Travel time	15	17	23	8	14	33	19	21	14	17	19
b) Automobile	Travel time	12	15	18	4	7	22	14	17	11	11	12
4. Congestion duration (minutes)	Travel time					Not applicable					80	72
5. Road quality index (percent of streets rated unsatisfactory)	Comfort	3	7	8	4	8	15	2	7	12	7	9
6. Citizen perception of comfort (percent satisfied)	Comfort	83	81	73	91	85	54	78	75	79	71	68
10. Noise levels (decibels - peaks)	Environ quality	48	45	50	40	55	75	60	80	75	60	56
Percent of households not owning an automobile[a]		31	23	15	53	11	5	28	3	34	20	22

a. This is not a measure of effectiveness. Instead, these data are intended to provide perspective on the degree of dependence on public transportation in each area.

the initial process when a local government makes the effort to spell out its own transportation objectives. Then, after choosing specific measures of effectiveness to match these objectives, the subsequent findings will form an orderly basis for seeing local conditions through an improved perspective. Community and citizen needs that currently may be overlooked or underestimated can then be given due consideration by officials before they assign priorities for further transportation developments.

PART THREE

CATALYSTS TO OUTPUT

HERBERT L. HABER

14 THE NEW YORK CITY APPROACH TO IMPROVING PRODUCTIVITY IN THE PUBLIC SECTOR

A discussion of labor relations involvement in productivity improvement requires some review and emphasis on several points:

First, while costs are rising about 15 percent annually, revenues are rising by only 5 percent. Even though labor's traditional position usually is "I don't give a damn how little money *you've* got, we want *ours*," responsible union leaders are well aware that the economic fortunes of their members are dependent upon the economic health of the employer.

Second, the taxpayer's revolt over rising municipal salaries and what he defines as poor services creates a climate in which the public servant feels defensive and, to say the least, unappreciated as a productive citizen.

And third, proceeding on the implications of the first two points, public employees see the handwriting on the wall: wage increases and even jobs are the inevitable victims of a budget squeeze and a failure of public confidence.

Reprinted by permission of Herbert L. Haber from his Address to the National Productivity Conference, March, 1973.

Increasing public employee awareness of these factors paralleled the Mayor's continuing moves to set the managerial stage for the productivity campaign in New York City. As a result, when we announced in December, 1970, that future wage increases would be conditional on increases in productivity, employee response was not *entirely* negative. This reaction was no accident.

Let us cover the steps toward developing this attitude and transforming it through productivity bargaining into reality.

What are the kinds of productivity that we bargain to achieve?

The most obvious, of course, is the kind most closely paralleling that in the private sector: increasing the number of units produced with the same or less time, manpower and resultant cost. This measure can be applied to such activities as garbage collected, equipment repaired, water meters read, potholes filled, inspections made, papers processed, buildings built.

Another kind of productivity increase that directly concerns employee representatives is the reorganization of service performance to eliminate or modify a program that has become traditional. In this category would fall revisions of response patterns to fire alarms and the conduct of welfare investigations by caseworkers.

Less obvious, but crucial in the public services, is the productivity that can only be measured in terms of *quality* of service offered; critical because service is municipal government's product. To the public, the way in which a service is provided—the speed, appropriateness and courtesy of the response—is often of greater importance than its cost efficiency. In pursuing improved quality of service, our major tool is establishing and enforcing performance standards; but in so doing we may have to depart from the private sector model in instances where the improvement in service may cost *more* but still be considered a necessary "productivity" increase.

Why Productivity Bargaining?

Having established the need for productivity and identifying some of the kinds of productivity on which we bargain, we come to the *how*—how do we achieve it? Why don't we just do it? Doesn't the control and responsibility of government operation lie wholly within management's ambit? Are not defining the mission of an agency or department and creating its operational tools processes entirely within the prerogatives of management?

Why, therefore, do we introduce these matters to the bargaining table? Why do we not cleave to a conviction of the sovereignty of government and make a stand with unilateral decisions and orders? Are we not risking our authority and ability to manage by permitting union involvement in the managerial process?

To take the last question first, yes, there are risks. But we believe they are justified and can be avoided or minimized. There are ways of approaching these subjects at the bargaining table that permit of their discussion without surrendering management's prerogatives. But why run these risks; why bargain on productivity at all?

First, we must face the impact of a century of history in labor relations and collective bargaining in the private sector, and a decade of developing strength among public employee unions. The reality of employees and their representatives as a force in governmental decision-making has, like consumerism, become a fact of life.

Second, the basic "product" of government is service; the essential ingredient in government service is people; and the ratio of people to product is enormous. Therefore, while technological improvement is important, involvement of people in any change process is critical.

How to involve them?

Of the 13 million people employed by government in the United States, 4 million are organized—2.3 million in unions and 1.7 million in associations, unions in fancy dress. More than a third of the nation's local and state government employees are union members. And in New York City, 95 percent of the city's 470,000 employees are organized by 156 different union locals into about 315 separate bargaining units. Obviously, it is helpful to use the employee organizations as a channel of communications, and hopefully, for involvement in change.

Third, there are certain practical restrictions on managerial control that have developed over the years, some of them in labor contracts that the courts imbue with the force of law. Although the city has made and continues to make efforts to reduce contractual encroachments on managerial prerogatives—a matter I will discuss more fully later—there still remain significant areas in which union concurrence is required before we can proceed. Also, attention must be paid to traditional work patterns that have emerged over time and that, in the minds of employees, acquire the force of law or become institutionalized as "past practice." Finally, in matters covered by legislation, amendments may have to be sought.

The fourth reason for productivity bargaining is that an understanding, cooperative attitude by employees and a willingness to accept and participate in new programs augur for effective implementation. I say flatly that without positive employee attitudes, the boss doesn't have a chance. There is no group of employees anywhere in the public or private sector that cannot succeed in disrupting operations even if only by strictly following the letter of their work rules.

To illustrate the point on the necessity of bargaining on productivity, I would like to quote two union officials who commented in the press last August on the Mayor's announcement of his productivity goals. An official of the city's largest union said: "Where there's no consultation, there's likely to be no cooperation. Where we're consulted first and a productivity program comes out as joint effort, we're more than willing to pitch in."

The president of that union's clerical local added: "We want to protect our members but we don't want to stand in the way of progress. We're not taking a featherbedding position."

Establishing Climate for Discussion

The first move in the journey to the bargaining table is to create an appropriate climate for discussions on productivity. It is crucial that employees learn early that productivity is not just another jargon word to make the employer look good in the media; the employer must establish without question that he means business.

To this end, we announced publicly in December, 1970, early in the round of negotiations now concluding, that the city was committed to the productivity course. In a statement I issued on behalf of the Mayor's Labor Policy Committee, we declared that "no salary increase is justified which is not necessary to offset inflation or is not tied to corresponding increases in worker productivity."

But even earlier, in the prior two rounds of negotiations, we had made clear to the unions that this was our long-range plan: that in the first two rounds, which began in 1966, we intended to iron out inequities and anomalies in the city's salary structure, and to move into the 1970s with written collective bargaining agreements for the first time in the city's history; and that once these goals had been achieved, the city was determined to move forward, hopefully jointly with the unions, toward increased productivity.

That is, any future wage adjustments would have to be

paid for by employees through commitments to more efficient delivery of services: increased productivity.

During the next two years, 1971 and 1972, we hammered constantly on the theme that bargaining is a two-way street; true give and take; not just that we give and they take. The traditional union attitude is that they make appeals to the employer to improve their wages, benefits and working conditions; but the concept of their working *with* management to improve operating procedures is unfamiliar and viewed as threatening and dangerous.

The best weapons in attacking these negative attitudes are *incentives* to agreement, as any experienced bargainer certainly knows. The primary incentive is, of course, money.

We were firm in our intention to make no wage adjustments beyond those justified by cost of living increases without agreement on productivity changes. Union negotiators soon learned that city wage offers would be severely curtailed unless they, and their members, were ready to cooperate in achieving the city's productivity goals.

Another incentive is giving unions an opportunity for input into productivity decision-making. For example, the union frequently can suggest alternative efficiencies that would be less difficult for employees to accept while accomplishing the city's aim equally as well.

And, in the parallel growth of union interest in job enrichment and promotional opportunities, members can participate in the creation of career development programs.

The union can also be offered involvement in working on the re-training, re-assignment, and protection of workers in cases where improved productivity leads to a reduction in the work force.

And a fifth incentive is, frankly, the chance for an improved image. Certainly, the taxpayer's current view of the civil servant couldn't be more jaundiced, and public employees suffer from their poor reputation. Given the public's serious concern, indeed despair, about the quality of government services, public employees can only benefit from whatever enhancement results from increased productivity.

Critical Prerequisites

Now, what about the risks to managerial prerogatives I mentioned earlier as being raised by these approaches. To minimize the risks, certain preconditions must be established. My conviction of their absolute necessity flows from the city's bitter experience that other jurisdictions would do well to heed.

The first necessity is the clear establishment of managerial prerogatives as non-bargainable matters that the employer cannot be forced to bring to the table. This is an imperative for the collective bargaining structure, whether or not productivity is an issue. Great care must be taken to avoid such ambushes as befell New York City in 1965 when an arbitrator imposed a welfare strike settlement giving the union, in effect, the right to veto top-level policy decisions. It has been a long road back from that settlement, as the city has doggedly worked—in three successive negotiations, involving two long strikes—to retrieve its managerial prerogatives from the welfare union.

The course we have pursued in the protection of managerial prerogatives is the establishment of three categories within the scope of bargaining—prohibited, mandatory and permissive.

Prohibited subjects are those where the obligation or duty is fixed by law, and a contrary agreement would be illegal.

Mandatory subjects such as wages and hours are those upon which the city is *required* to bargain. If agreement cannot be reached through negotiations, these matters are subject to determination by outside fact-finders.

Permissive subjects are those on which we cannot be required to bargain, but may if we wish. If agreement cannot be reached on *these* matters, they cannot be taken to fact-finding. Their inclusion in a contract does not convert them into mandatory subjects for a subsequent contract. The city may move to have the matter removed from the contract without making it subject to a grievance or arbitration.

Productivity bargaining unquestionably belongs in the permissive category. Since productivity is accomplished with management's tools, we must not be *required* to bargain on its terms. But we *do* want union cooperation for the reasons I have indicated. Failing cooperation, however, the city must be able to proceed unilaterally with its programs.

Our efforts to establish management's essential right to run the business may seem bizarre to representatives of government units that have not yet been confronted by strong union demands that encroach on management's rights. I say "not yet" seriously. The time will inevitably come. It came in the private sector; it came to New York City government and to other major cities and it will come to others in time.

Being one of the first public employers to be burdened with this issue, necessity has fostered invention. We are the first employer—I believe in either the public or the private sector—to obtain clear and strong contract language in which the union recognizes the need for productivity, and acknowledges management's right and commitment to secure it. The language appearing in our current major contracts is as follows:

Delivery of municipal services in the most efficient, effective and courteous manner is of paramount importance to the City and the Union. Such achievement is recognized to be a mutual obligation of both parties within their respective roles and responsibilities. To achieve and maintain a high level of effectiveness, the parties hereby agree to the following terms:

Section 1. Performance Levels

(a) The Union recognizes the City's right under the New York City Collective Bargaining Law to establish and/or revise performance standards or norms notwithstanding the existence of prior performance levels, norms or standards. Such standards, developed by usual work measurement procedures, may be used to determine acceptable performance levels, prepare work schedules and to measure the performance of each employee or group of employees. *For the purpose of this Section, the Union may, under Section 1173-4.3b of the New York City Collective Bargaining Law, assert to the City and/or the Board of Collective Bargaining during the term of this agreement that the City's decisions on the foregoing matters have a practical impact on employees, within the meaning of the Board of Collective Bargaining's Decision No. B-9-68. The City will give the Union prior notice of the establishment and/or revision of performance standards or norms hereunder.

(b) Employees who work at less than acceptable levels of performance may be subject to disciplinary measures in accordance with the applicable law.

Section 2. Supervisory Responsibility

(a) The Union recognizes the City's right under the New York City Collective Bargaining Law to establish and/or revise standards for supervisory responsibility in achieving and maintaining performance levels of supervised employees for employees in supervisory positions ... [the section continues as in Section 1 from the asterisk above].

The Board of Collective Bargaining decision referred to in the quoted language defined the term "practical impact" as an unreasonably excessive or unduly burdensome workload as a regular condition of employment. Whether or not a management decision has had such an impact is for the board to determine. If an impact is found, the city may act unilaterally to relieve it or may seek to relieve it through a negotiated agreement with the union. If an impasse is reached, a fact finder may make recommendations for relief.

The significance of the language is its clear delineation of an attitude, a frame of mind. Employees are put on notice that their union acknowledges management's right to define the job, judge the performance and hold employees accountable.

The fact that an additional section establishing the accountability of supervisors appears in the supervisees' contract signals the second critical precondition to a successful productivity program: the establishment of a management cadre.

One result of the original crazy-quilt certification of

bargaining units in New York before 1966 was the inclusion in some of these units of managerial-executive personnel. This has led to a situation in which all supervisors except those in the very highest echelon of management are union members and subject to collective bargaining. In the Police Department, for example, only 18 of the department's 31,000 members are not in the union; and in the Fire Department, only 22 out of 13,000.

The implications are obvious. Supervisors tend to make common cause with their employees and are subject to union discipline during job actions. Employees view their supervisors more as protectors and advocates than as enforcers of performance standards; and supervisors identify with their employees rather than with management. The contract language I have cited puts employees on notice that their supervisors—whether they are union brothers or not—cannot continue the cosy relationships of the past. For unionized supervisors, however, the road to appropriate managerial attitudes is longer.

Establishing a management orientation among top supervisors depends on the city's ability to exclude or remove them from bargaining units and to provide benefits commensurate with those they would receive as a result of collective bargaining.

We have, over the past five years, been petitioning the certifying agency (OCB's Board of Certification) to deny certification to units of managerial/executive personnel and to remove from certification those who were covered in the past. Our most recent submission involves high officials in the police and fire departments, but the decision is not expected for some time.

Insuring salary improvements is an even more difficult problem. The unilateral granting of wage increases to top officials places the city in a vulnerable position publicly when our fiscal plight is so well known and the erroneous view that city salaries are already high is so deeply embedded. The fact is, however, that we cannot expect managers to identify with management if they are making less than the people they supervise. And managers *must* identify with management if a productivity program is to succeed.

Having established our terms, intentions, and preconditions, we come to the table, ready for long, hard bargaining despite the long, careful preparation. Every productivity improvement required extensive discussion with the union or unions involved.

It is essential, of course, that the negotiator brings to the table clear, sharp specifics. Ours have been carefully designed by the Bureau of the Budget with the departments and we remain in close consultation with both budget and our operating departments throughout the bargaining process, involving them directly when appropriate.

Productivity Approaches

In our six major approaches to productivity improvement, there are labor relations aspects that become immediately apparent.

The classical approach is the introduction of more modern and efficient equipment: larger trucks in sanitation, improved communications devices, rapid water in smaller hoses in fire-fighting, more sophisticated computers in tax and welfare administration. Here changes in personnel deployment and training are necessary and require union cooperation. Employee apprehension about job safety and the fear of job loss through automation must be confronted.

A second approach is the rescheduling of hours and days of work. Establishing night tours for road crews; smoothing vacation and changing off-time schedules in sanitation so heavy work days have more manpower; rearranging duty tours in police, youth services, corrections and computer operations to achieve better coverage and use of equipment are examples with obvious employee impact.

A third productivity approach is the contracting out of

functions better performed outside the city departmental structure, usually for short-term projects. Eliminating work is of course a burning issue with employee groups and is a touchy matter for bargaining.

The development of increased productivity through the reorganization of an agency operation requires substantial, and continuing, employee involvement. Even the most carefully planned modification of ways in which employees have long functioned creates anxiety and, perhaps, physical disruption. These responses should be respected and certainly deserve discussion with employee representatives.

A major example of this, the separation of income maintenance and social services in the city's public welfare operation, brought radical changes to staff that have been continuously discussed for several years. Briefly, the approach was to analyze components of the caseworker's job, separate the two main functions of eligibility determination and service delivery, assign the former to clerical personnel, and retrain and redeploy caseworkers to provide services only. One result has been an increase in lower-salaried clerical workers, the attrition of college-graduate caseworkers and the requirement that they function on a more independent and challenging level. Particularly in this department, where union involvement is still often demanded—though not necessarily granted—in such matters as transfer policy, level of supervision and the like, the labor relations activity has been enormous.

A fifth productivity approach, the general tightening of employee adherence to time requirements, often involves upsetting arrangements that employees have come to regard as traditional. Enforcing time and leave rules, requiring full scheduled time to be spent on the job—such matters demand the exercise of supervisory and administrative responsibility. But because they trespass on employees' notions of hallowed past practices, labor relations attention is appropriate.

Finally, and probably most critical, is the development, establishment and enforcement of performance standards as they relate to both the quality and quantity of work. This approach is particularly open to union contention of practical impact and requires extensive discussion in order to gain union acceptance and cooperation.

Supervisory responsibility for meeting such standards also becomes a matter of contention. But the acceptance of the principle of disciplinary action for non-performers must be secured. It is in this area that the necessity for a management cadre becomes most obvious.

The establishment of standards and norms for performance is an empty gesture, a waste of professional time and, indeed, a farce unless adherence to those standards is enforced through a system of penalty and reward. Employees must have the evidence that failure to meet standards automatically means disciplinary action and performance beyond the standards is consistently recognized. Since it is only through proper supervision that such a system can function, every possible means must be sought to insure that supervisors identify with management's productivity goals.

Initiating productivity discussions with the unions in all these areas has eased the introduction of methods and programs that would inevitably have generated disruptive concern if introduced unilaterally. Even when the city must proceed over union objections, a union representative with prior notice and comprehension can at least respond to complaints from his members armed with knowledge and understanding of the moves being made, and a commitment that the union will continue to be alert and concerned.

As for the future of productivity bargaining, we are committed to continuing on the same path; making wage settlements that include a productivity return while staying within prevailing wage patterns. We will again notify our unions as we enter the new round of negotiations that we will not automatically offer wage and benefit improvements. Increases will continue to depend entirely on the city's ability to pay and the degree of productivity improvement employees can commit themselves to achieve.

We have had a reasonable degree of success in our productivity bargaining strategy so far; and after the experience of the past three years, I am more than ever convinced that collective bargaining is the most appropriate way to establish the terms and conditions under which government employees can provide improved public services.

WALTER L. BALK

15   DECISION CONSTRUCTS AND THE POLITICS OF PRODUCTIVITY

The traditional purpose of collective bargaining is to establish decision-making units that will maintain an effective balance of power between management and employees. Traditional objectives of productivity increases have been to demonstrate improved output for resources used. Along with the spectacular rise of membership in unions and employee associations in the public sector, collective bargaining and productivity have taken on increasing importance. Consequently productivity has recently become a central consideration in collective bargaining between New York State and its employees.

Technically, it is quite interesting to try to understand what government productivity is and how to bring about improvement within public agencies. Yet, most of us tend to accept industrial labor-management tradition and give scant attention to the "open system," or political influence processes that place constraints upon or encourage improvement. There is also a good amount of confusion regarding the conceptual underpinning of "productivity bargaining." One

---

Reprinted by permission of Walter L. Balk.

173

purpose here is to better understand the productivity improvement concern in the public sector and the meaning of the concepts involved. Another is to review recent history in New York State in order to analyze political influence processes in relation to the productivity problem. This suggests approaches which may have general application to a number of public sector collective bargaining problems.

Scarcity as a Core Assumption

The November/December 1972 issue of the *Public Administration Review* gives a good idea of the concern over the matter of government productivity. Improvement is perceived as fundamental to the success of the national economy. The public is depicted as filled with wrath at its increasing tax load and the wastefulness of bureaucracies. "Budget crunches" are seen as continuing, if not increasing, at every level of government. Aside from these harbingers of urgency, several interesting facts emerge. One is that the term "productivity" is highly elusive. Also, only in the past few years have any government agencies made any coherent attempt to communicate an overall economic sense of value received for their activities. An initial effort was started two years ago in the federal area at the bidding of Senator Proxmire when he found it "distressing that we have no real measures of the efficiency of the federal government." The result was an intensive study by the Office of the Controller General which concluded that (a) the measurable functions of public services were increasing "consistently and at a modest rate"; (b) there is considerable exposure to misusing productivity indices; and (c) a good deal of research must be undertaken to understand what is the nature of productivity problems.[1] In this same issue of the *Review*, the efforts of some city and state agencies are described. Yet the conclusion is that the efforts of state and local governments, representing 80 percent of all government employees (about 10 million persons), are largely unmeasured.

This is not to say, of course, that everyone is in accord with and supports the idea of measuring and trying to improve government productivity. Some see the current efforts as a type of "Taylorism revisited."[2] The line of reasoning is that public agencies are not factories turning out hardware. Productivity studies, they feel, tend to emphasize heartless efficiency and an obsession with quantity rather than with quality or social mission. Suppose you are doing something poorly, they say; being more productive means you only continue to do more of the same inadequate work. Another attack is that the social consequences of increasing productivity are often ignored. Why should we find ways to lay off government workers in times of high unemployment? Finally, some feel that the emphasis upon increased efficiency is misplaced as a social priority because the first consideration should be to better distribute the resources we already have. These arguments are interesting and worth pursuing, but here I will take the position that there is a critical need to gather facts about the efficiency and effectiveness of government operations and take cost improvement action. The reason for this is that all societies are faced with the necessity to make intelligent decisions about the generation and allocation of scarce resources. In most cases this affects the arrangement of people, materials and equipment in large public agencies created to satisfy social needs. Hopefully, productivity studies will make it possible to better know when and where these resources are being well managed and mismanaged. In some ways productivity knowledge may serve as an integrating force between the state and its employees. In other ways it can help demonstrate that some elements of the public sector deserve public support, thus blunting the efforts of some of the regressive forces in our society.

The core assumption in the perceived necessity to study

and improve productivity is that of a continued, overall and generalized scarcity of resources. As already mentioned, some see the affluence of this nation and cannot accept the ideas of general scarcity. Thus, the key issues are not productivity-oriented but, rather, ones of distribution. Without minimizing the seriousness of the gap between the well-to-do and the poor, it appears that the basic assumption of an overall, increasing scarcity of government resources is valid. As an example, even in the short run, numerous cities (e.g., New York) appear to have no clear way out of their financial crisis. Political leaders at all levels, purportedly responding to public backlash, are drastically curtailing government spending—or at least announcing their intent to do so.[3] The longer-run, world-wide scarcity problems that should increasingly impact our society do not seem to be diminishing. It is difficult to envision the more developed countries, with a fraction of the world's population, continuing to consume about three quarters of the available resources. There is also increasing recognition that there are limits to the exploitation of the planet and that people must exist in a symbiotic manner with nature's environment. The point of all of this is that productivity—or how to do more with less—is likely to be a sizeable and continued concern of society in as well as out of government.

What Is Productivity?

Economists have used the term "productivity" to relate the quantity of goods produced to the quantity of resources used. Another common definition is "real output per hour" of work.[4] Neither of these descriptions is practical for many analysts attempting to improve government productivity because of the emphasis upon units of tangible output (quantity) at the expense of the *content* of output.

A more fruitful way to understand productivity is to

consider it as a process. Any large organization, public agencies included, can be considered as a converter of resources, from one form into another. In this manner we can conceive such factors as money and manpower (input) being turned into "services" (output). Intellectually, this chain of events can be called a production process. Productivity consists of two sets of relationships. The first is called efficiency, and the other effectiveness. Efficiency is the relationship of *quantity* and *content* of output to input. Basically, if the relationship can be established, it answers the question, "What is 'the public' getting for the resources being used?" Effectiveness is the relationship of output to goals or desired standards of quantity and content of service. This helps answer the question, "Is what is being produced living up to the expectations of the public?" Output, then, is central to any concept of productivity. One goes about improving productivity by increasing the quantity and/or content of output by:

- Rearranging timing, flow or position of work elements (working smarter)
- Increasing individual and group effort (working harder)
- The use of new materials and equipment (technology)

But there are great difficulties in understanding "output." This depends upon the ambiguity of the tasks being performed.

For example, key punching operations are highly programmed. Quality is controlled by the card verification operation. In this case, scientifically engineered standards can be set for the job that define the "normal" amount of output per operator. One can, therefore, say that the productivity of a keypunch operation is the number of cards punched and verified over a period of time compared to engineered standards of output. In other words, quantity of cards produced per working hour is an adequate productivity statement because standards and quality factors are controlled (assuming that the costs of overhead, materials and equipment are held constant). But few tasks in government are as programmed as those of keypunch operators.

The more usual situation is one in which a group of employees contributes to a product, for example, vehicle registrations. In this case, multiple operations by different people are required in order to issue licenses. This is different from key punching in that the tasks are more interrelated and complex. Therefore, efficiency and effectiveness must be measured by looking at the output volume and output quality of the group as compared to desired standards of accomplishment. The process is considerably less incremental and scientific than is that of engineered standards; therefore, the data is less "hard" or reliable, even though it has decision-making utility. (Other examples of group effort are rehabilitation counselling, ward attending and highway maintenance.)

Finally, there are a number of operations for which output volume, or units produced, has little or no significance. The performance of a legal staff function cannot generally be gauged by the number of cases handled. A public relations effort cannot be evaluated by the number of pages of copy sent to the press. In each of these cases, content is the essential indicator, and ways must be found to express this as some type of standard of accomplishment against which performance is gauged.

It is apparent, then, that the specific nature of any given set of tasks determines the appropriate type of productivity measurements. In most public sector cases, it is impossible to obtain a full, rational, engineered indicator of the productivity situation. Therefore, employees must contribute to the analysis and development of information. This becomes increasingly vital since, as tasks get less programmed and more complex, our information becomes more subject to being misinterpreted unless we know what assumptions are being made as the data is gathered and evaluated.

Another major factor in the consideration of productivity is that of time. Short-run gains may result in long-term losses.

Short-run losses are often essential to long-run gains. To illustrate the first condition, people can be motivated to work at a fast, unnatural pace for a short period of time; however, this can result in a general lowering of quality and quantity because fatigue may cause a drastic loss of productivity at a later time. Considering the second condition, it is usual, when introducing a new computer system, to overlap the old and new systems for a period of time. This insures control while working out the problems of introduction. During this period efficiency drops, but the long-term advantage of the computer will be felt at a later time.

It is interesting to note that many explanations of the intricate term "productivity" apply to either government or business activities. However, business has an analytical advantage when it goes about understanding output in that its production has a market price. Therefore, even in the service industries, there is a sense of monetary value, or demand for the product which can be compared to the value of other outputs. Business managers, as we know, also have a decision-making advantage in that they report to a small group of policy makers who have a more narrow perspective of what is a favorable output result (i.e., profit, competitive advantage) than do policy makers in the public sector. Unfortunately, a number of people, including some government employees, fail to understand these crucial differences. In their eyes, every public agency is, indeed, a paperwork factory manned largely by malingerers and incompetents who only require a good dose of business-style management to shape them up. (There are also, of course, outstanding problems with business controls. The dysfunctional consequences of performance measurements have been dealt with in organizational literature at some length.[5,6] Industrial relations experts also recognize that there is little specific attention in negotiations given to techniques and plans to measure and increase plant productivity.[7])

In summary, the conceptual nature and measurement of productivity in the public sector is a highly complex and technical matter. Ambiguity of tasks frequently puts severe limitations on all-inclusive scientific investigation and unilateral evaluation of work by "management." This means that employees must become intimately involved in the design of the more ambiguous work and the measurement of results, including the long-range and short-term consequences of attempts to bring about change. All of these factors are a crucial part of the setting between government administrators and employees when they go about improving productivity.

Three Constructs of Governments and Their Employees

Influence processes and decision outcomes depend upon how those involved perceive events. Three paradigms, or decision constructs, will be used in the following analysis. These are derived from Graham Allison's book, "The Essence of Decision."[8]

We can think of a set of rational actors engaged in productivity bargaining, in which "the government" is a unitary actor dealing with its "employees" as the other actor. Each has a set of specified goals that are pursued through rational choice after benefits and costs have been determined for each party. Each is strategically attempting to maximize its benefits and minimize its costs. This, essentially, is the conventional adversary model of management and employees in collective bargaining in which "each party tries to maximize its capacity to inflict costs upon the other."[9] One consequence of using this paradigm is that the public interest is perceived as identical to that of management, or the government, or the state. For, after all, taxpayers foot the bill and are, in effect, stockholders. And it follows that it is to the advantage of the public to get more productivity out of its employees. While there is some surface utility to this way of perceiving "the" problem, it does not readily lend itself to the resolution of productivity issues. One reason is that it implies employees are generally nonproductive, and reinforces some unfortunate attitudes against public employees as a category. The major reason, however, is that it is basically an adversary model that assumes a common understanding of concepts, a clear delineation of facts and a common agreement of output. Hopefully, the point has already been made that concepts, facts and definitions of output are extremely difficult to arrive at in many government operations. When the world is perceived in a unitary style without pertinent and essential facts, each side is liable to concentrate upon strategies of manipulating the other. The outcome may or may not have anything to do with actually bringing about increased productivity.

A second manner in which to perceive productivity issues is to think of the actions of government and employees as organizational output. This involves subdividing "government" into various units such as legislatures, executive offices and public agencies, each with differing outputs, goals and constraints. Employee organizations are considered as composed of bargaining units with differing reward systems. "The" public consists of diverse constituencies. One advantage of this method of analysis is that it gives proper attention to parochial priorities and perceptions along with the administrative feasibility of change. Action is not emphasized as a matter of limited choice and strategy, but rather as incremental behavior with various alternatives. While it can lead to more constructive resolution of issues, the problems in using the paradigm for policy purposes are ones of complexity as well as accessibility of information to those affected.

The third method of analyzing productivity decision-making is to consider key actors, strictly as individuals engaged in bargaining and exchange. Again, parochial priorities are taken into major account, but these seem as more dependent upon the gratification of individual needs rather than associated with the nature of organizational output. Pressures of the job, deadlines and personality characteristics are given attention by the use of this model. In this way different events may be better accounted for. One limitation to the construct is that it is difficult to get at the essential data. The process of power and exchange between political actors tends to be culturally covert. Society appears to value policy and action if it is "rational" and independent of the personalities involved. Therefore, since actors are not prone to discuss or volunteer information, much of this has to be inferred by the analyst.

Allison states that the above constructs are like "alternative pairs of spectacles" that facilitate the generation of hypotheses and help in the analysis of problems. The reason is that they ask different sets of questions. The first approach (unitary actors) is concerned with defining the problem, and considering broad alternatives as well as strategic costs and benefits. The second (organizational output) considers the organizational components of the problem, their different ways of doing things as well as their potential constraints upon implementing change. The third paradigm (key actors) specifies which positions are centrally involved, the characteristics of the actors and the nature of deadlines which force issues to resolution. The models are commonly concerned with the processes of influence (or "politics"). They complement each other and deal sequentially with broad context, organizational routines and leadership.

Some psychological aspects of these ways of perceiving issues are of interest. The unitary actors construct appears to have advantages when long-term policy is generated. In order for people to have a "vision" of what is ahead, they must stereotype and do violence to the complexity of the world. However, when it is necessary to *implement* change, the organizational output and key actors' paradigms have utility in that they enable analysts and actors to conceive of short-run actions which may be consistent with the "visions" of the unitary actor construct.

The next section is an attempt to review some recent events in New York State using the above paradigms as an analytical device.

Some Events in New York State

Almost 190,000 positions are under the direct jurisdiction of the New York State Department of Civil Service. Of these, about 70 percent are represented by the Civil Service Employees Association (CSEA), which is divided into four major bargaining units. (Associations historically differ from unions in that they (a) usually include a high number of professionals, (b) prefer broader groupings of employees rather than the narrow bargaining units favored by unions, (c) include supervisors and (d) generally reject the strike in favor of political pressure and lobbying.[10] Admittedly, these distinctions have become more blurred with the passage of time.) Negotiations are conducted on behalf of the government by the Director of the Office of Employee Relations who has the responsibility for conducting collective negotiations with recognized or certified state employee organizations.

During the years 1971 and 1972 the state went through a particularly severe budgetary crisis. The result was that thousands of employees were laid off by the state. In the aftermath of these traumatic events, an act was passed in April, 1972, under the provisions of Article 14 of the Civil Service Law that permits negotiations between the executive and state employee organizations for programs of productivity improvement.[11] A major proviso is that a 1½ percent bonus will be paid in April, 1973, "conditional upon agreement between the executive branch and the employee organization being reached upon criteria and procedures for the measurement of savings resulting from such program of productivity improvement and criteria and procedures for allocation of such savings." Agreements for productivity improvement programs, procedures and criteria for measurement and "allocation of savings resulting from such programs" must be submitted to the legislature and authorized by law. Finally, all increases of salary and compensation, based on time in service, are subject to negotiation.

The next development, in June, 1972, was the writing of an article in a contract between New York State and the Civil Service Employees Association.[12] This stated that the actors "agree on the need for cooperative efforts toward increasing productivity in state operations, thereby providing improved efficiencies and service to the public and job enrichment and economic benefits arising from such improvements to employees." A joint committee was established to study and seek agreement upon such things as increased flexibility in work assignments, working hours and a four-day work week. Attention would also be given to charging tardiness against leave time, job security and the establishment of a 40-hour work week. (The present work week is 37.5 hours.)

A statement in the contract (Article 8, Section B.7) stated that the joint committee would study

> criteria and procedures for measurement and criteria and procedures for allocation of savings resulting from implementation of proposals. . . . Such allocation shall include 25 percent for across-the-board adjustments in compensation for all employees; 25 percent bonus for those units and employees who most contribute to productivity improvements and 50 percent for the state.

A close examination of the proposed study items show that all are *means* for helping to improve productivity. They have to do with either distributing load, increasing input, time controls or motivation. There appears to be a conclusion that their impact can be measured. This is a very tenuous assumption, since measurement depends upon an agreed-upon definition of *output*. As already mentioned, there are sizeable technical and conceptual barriers to the finite measurement of work in the public sector. The kind of measurements employed, along with their validity and reliability, depend upon the ambiguity, or complexity, of the tasks being performed. This is not to say that work with a high ambiguity content cannot be evaluated; but there is no doubt that bringing about productivity improvement in these tasks requires a common investigation and understanding of the origins and meaning of evaluative data between managers and the employees. In turn, improvement cannot occur without a high degree of flexibility, risk-taking and mutual trust. Therefore, a basic problem was that the contracting parties did not clearly agree to study the nature of the work involved, nor the measurement of output. Precise allocation of "savings" was also considered. Of course, it is impossible to know if improvement has occurred without a knowledge of increased output in quantitative or qualitative terms. In addition, how is each case of increased productivity to be judged as to the impact of employees? For example, let us say a new computer system is installed. Are the gains, when measurable, to be attributed to employees because they cooperated in the installation? Or is this a management change for which employees can take no credit?

The establishment of a joint committee was a response to working out legislative intent. The group addressed itself to short term means to increase productivity. The problem was that there was no clear recognition of the centrality of knowing more about output. Expectations may have been raised for the imminent possibility of sharing savings. There could be no solid, rational basis for this until "output" was defined along with the perogatives of administration and employees. Predictably, then, if the committee members had no common referent as to what productivity was and in which cases "credit" would be given to employees for improvement, each side would deal in broad strategy. Negotiations would proceed on purely an adversary model. Each side would attempt to pressure the other to its perceived advantage with a minimum of common understanding of the situation. While some of this is inevitable in any negotiation, the scene was set for a minimal concern with productivity improvement and a maximum attempt for short-term bargaining advantage as an objective in itself.

The next development was in December, 1972, at which time a supplemental agreement was signed with CSEA.[13] It is a rather unique document in that a major section (Article 2) is devoted to what might be called a philsosphy of measurement of productivity. This reviews some of the basic problems of measurement, controls and motivation. Section D states:

> The State and CSEA reaffirm their commitment to the need for improved efficiency in state operations. A cooperative effort in this area is likely to provide improved service at reduced cost to the public, together with job enrichment and economic benefits arising from such improvements to state employees.
>
> The determination and measurement of output should be a first area of concern. Without reliable and objective criteria for the measurement and evaluation of output there can be no meaningful efforts at productivity improvement. This task will not be an easy one and requires the mobilization of resources within the state and a review of experience in the private sector.

The contract, then, goes on with another unusual provision. In Article 3, both parties agree to jointly employing (expenses to be shared equally) a consultant who has the responsibility

- To provide research data on the present state of the art concerning productivity data in both the private and public sectors
- To develop an inventory of New York State services and functions to determine which services and functions are measurable and the appropriate method of measurement
- To provide research data concerning methods of solving problems of job security related to productivity
- To recommend output criteria.

The contract was the basis for the consideration by the legislature of a 1½ percent increase for all state employees. What we now must ask ourselves is, how good are the prospects for productivity improvement to occur as a result of this chain of events?*

Interpretation of Events

Using the unitary actor paradigm, we perceive three principals in the decision-making process. The first is the legislature, which indirectly defines the public interest. It posits that discontinuing the automatic nature of time-in-service increases and trying to replace these by wage adjustments backed up by improved productivity are to the public benefit. The allocation of some of the savings gained as a result of productivity improvement back to the employees is considered as having favorable motivational aspects. In fact, the legislature feels strongly enough about this to consider a 1½ percent bonus if management and employees agree upon a general improvement program. The working out of a joint plan to increase productivity is left to the traditional adversaries, management and organized employees.

These rivals met and at first made a contractual agreement which does not appear to face some of the dilemmas of measuring output of work. A subsequent agreement was reached which (a) clearly states the nature of mutual dependence of management and employees, (b) recognizes the complexities of measuring productivity, and (c) takes positive action to start an inventory of the measurement of state agency functions. Hopefully, then, future negotiations will occur based upon mutually understood facts.

Turning to the second mode of analysis, organizational

---

*Editor's note: A few months after Dr. Balk made this study, the matter of mutual investigation of productivity factors by employees and New York State management was abruptly dropped at the suggestion of CSEA. This demonstrates how threatening and loaded with uncertainty productivity issues can be for employees.

output, it would appear that the executive branch is not a unitary concept. While bargaining is focused through the Director of the Office of Employee Relations, "the" output of public agencies involves that of a multiplicity of large bureaucracies ranging in degree of work ambiguity from that of the Department of Motor Vehicles to the Department of Mental Hygiene. The operating style and goals of each vary markedly. Each department is convinced of the urgent priority of its mission which, in turn, is substantially affected by size of input, or operating budget. While increasing productivity (assuming this can be proved) can have a return for employees, what are the advantages to management and administrators? Unlike in business, there is no direct reinforcement or reward system to public bureaucracy management for increasing productivity. In times of tight resources, if an agency announces a million dollar savings in year one, the chances are that it will be cut from the budget in year two. Generally, it appears that agencies gain their major advantages by strategic abilities involving prediction and timing, such as responding to perceived needs of constituencies, carefully gauging what the executive wants and how to influence legislators; emphasis upon this by top administrators currently brings more rewards than the difficult, anxiety-provoking and minimally rewarding efforts to clearly define agency goals and output. Apparently, the productivity bargaining fact base will depend upon the close cooperation of agency management. The cooperation required is that of creative involvement. It is difficult to force this by threat or sanction. What will be needed are institutional incentives or reward systems involving agency managers for making productivity improvements.

The employee association is also not a unitary concept when viewed in this second mode of analysis. CSEA, for example, consists of four bargaining units (Administrative; Institutional; Operational; and the Professional, Scientific and Technical Services Unit), each with a different type of output. The association has an identity problem in that it is seeking to show improvement for all of its members, while satisfying the particular needs of each unit. (Regarding labor organizations, Raskin says they are "comprised of members with a conglomeration of conflicting and common interests. A gain to one may involve a loss, or preclude a gain, or distant past relationship with another."[14] It would appear that the same reasoning applies to the legislature as well as components of the executive branch.)

Pacing salary improvement to productivity increases raises a paradox since one of the classical objectives of employees in a bargaining unit is parity for its members, just by virtue of paying dues and being represented in the union. Therefore, the Association could be placed in an awkward position if small groups within a unit are differentially rewarded for productivity improvement. A more serious problem is that of job security. An employee organization cannot be expected to join in an effort that will cut its members out of jobs. If productivity "savings" are perceived by elements of the public, by legislators and the executive as cutting back on the total number of government employees beyond normal attrition, then the prospects for cooperative productivity bargaining on the part of the employees' representatives appear very dim, indeed.

Legislators form coalitions with differing goals, outputs and exchange arrangements. While "keeping costs down" can be perceived as an abstract, desirable goal in the public interest, it is the specific translation into productivity action which will present dilemmas. Such tensions of "cost cutting" for specific programs are already evident in legislative budget negotiations, which is only on the "input" side. Also productivity improvement action requires a sophisticated knowledge of the general nature of the output problem, long-term investments of legislative resources and time as well as the restructuring of some basic institutions. For example, consider the question of job security. It is conceivable that productivity improvements could result in no need for several thousand existing employees in agency A while agencies B and C have to hire people with different qualifications. Retraining the surplus people in agency A could require a large investment. In addition, Civil Service job classification systems might inhibit such flexibility, calling for a change in legal environment. The question remains if legislators will organizationally be motivated to engage in such complex and long-term effort in order to ensure eventual improvements in efficiency and effectiveness.

Finally, there is the viewpoint of key actors in which players occupying central positions are involved. These, in the case of state productivity, are key legislators, the governor, the director of employee relations, employee association officials, public agency executives and consitituency leaders. The players are linked and clustered by a maze of ongoing exchanges of concrete and emotional resources such as information, status, services and interpersonal attraction.[15] These emphasize short-run decisions, deadlines, past stances, and immediate pressures that encourage the stereotyping and broad categorizing of decisions. Yet the effect of productivity studies and action is to differentiate situations, especially in terms of the ambiguity of employee tasks and long-term solutions. Again, the question remains open if the key players will be motivated to adjust and restructure their perspective and present exchanges in order to improve the long-term productivity of government employees. Their problem will be one of tolerating the lack of unilaterally derived, totally scientific knowledge of productivity in government, supporting long run action at the expense of short run decisions and modifying past stances.

To summarize, it appears that improvement of productivity in government is very much dependent upon political factors in the environment of public agencies. An effective, comprehensive approach will require major changes in policy, institutions and vested interests of decision makers.

Toward Government Productivity Policies

The New York State case is interesting in that it suggests a way to generally approach the improvement of the productivity of government operations. One sequence could be:

- Definition of the resource scarcity situation
- Orientation of major players in the political environment
- Definition of the public interest
- Passage of motivating legislation
- Contractual agreements with employees
- Fact gathering
- Development and revision of institutions

To consider the first point, while the existence of resource scarcity is evident, several problems remain in integrating and understanding the situation. Some reconciliation has to be made with the point of view that recommends improved distribution as *the* priority problem, to the exclusion of scarcity considerations. The long-term prospects and limitations of tax loads need to be more clearly made. This will have a connection with the national economy as well as voter attitudes. In turn, the nature of resource scarcity requires better definition. Since government operations are "labor intensive" by nature, and no shortage of people is foreseen, why is there a feeling of long-run scarcity? The answer at present centers around finances and the economy. But how does this extend into the long run?

Assuming that the case for scarcity can be made in an integrated fashion, then this has to be communicated to policy makers, or "key actors" in the political environment. This includes, as already mentioned, people in government, employee associations and constitutency groups. They will have to be oriented to better understand the fundamentals of productivity. This would include some knowledge of the process, how this differs from business orientation, and a recognition of the limitations of our knowledge as agency tasks become more ambiguous. Programs should be seen as evolutionary, long-term chain of events that will entail the major revamping of some institutions. For example, it is difficult to conceive of steady improvement in productivity without more stable and longer-term budgeting commitments in order to do more effective planning.

The next step would be to generate a statement of public interest. As has already been mentioned, the interest of business in productivity is quite specific and understandable since it directly ties into the concept of profit and the national economy. A counterpart must be developed in the public sector. This should include a recognition that *content*, or social significance, of work, is frequently more important than the volume of output. Part of the statement should highlight the importance of job security for capable government employees in terms of providing a dedicated population of civil servants. Also, it would appear that the viability of rewarding civil servants for increased productivity would be a central theme, with the stipulation that all increases cannot be matched by an equal increase in pay. There are two reasons for this. The first is all increases will not be attributable to employee action. The second is if each increase in productivity was matched by an increase in salary to employees and managers, then the net result would be a zero increase. It will be important not to raise the expectations of the public unrealistically. Recently, for example, the United States Civil Service Commission announced that it will embark on a program to develop a "new performance evaluation system that will measure the productivity and effectiveness of each federal employee."[16] Such a move appears doomed to failure. Not only is there a dearth of techniques to measure individual performance, but the movement leads away from broad productivity improvement since it will take away effort from group improvement in order to generate detailed, uncontrollable, centralized paperwork and promises to water down the authority and responsibility of immediate management to improve performance results. Emphasis upon *group* results is often a shortcut to increased performance. The Civil Service effort forces attention upon individuals.

Motivating legislation is necessary since it begins the implementation of statements of public interest. It should include, as did the New York State laws, provisions for joint councils of management and employees with the responsibility to generate approaches to the improvement of productivity along with devising criteria for the measurement of output. A bonus incentive to encourage an agreed-upon plan appears desirable as well as the retention of legislative control over future patterns of agreement to reward employees for productivity increases. The legislation should clearly state that it is the responsibility of individual agencies to develop output criteria and relate these to productivity data. The reason for this is that it will (a) strengthen the management-employee improvement function, (b) develop a more rational setting for productivity negotiations, and (c) increase the ability of the legislature to make budgetary allocations.

When contracts are written between the executive and government employees, the necessity for joint investigation of the meaning and generation of productivity data should be emphasized. In the case of New York State, the equal sharing of the expenses of a consultant was tangible evidence of this intent. Care should be taken to recognize that the rewarding of employees for savings involves having definite knowledge about output and the part employees play in bringing about productivity gains. This should lead to tolerating an evolutionary approach rather than prematurely and abstractly trying to decide how to divide productivity profits.

The sequence of scarcity-recognition, orientation of policy makers, statement of public interest, legislation and evolutionary contract negotiations should help generate pertinent facts. From these can be derived the necessity to change major, existing institutions in order to bring about productivity improvement. Some possible changes have already been mentioned such as establishing management rewards, changing job classification systems, commitment to long-term budgeting and the emphasis upon the development of criteria by agency management. Most fundamental is the possibility of going from an adversary model of collective bargaining to a more collaborative model. In order to do this, a less punitive atmosphere will have to be created, in which numbers and data are used to bring about improvement rather than locate malefactors. This means finding ways to reward rather than punish. (A prime example of a non-rewarding system is that of mandatory, across the board decreases. This tends to limit cooperative, creative management-employee action which could result in higher savings.)

A good number of applied scholarly research prospects have been implied throughout this chapter. One of the first priorities is to find better methods of gauging agency output so that this incorporates the more ambiguous tasks. Ways have to be devised that emphasize content of work and social mission as well as counting the numbers of units of things people do. In this general vein, understanding the degree of task ambiguity and relating this to appropriate management climates should provide an immense return.

How to go about changing institutions based upon the nature of influence and exchange systems will have to be explored. The basic questions of what is the public interest in productivity improvement, and what is the nature of scarcity, require a good deal of intradisciplinary research.

Specific ideas might crop up. For example, if "the public" is the equivalent of "stockholder," does it not merit the equivalent of individual, corporate statements from public agencies? As another example, it is often said that immense numbers of public employees just sit around with nothing to do, leading lives of quiet desperation. Could some institution-alized way be found for these people to find worthwhile employment without branding them as trouble-makers? As a third instance, it appears that the very term "productivity" turns people off.[17] This probably because of associations with sweat shops and with what is seen on the part of employees as punishing action by management. So is there a possibility that an entirely new set of concepts and language can be devised for the public sector that will better free those involved from past associations?

In conclusion, there exists a tremendous opportunity to investigate the question of productivity improvement in government. The task will be to do this in an innovative and humanistic way, retaining the essential cumulative knowledge while freeing ourselves of outmoded or, if you will, "unproductive" perceptions.

JOHN W. KENDRICK

16 PUBLIC CAPITAL EXPENDITURES AND BUDGETING FOR PRODUCTIVITY ADVANCE

Having helped to spark the initial pilot study of productivity in selected federal government organizations,[1] it gives me particular pleasure to see the successful completion of the new interagency study of productivity covering more than half of the 1.56 million man-years employed in civilian functions by the 17 participating executive agencies.[2]

The measurement of past productivity changes has value as a background for budgeting and longer-term projections of resource requirements and costs within organizations. But I believe that productivity measurement is even more important in increasing "productivity-mindedness" and focusing management thinking on ways and means of cutting real unit costs and thus enhancing productivity advance in the future. Accordingly, I was pleased that the Joint Project report gave equal billing to measuring and to enhancing productivity. This chapter deals with one of the chief means by which productivity is raised: by investments in new and improved

Reprinted from *Measuring and Enhancing Productivity in the Federal Government*, Summary Report, Joint Federal Productivity Project, 1973.

capital goods, chiefly structures and equipment, and by the "intangible investments" associated with tangible outlays.

Although output per man-year increased at an average annual rate of 1.9 percent in the measured government functions between fiscal years 1967 and 1971, a bit more than the increase in the private economy, this is no reason for complacency. The private economy rate was affected by a slowdown after 1966, reflecting in part, at least, the retardation in economic growth and the cyclical contraction of 1969-70. The secular trend-rate (since 1948) of growth in real private product per man-year is close to 3 percent, well above the figure shown in the joint project report. Accelerating the rate of advance in public sector productivity will enable the public to obtain more services for the same resources, or the same level of output for fewer resources, or some of both, than would otherwise be the case. In this era of heightened sensitivity to the tax burden, heightened productivity-consciousness on the part of public administrators is very much in order.

The Concept and Measuring of Productivity

The broadest and most useful concept (and measure) of productivity is one in which output is related to *all* associated inputs, in real terms—labor, capital, and purchased materials, supplies and outside services, combined (weighted) in proportion to their relative costs in a base period. Such a "total productivity" measure reflects increases in productive efficiency as a result of net savings in real (constant dollar) costs per unit of output.

Increases in productive efficiency over the long run largely reflect cost-reducing technological advances. Technological advance in the first instance stems from investments in research and development designed to develop new and improved producer's goods and processes, and from investments in the tangible capital goods in which the improvements are embodied. Also important are the "intangible" human investments, particularly in education and training, not only to prepare the scientists, engineers, and managers who make the inventions and innovations, but also to train the work force generally to operate the increasingly complex technology.

Other forces also affect total productivity. In the short run, changes in rates of utilization of capacity, and the speed with which an organization adapts to, or "learns," new technology are important. Also, there may be various internal and external economies of scale. But my own research, and that of others, shows that the most important factor influencing productivity over the long run is investment, both tangible and intangible.[3]

"Partial" productivity measures, which relate output to one class of inputs, usually labor, are affected by factor input substitutions, as well as by changes in efficiency. The partial measures are also useful in revealing the unit savings achieved in the particular class of input, and the labor productivity measures are particularly useful since labor is generally the largest single cost item, particularly in the services sectors, private and public. But I am pleased that the federal interagency study group plans to attempt to measure non-labor inputs and productivity during the second year of the project, in order to get at net savings in total unit real costs. A reduction in total unit real cost, may, of course, be associated with an increase in current dollar costs per unit of output, to the extent that price increases of the inputs exceed the productivity increases—which is generally the case.

Unit Cost-Savings and Capital Budgeting

The unit cost aspect of productivity advance is particularly

important from the viewpoint of budgeting capital investments for productivity advance. That is, the cost saving (or
the net increase in revenues or the value of services rendered
in the case of capacity expansion) resulting from new
investments can not only amortize the initial outlays for the
capital goods by the end of their lifetimes, but can also yield
a net return on the invested capital equal to or exceeding the
interest cost. To state it differently, the present value of the
expected future income stream resulting from cost-savings (or
increased revenue), discounted at an appropriate rate, should
equal or exceed the cost of the capital goods.

This may be expressed in terms of the familiar formula, in
which V = the present value of the capital good, R = each
year's additional revenue due to cost-savings or increased
value of services rendered, i = the interest rate, and n =
number of years of economic life of the capital good:

$$V = \frac{R_1}{(1+i)} + \frac{R_2}{(1+i)^2} + \ldots + \frac{Rn}{(1+i)^n}$$

If the present value of the capital goods exceeds its cost, then
its purchase is justified. In the alternative statement, instead
of V, one enters C, the capital cost, and solves for the rate of
discount (r, which replaces i in the formula), which causes
the future R's to equal C. In this formulation, if $r > i$, then
the investment is economically justified.

There is quite a literature on the appropriate interest
(discount) rate to use in estimating present values of public
investment. There is not space to treat this issue, and it
remains controversial in any case. I personally believe that
the long-term interest rate at which the federal government
borrows is too low; rather the opportunity cost of capital

employed in the private economy, as reflected in the average rate of return on new investment, would be more appropriate, since I believe that public investments should generally yield as much as private.

Private firms typically go through a systematic capital-budgeting exercise involving the sort of analysis just outlined in deciding which proposed investment projects to include in the capital budget. Capital budgeting is usually confined to tangible investments, although a similar type of analysis should also be applied to the intangible investments in R & D, and education and training. Even though these outlays are generally charged to current expense, they are also investments in that they increase income over a number of future yearly accounting periods.

It should also be noted that the accounts of private firms include the depreciation and interest charges on the tangible investments, as well as maintenance and repair, as current costs. This is important, since it is the net saving in all costs, including capital charges, that must be taken into account in the decision to make productivity-increasing investments. If the investments are judged to be economic, then it is perfectly appropriate to finance them by debt (or new equity issue in the private sector), as well as by retained earnings (which could otherwise be used to reduce debt), since the return would both amortize the debt and cover the debt-service, and possibly also yield an implicit "profit" or "surplus" to the government.

In the federal government, however, even tangible capital outlays are budgeted and accounted for as current expenses, and they are financed from current revenue. To the extent that the government uses debt financing, it is not linked to productive capital outlays, the returns to which will cover interest and amortization (which *should* be charged to current account); rather, increases in debt are linked to deficits in the balance between revenues and total expenditures of both a current and capital nature, with no direct relationship to the latter.

Deficiencies in Government Capital Review
and Budgeting Procedures

The lack of a capital budget in government, and the related practice of not charging capital costs to current expense, have several unfavorable consequences. In the first place, it is my impression that proposed internal agency investment projects (as distinguished from public works and other investments designed to enhance the productive capacity and efficiency of the total economy) are not universally subject to a systematic review procedure designed to establish their economic desirability, according to the criteria outlined above. In fact, not only should rates of return be computed on proposed projects, but an organized procedure should be developed to uncover possible capital outlays, either for replacement of, or additions to, existing stocks of capital, which would appear to have a high enough return to qualify for review. I should add that proposed public works and other investments designed to enhance the social infrastructure are generally subjected to some kind of cost-benefit, or rate-of-return, analysis. Such investments are far more important, in aggregate, than the internal, productivity-enhancing investments which are the subject of this chapter.

Secondly, the charging of capital outlays to current expense and their cash financing out of current revenues probably reduces the volume of internal investment below that which would be economically justifiable, particularly in years of budgetary squeeze resulting from executive or congressional pressures for "economy." The Joint Project report adduces various examples of proposed investments with short pay-out periods and presumably high rates of return being shelved due to such pressures. In many cases, the capital outlays are cut out during internal agency reviews in order to hold total spending within ceilings established by the agency and the OMB. In other cases, capital items are often the first casualty of cuts in congressional appropriations and new obligational authority. That is, current expenses necessary to carry on the functions of government organizations get the first call on limited funds, even though the rejected investments would more than pay for themselves in cost-savings over their lifetimes and provide a return on the capital in excess of its cost. It seems clear that it would be desirable if productive, economically justified public investments could be specifically and directly financed by borrowing. This is accepted as sound private industry practice; it is no less so in the public sector.

Third, the absence of capital budgeting in government may lead to more costly methods of obtaining the capital services.[4] The alternatives in certain situations are leasing, renting, or lease-purchase; and contracting with private firms for goods or services (such as computer services) which would by-pass the need to acquire certain capital goods. Obviously, the annual rental of capital goods, or the annual payments for capital-intensive services, would be much less than the capital outlay itself in any one year. But in many cases where the alternatives are available they would be more expensive over a period of years than the costs associated with agency acquisition of the capital goods. The point is that with capital budgeting and financing, government agencies would be free to decide, as do private firms, whether it is more economic to make the capital expenditure, or obtain the capital services by the alternative means.

Finally, government accounting practices do not charge annual capital costs (depreciation plus actual or implicit interest on accumulated net investment) to current expense and therefore do not properly reflect the total and unit costs of producing various types of services. It thereby becomes difficult to estimate cost-savings that have resulted from given investments. Omission of current capital charges (as distinct from capital outlays) also makes it more difficult to estimate total productivity, which includes capital input (i.e., real capital charges) in addition to labor and intermediate inputs.

Recommendations

As a result of the above considerations, I make the following recommendations:

• A systematic procedure for developing cost-reducing innovations and related investment projects, and reviewing the economic rationality of such proposed projects, should be instituted within all federal government organizations. The Office of Management and Budget could aid in developing procedures and establishing criteria for selection of new investment projects.

• Agencies and existing revolving funds should have separate capital budgets for both internal investments and investments designed to increase the capacity and/or productivity of the outside economy. It should be accepted practice to finance these outlays through borrowing, unless budgetary surpluses on current account should make possible to some extent internal financing (or debt repayment in advance of full amortization).

Because of traditional opposition to government capital budgeting, the Joint Project Report recommended that a "productivity bank," or other special fund, be created to finance projects with high potential for increasing productivity and thus cutting costs of governmental operations. As outlined in the report, there are some advantages in financing through a specialized fund of this type, rather than through the general borrowing power of the Treasury Department. Unless the capitalization of the "productivity bank" were adequate, however, it could perpetuate underinvestment within the government.

The bank, or fund, should also, of course, be empowered to invest in general obligations of the federal government in case its loanable funds exceeded the justified demands for capital financing by federal agencies. Representatives of the OMB should sit on the board of the bank or fund, since it would, in effect, take over a small portion of the budget review function now exercised by the office. Since the new financing agency would be a creature of Congress, the ultimate authority of Congress is not at issue.

If the bank idea works well for financing internal investments by public organizations, the concept might be extended to public works, as well.

• The interest and depreciation (or amortization) charges on agency investments, which would be paid into the bank or special fund, should be carried as a current expense of the agency. This would bring government cost accounting more closely in line with private practice, and permit better estimates of total productivity and cost-savings resulting from investments that promote technological advance.

• Post-investment audits should be made by all government organizations and spot-checked by the General Accounting Office to determine whether the anticipated cost-savings were in fact realized. Such post-audits should help improve investment-review and capital budgeting procedures as experience is accumulated.

I am convinced that the basic ideas underlying this chapter are sound. But the precise forms of possible institutional implementation will require some further research, and, above all, further creative and innovative thinking. The National Commission on Productivity is in a position to play a key role in formulating final proposals to Congress in this area. The final task of securing legislation incorporating the proposed institutional changes to facilitate productivity-enhancing public investment will require some creative politics!

17 IMPROVING PRODUCTIVITY THROUGH CAPITAL INVESTMENT

Another area of interest to the joint productivity team principals was the role of capital investment in increasing productivity. New and improved capital goods—and the research and development and education and training required to create and use them—is estimated by leading economists to have contributed from about 40 to 60 percent of the productivity increase in the private sector.

Because of the important role capital investment plays in productivity improvement, the principals asked the joint productivity team to study the need to facilitate capital investment in equipment and facilities that will increase Federal employees' productivity.

Scope of Study

The joint productivity team's first year's work indicated that there were several disincentives to the timely acquisition of equipment and facilities that would increase productivity and that many agencies were having problems financing such acquisitions. To attempt to establish the nature and magnitude of the problems, the team asked 10 cabinet departments and five independent agencies to provide information about their experience in obtaining funds for labor-saving equipment and facilities. These 15 organizations were asked to provide lists of the equipment and facilities for which funds had been obtained or of those for which funds had not been obtained. In reporting unfunded projects, the agencies were asked to list separately (1) the existing backlog of projects that had been proposed for inclusion in the budget and (2) any projects that may have been identified but for which funds had not been requested through official budget channels.

In reporting projects, agencies were asked to report only labor-saving equipment, facilities and systems costing over $10,000 and which are self-amortizing within five years. The Department of Defense limited its response to projects over $50,000.

The joint productivity team also made on-site studies at selected agencies to compile a list of unfunded opportunities identified by the agencies for investments in equipment or facilities whose cost could be quickly recovered through savings and to study agency capital investment programs. (This work was primarily accomplished for the Joint Project by the Norfolk Region of the General Accounting Office.) An engineering study was arranged at two activities to test for the existence of profitable investment opportunities that had not been identified by activity personnel.

Inventory Results

Of the 15 departments and agencies asked to provide data, nine responded with information on funded projects and 10 provided data on unfunded projects (but the data for two were incomplete and were excluded). Four reported no problems in financing productivity-increasing projects and one was excused from participation.

The joint productivity team did not verify the inventory results reported by the agencies, but it scrutinized the supporting information provided for each unfunded project and excluded projects not meeting the $10,000 and five-year pay-back criteria. The results showed that funded projects for fiscal years 1972 and 1973 were $347 million and $276 million, respectively. The reports also showed that 392 projects estimated to cost $242 million had *not* been funded. These 392 projects would produce recurring annual savings of $66 million and some $62 million in one-time savings. One-time savings arise, for example, from the use of better handling and storage methods that permit a one-time reduction in inventory levels.

Table 17-1. Plans for Funding Unfunded Projects

	Number of projects	Estimated cost	Pay-back period (years)
		(000,000 omitted)	
Funding expected in 1973	29	$ 17	2.6
Deferred or included in future budget plans	338	220	2.8
Not budgeted	25	5	1.4
	392	$242	2.7

Although the cost of unfunded projects is substantial, the joint productivity team believes this figure is far lower than would be the case if government organizations were actively searching for areas in which additional investment could improve productivity.

To test this belief, the joint productivity team engaged a team of engineers from AMETA to visit two government installations (one defense and one civilian) to look for such opportunities. In a matter of a few weeks they identified five projects estimated to cost $590,000 that would produce annual savings of about $362,000. The joint team believes that, if each agency adopted an active program, such opportunities might be several times those identified by the survey.

The difficulty of financing productivity improvements seems to have been a factor in stifling the initiative of many organizations to identify such opportunities. An illustration of how available funding can stimulate money-saving investments is provided by the Army. (The Army plan was developed by Mr. Eckhard Bennewitz, Deputy Assistant Secretary of the Army [Financial Management] in conjunction with the Army Materiel Command.) The Army gave one of its subordinate organizations $400,000 to finance fast pay-back investments. After seven months, this money had stimulated investments of $286,000 from which the Army estimates it will realize savings of $1,100,000 during the first full year the new equipment and facilities are in use. Agency officials believe that most of these projects would not have been initiated without this approach, and the savings have reportedly inspired one or two of the local plants to express a desire in hiring an industrial engineer to help identify additional money-saving investment opportunities. Some examples of the items funded follow:

• Acquisition of a $25,000 clothes dryer to replace a manual drying tunnel procedure should save $50,000 a year by reducing the need for laundry employees from 12 to seven.
• Acquisition of a $38,200 heavy-duty nailing machine for making pallets is projected to permit a 20-man reduction in carpenters and an estimated annual saving of $241,000.

Improvements Needed Relative to
Agency Capital Investment Programs

During on-site studies, the joint productivity team concluded that the capital investment programs of most of the agencies visited needed significant improvements. Based on discussions with officials from the participating agencies, and in view of the large backlog of unfunded projects and potential unidentified projects, the team believes that other agencies may also need to adopt more aggressive programs for seeking out and implementing profitable projects. Specifically, the team believes there is a need for:

- Greater visibility to be given productivity-increasing investments.
- Increased emphasis on identification of productivity-increasing projects.
- Improved credibility of productivity investment programs.

Need for Increased Visibility of
Productivity Investments

The team sees increased visibility as one of the most important ways to improve the competitive advantage of productivity investments because it is believed that the cost savings associated with such investments will permit them to attract a greater share of funds on their own merit. Therefore, visibility is needed from the lowest management level within an organization up to and including final authority for fund approval. Under current budget procedures, investment proposals are commingled and agencies can not readily determine how much is budgeted or spent for such projects or the number of proposed projects that have not been funded.

A simple first step in providing this visibility is to classify investment proposals by primary purpose; for example, health and safety projects, pollution abatement projects, and productivity-increasing projects. Such classification not only provides separate identification for productivity investments, it also provides information to management which will permit a meaningful evaluation of competing types of investments and it identifies investments for possible special funding. To provide visibility to upper levels of management, such a classification system could be incorporated in agency budget submissions. Or, if separate identification were limited to productivity-enhancing projects, it could be accomplished by providing a separate line item in agency submissions as is done for automatic data-processing investments.

Need for Increased Emphasis on Identification of Productivity-Increasing Projects

A well-staffed centralized organization oriented toward the identification of productivity-improving investments on a continued basis is considered the key to a good capital investment program.

Only one of the activities visited by the joint team had a centralized staff and few of the activities appeared to be well-staffed with qualified personnel to do a thorough job of investigating all of the potential investment opportunities for increasing productivity. In most activities visited, the investment programs were add-on duties and efforts in identifying profitable investments seemed to coincide with the budget cycle.

The lack of qualified personnel was attested to by many of the activities visited by the team; in fact, headquarters officials responsible for the equipment programs at eight activities told the team that the shortage of personnel (engineers) was more of a restrictive factor in acquiring productivity-enhancing items than the level of funding.

As previously mentioned, the benefit of having qualified personnel devoted to identification of profitable investment opportunities was demonstrated on a very small scale by a special experiment made for the joint team where a team of industrial engineers conducted a systematic study at two government activities to test the need for capital investments to increase productivity.

The joint team observed that management of the activities visited tended to rely on operating personnel for identification of investment needs and that the primary emphasis was on replacement of isolated items of deteriorated equipment and facilities. Increased productivity did not seem to be a primary motivation factor. Although the activities, in most instances, were preparing cost-benefit analyses that showed self-amortizing savings, it seemed that they were justifying the projects primarily on the basis of being needed "to get the job done" and that increased productivity or cost savings was a secondary consideration. It did not seem that investments in productivity-improving items were being made as part of a deliberate means to achieve specific cost reduction or productivity-increasing goals (a practice we found quite prevalent in the private companies we contacted). From our discussions with participating agencies, this seems generally to be the prevailing approach in most Federal activities.

Need to Improve the Credibility of
Productivity-Enhancing Investment Programs

Continued support and funding, both by the organization and higher management levels, for an aggressive investment program directed at increasing productivity is seen by the team as being dependent on the credibility of the investment program and its results. The joint team identified two major areas where improvements can be made to improve such credibility: justification of projects and feedback on completed projects.

(1) Justification of projects. Good investment decisions depend, in large part, on the adequacy of project justifications; adequate justfications depend on good cost-benefit

analyses. A good analysis is needed to evaluate competing projects on an equal basis, to rank them in order of priority according to economic desirability, and to permit post evaluation of the actual results.

The joint team generally found that the activities visited had little or no documentation to support proposals for projects and that the cost-benefit analyses were often poorly prepared. Contributing to the inadequate justifications were:

- A general lack of emphasis on preparation of cost benefit analyses.
- Inadequate training.
- Lack of basic management data.
- Inadequate review.

(2) Feedback of information on completed projects. Feedback of information on completed projects is essential to establish whether the projected benefits were achieved and for identifying problems in an organization's investment system. Without reliable supporting evidence, acclaimed investment benefits will become suspect. Follow-up of implemented projects was virtually nonexistent in most agencies visited by the joint team. This appeared to stem from a lack of appreciation by managers of the value of such information, the lack of a system to generate the necessary data for such follow-up, and the absence of requirements for follow-up.

Basic Problems in Financing Capital Investments

Under normal federal budget procedures, virtually all capital investments are financed on a cash basis. Purchase of capital assets often requires large initial cash outlays that can impose significant demands on available budget resources. This is referred to by managers as the "lumpiness problem." In this financial framework, the usually high initial outlay required can often result in deferral of capital investments.

Since agencies usually can fulfill their missions without investment in productivity-improving technology, there is a strong tendency to allocate their limited cash resources to the requirements imposed by new workloads and legislative mandate. This potential for deferral of capital assets is further increased by the fact that the life of existing capital assets can often be extended by spending only slightly more for maintenance or by simply letting the assets deteriorate. Thus, in competition for cash resources, capital expenditures tend to receive lower priority than operational requirements and productivity-enhancing investments receive the lowest priority of capital expenditures. Since the budget is developed in a bottom-up fashion, productivity projects often lose out in the competition for budget dollars at relatively low levels in the organizational structure.

The long budget review cycle limits opportunities for increasing productivity. It not only delays the realization of the potential cost savings but also often reduces the amount of the savings. Even worse, it tends to discourage formal submission of self-amortizing projects. In fact, the inventory results contained numerous investments that could have been acquired and installed and the cost recouped within the time spent awaiting budget review and fund approval. This often takes as much as two years or more.

In view of these basic funding problems, efforts to increase the competitive position of self-amortizing investments need to elevate the level of funding consideration and to reduce the high initial cost impact and the long budget lead-time. Elevating the level of funding consideration could be accomplished by separately identifying internal productivity-enhancing investments in budget submissions.

Reducing the high initial cost impact and the long budget lead-time would require the use of either lease or lease-purchase arrangements or a special financing arrangement.

Since lease and lease-purchase are accepted forms of financing in the federal government, the team devoted its efforts to evaluating special financing techniques.

A large number of possible special financing techniques could be adopted. The team evaluated only four: (1) capital budget-borrowing, (2) a "productivity bank," (3) revolving funds, and (4) decentralized omnibus funds. As mentioned previously, use of a decentralized omnibus fund has proven very successful in one Army command.

The team does not feel that any one method of financing self-amortizing investments is best suited for all agencies. An agency's choice should depend on its individual circumstances. The team suggests that immediate efforts be directed at elevating the level at which decisions on fund allocation for such projects are made and at adopting budget and financing arrangements that will reduce the long budget lead-time, since these can be more easily accomplished. Use of decentralized omnibus funds, such as that used by the Army, is suggested as a proved means for reducing the long budget lead-time. Lease or lease-purchase can be used, when appropriate, as an immediate means to reduce the high initial cost.

Should experience prove these arrangements inadequate, long-range goals should focus on adopting financing arrangements that will provide more flexible and direct means for reducing the high initial cost impact. The productivity bank is suggested as the most desirable and useful arrangement for financing self-amortizing investments that will reduce the cost of government operations.

18 PROCEDURES FOR IDENTIFYING AND EVALUATING INNOVATIONS

This is part of a study that was aimed at the development and testing of procedures for identifying and then evaluating potential innovations that are currently being tried out in at least one local government.

Findings on the Search and Evaluation Procedures

(1)   There does not currently exist an adequate mechanism in the United States for:
• Identification of existing local government innovations
• Their thorough evaluation as to productivity potential
• The rapid dissemination of such findings to other local governments throughout the country.
(2)   Professional urban administrators rely on a rather vast but ill-defined and incomplete network to bring to their attention new approaches and new ideas.

Reprinted from *Improving Productivity Measurements and Evaluation in Local Government*, June 1972, prepared for the National Commission on Productivity by the Urban Institute and the International City Managers Association.

This private network consists of people whom the administrator is comfortable with and through experience has learned that he can rely upon. These personal networks are valuable in discovering and assessing technical innovations. While there is no doubt that this system will continue to operate, the inherent lack of scope and depth certainly has prompted administrators to look elsewhere for information on innovations.

(3) Some formal dissemination mechanisms for innovation do exist. Among these are certain federal government programs, state and local government programs, public interest groups, functional professional associations, national, municipal and professional journals, and the newly formed Public Technology, Inc.

(4) The typical published material in professional journals and national municipal magazines is lacking in adequate evaluation data, including full cost, favorable and unfavorable effects, and social and institutional implications.

(5) There is a considerable lack of readily available evaluative information on the innovations examined.

Data on both total costs and effectiveness impacts were inadequate to evaluate the innovations properly without extensive effort—more than available to this project.

(6) In none of the cases examined had attempts been made either by the local government or some other organization, such as the federal government, to provide for evaluation before the innovation went into effect. The lack of such preplanning precluded extensive "before" versus "after" comparisons of innovative programs. However, in a few cases, federal agencies supported evaluations after the introduction of the innovation.

Yet even in these instances, much was left to be desired in the way of adequate cost and effectiveness information, especially that which would be relevant to other governments.

(7) While the lack of control groups and preplanned

evaluation precludes isolating all of the variables in a case study, after-the-fact evaluation still seems useful.

(8) Despite considerable interest among local government managers in municipal productivity, an indication of the undeveloped state of the art is that there is no agreed-upon definition of municipal productivity.

(9) There is little uniformity in the type of measurement data presently collected by municipal jurisdictions.

(10) Because citizens are the recipients of municipal services, citizen feedback should be included in productivity measurement. Local governments have few systematic mechanisms to obtain and sustain citizen feedback.

Findings Relevant to the Specific Innovations Evaluated

Twelve solid-waste collection and thirteen police function potential innovations were identified in the initial phase of this work. From these, six were selected that seemed to lend themselves more readily to a one-to-two-week evaluation and that appeared to be of most interest to other local governments, assuming that their impact on productivity proved favorable. Their inclusion in this study does not necessarily mean that the innovations had resulted in increased productivity in the subject cities. Following are our findings based on the abbreviated evaluations.

(1) Nonmechanized, one-man refuse collection in Inglewood, California, has resulted in a 33 percent reduction in manpower while the city has experienced a 55 percent increase in the annual tonnage of refuse over a 10-year period. Also, productivity in tons per man now increased 100 percent. This increase in productivity has compensated for part of the rising cost of labor.

(2) The Bellaire, Texas, and Scottsdale, Arizona, one-man mechanized, containerized collection systems have reduced

the collection manpower force and have resulted in a potential lowering of the cost of collection service in each of those communities.

(3) The two computer-assisted solid-waste collection systems evaluated in Wichita Falls, Texas, and Baton Rouge, Louisiana, both claimed savings—one in cost, the other in manpower. However, the data presented was not sufficient to fully substantiate either savings. The equalization of employee task assignments in both communities, however, has had a beneficial impact on employee morale.

(4) The use of nonprofessionals in the Dallas police department is closely modeled after the recommendation of the President's Crime Commission. There is no clear indication that the program has actually resulted in a cost reduction for the department. However, the program has increased the number of minorities in the department by 15 percent.

(5) The evaluation of use of helicopters in Operation Skyknight in Lakewood, California, and air support to regular operations in Los Angeles points up the requirement for additional research in order to estimate the full cost and effects of such programs. Apparent substantial crime reduction was reported for both these tests—but at substantial cost.

(6) The Kansas City, Missouri, police department originally used the manpower resource allocation system to predict peaks in calls for service and design differentially manned beats. With an increase in police manpower, the department shifted to even manning and appears to be using the prediction capability of the system for tactical deployment only. A serious drawback in evaluating this program has been the lack of response time data. A closer analysis of the arrest rates before versus after the implementation is also required.

Recommendations

Major recommendations are presented below.

(1) It is recommended that the federal government and the state and local government public interest groups encourage and sponsor the development of a three-phase process:
- identification of possible local government innovations
- thorough evaluation of each and its potential effect on productivity
- provision for the rapid and effective dissemination of the evaluation findings to other local governments in the United States. The procedures outlined in this report can be utilized in this process.

Not all new ideas or new technology will increase productivity. Thus, dissemination of purely descriptive information on new ideas *without thorough evaluative information* would have the danger of encouraging further waste. Potential innovations to be examined should include not only hardware-technological advances but any type of program that may contribute significantly to productivity—including management systems, software, procedural changes, motivational programs, variations of existing programs, etc.

(2) The evaluation of potential innovations should emphasize: (a) all relevant costs; (b) impacts, both intended and unintended, both beneficial and negative; (c) impact on productivity based on the information obtained in (a) and (b); (d) implementation problems likely to arise in other governments including legal, political, personnel, labor management relations, etc.

This evaluation should attempt to translate the cost, effects on productivity, and problems in the innovating jurisdiction into the likely costs, effects, and problems in other potential implementing jurisdictions.

(3) Special approaches, such as the use of technology transfer teams, regional workshops, and mixed media, should be tested as means to rapidly and effectively disseminate the findings of the evaluation. This would provide an added spur to innovation in local governments.

(4) Local governments should be encouraged to collect relevant data on costs and effects to improve their own

evaluation and analysis capability to evaluate their own programs.

An important component that is lacking is a formal method, such as citizen surveys, for obtaining citizen feedback.

GEORGE A. GUSTAFSON

19   MANAGEMENT-TYPE AUDITING

Much has been written and spoken about a type of auditing often called "operational audits," "functional audits" or "management-type audits."

The terms are synonymous.

This type of auditing can be defined and illustrated by contrasting it with the more conventional financial-type auditing, sometimes referred to as fiscal or administrative auditing.

Conventional definition

The art of recording, classifying and summarizing in a significant manner and in terms of money, transactions and events which are, in part at least, of a financial character, and interpreting the results thereof.[1]

Expanded definition

The work of assembling, analyzing and interpreting the essential dollar-and-cents information about the

Reprinted by permission from the *Internal Auditor*, November/ December 1970. Copyright by the Institute of Internal Auditors, Inc.

operations of an organization; to supply the facts and the interpretations which the organization must have in order to plan and control its operations effectively.

The expanded definition (see above) does not emphasize procedural record-keeping functions. It accents operations. A description of management-type auditing, as contrasted with financial-type auditing, can be cast as follows: Management-type auditing means the auditor goes beyond financial controls into operating areas. While financial-type audits look only at the history of transactions, management-type audits aim to improve future business operations.

The scope of management-type auditing goes beyond accounting, financial and compliance matters. It also focuses on operations to determine if they are carried out in an effective, efficient and economical manner. To accomplish these objectives requires going behind the accounts into non-accounting areas and beyond accounting records, analyzing and interpreting results of operations in terms of fundamental business policies and procedures and relating expenditures to the accomplishments.

An example of going beyond accounts and accounting records is the selection of one significant operation (or several related operations), obtaining background information, and analyzing, evaluating and reporting the findings. Inquiries which might be used in an audit questionnaire are:

• How were operations planned? What justifies these particular plans? Are there more effective and efficient methods which might be used?

• What objectives are to be accomplished? Why are these objectives chosen? Are there alternative objectives?

• What procedures, practices and processes are relevant to achieving these objectives? Why were they selected? Are there more effective and efficient methods?

• What were the results of operations planned in relation to defined objectives? Why were (or why not) they considered satisfactory?

If operations are included in the audit scope, it is evident the concept of internal control should also be broadened to include operational efficiency as well as accounting procedures. The management control chart (Table 19-1) indicates objectives of promoting operational efficiency and adherence to prescribed managerial policies and procedures. Additionally, objectives of providing accurate and reliable data (accounting control) and safeguarding assets and other resources (internal check) are included.

The table groups the components of internal control and the related principles under organization, accounting, reporting and review. Expansion, of course, is possible. Internal control comprises not only the organizational structure but also the development and implementation of management policies, administrative regulations, manuals, directives, decisions, internal check, internal auditing, reporting, employee training, etc. A relationship exists between all components. They apply not only to accounting and financial departments, but to all other departments of an organization. Viewed in this manner, and accepting the argument that internal control is a function of management, the components can be designated as "management control."

Audit Standards and Procedures

It is generally conceded that management is primarily responsible for the substance and accuracy of financial statements and that accounts reflect the financial condition and results of operations. Generally accepted guidelines have been established for financial-type audits. These include auditing general standards, field work and reporting standards and audit procedures.

Auditing standards deal with the quality of auditor performance that might be viewed as professional policies. Additionally, they relate to judgment exercised in the audit and subsequent reporting.

Audit procedures relate to work to be performed and the method for accomplishing objectives. Failure to apply the procedures where practicable and reasonable should be considered in the reporting process. Table 19-2 compacts and classifies these data.

Achieving efficient, effective and economical operations is also a basic management responsibility. In both profit and nonprofit operations, costs can be related to work accomplishments. Results can be evaluated in terms of budgeted and actual costs and in relation to planned objectives. Efficiency and productivity can be based on work standards and budgets.

Formulation and implementation of auditing standards and procedures for management-type auditing is also important. Since the scope of management-type auditing is an extension of conventional auditing, auditing standards and procedures previously mentioned also apply.

In management-type auditing, the internal (management) control over operations should be studied and evaluated to determine reliance and the extent to which audit testing procedures are to be restricted in discovering and evaluating apparent weaknesses and reporting on conditions found, together with the appropriate conclusions and recommendations.

In all cases, two very useful standards are that the work should be sufficiently *intensive* to assure validity and usefulness of findings; and sufficiently *extensive* to support opinions, conclusions and recommendations. In this connection, we might expand on Robert Mautz's article[2] that grouped audit techniques, such as physical examination, confirmation inquiry and examination of documents under three kinds of evidence, namely: (1) real (physical) evidence; (2) testimonial evidence; and (3) indirect evidence.

We might add a fourth evidence category called "analytical evidence," which might be thought of as applying (in management-type auditing) analytical or verificational techniques to information obtained by physical, testimonial and indirect evidence; for example, comparison of prescribed standards with results of actual operations.

The auditing procedures important in management-type auditing are testing the control system and focusing attention primarily upon apparent weaknesses in management policies, procedures and practices. This is often referred to as management-by-exception. The criteria are effectiveness, efficiency and economy of operations. They apply to management decisions including, of course, financial matters.

Naturally, audit procedures vary with circumstances. The auditor should determine whether the operational policies, procedures and practices are generally satisfactory, weak or wasteful. By examining organizational structure, plans, policies, methods of operation, and use of human, physical and financial resources, the auditor should be able to evaluate, at least in summary manner, management's 3 E's:

- Effectiveness—accomplishing goals selected after considering the alternatives.
- Efficiency—accomplishing goals by incurring the least cost, in terms of resources.
- Economy—eliminating waste, extravagance and duplication.

This approach applies to most management decisions, including: (1) evaluation of how well management is using equipment, money and other resources (such as adequate use of EDP equipment); (2) whether physical facilities are planned to meet operational requirements (such as adequate and approved feasibility and application studies prior to acquiring EDP equipment); and (3) soundness of selecting the most profitable methods of selling the product.

Rationale of Management-Type Auditing

The objective of management-type auditing is "to improve future business operations." To accomplish this, the auditor must examine the organizational structure and its components, plans and policies, methods of operation and the use of human, physical and financial resources. Essentially this evaluates management's 3 E's in using the methods, procedures, equipment, people and money at its disposal to carry out objectives.

Critics of management-type auditing have questioned whether engineering, production, purchasing, research and other diverse operations can be realistically evaluated by auditors with accounting and financial backgrounds. Their inquiry has centered around the accountants' competency to examine these highly technical areas. It is this author's opinion that an auditor does not have to be an expert in a field to raise significant management questions about how operations in a field are being conducted.

Robert N. Anthony's discussion is germane:

> The approach to conventional accounting used here is something like that used by an airplane pilot in learning to use his instruments. The pilot needs to know the meaning of the message conveyed by each of his instruments . . . that the flashing of a red light probably means that a certain part is not functioning. . . . On the other hand, the pilot does not need to know how to design airplane instruments, how to construct them, how to check them for accuracy, how to maintain them, or how to repair them.[3]

Similarly, an auditor does not have to be a construction engineer to determine facts and ask questions that will lead to reasonable, sensible conclusions on an operation's soundness. Common sense, alertness, imagination, initiative, inquisitiveness, persistence, sensible degree of skepticism, objectivity and an educated curiosity will enable the auditor to probe for apparent weaknesses and report on conditions.

The following citation is also in point:

> A number of auditing departments are currently conducting a broad program of operational audits without having engineers or other experts on their staffs. In technical areas they direct their reviews largely to the question of administrative controls, and avoid any appearance of attempting to appraise the end products of functions for which they are not technically qualified. . . . For example—in an organization preparing engineering specifications, the auditor can ascertain whether there is a prescribed system of reviews and approvals and whether they are made promptly, whether the work is being scheduled to meet requirements, whether the working papers or source material used are adequately indexed and filed for future reference, and whether the specifications are written in such a way as to be readily understood by the users. . . . A large portion of common sense, the ability to ask intelligent questions and the administrative viewpoint are much more pertinent qualifications than techincal education in any particular field.[4]

The basic approach in performing management-type audits is accumulating evidence and asking questions about management decision-making. As Eric Kohler remarked over a generation ago, the auditor studies management and observes the interplay of relationships between organizational units. He notes business policies that emerge at different levels. How do they originate? How are they given expression? Who is responsible for their operation? Who follows up, enforces and reports on them? How are they periodically reviewed and coordinated, if at all, to top management?[5]

In many cases, the auditor may find obvious deficiencies—controls established but not enforced, policies misinterpreted, policies originating at too low a level and not reviewed at a higher level, policies or controls needed where none exist and policies needing revision. Also, management standards may have to be altered or increased.

In short, the management-type auditor is a business (or management) oriented individual and an advisory staff man with a principal objective of rendering professional assistance to management in solving problems.

Typically, the auditor who has breadth of educational background, frequently can do, among other things, the following:

• Review operations, expenditures and employment of property and personnel from the standpoint of effectiveness with which funds and other resources are being made. In this connection, decisions and actions of management can be related to results obtained. For example, were the physical facilities properly planned? Is the work load properly scheduled? Are there any bottlenecks because of human or mechanical failures? Are the expenses reasonable for this type of operation? Was that expenditure necessary?

• Perform analytical and critical examinations into the authority and responsibility, organization and procedures and practices, including accounting systems and methods.

• Disclose any wasteful, extravagant, ineffective, inefficient and uneconomical practices and expenditures.

Approach to Management-Type Auditing

Two approaches to performing management-type audits will be described. One approach is extending testing and analysis of financial transactions to non-accounting areas and lines of inquiry. The other approach is selecting, analyzing and testing transactions of the non-accounting areas based on review of the organization, responsibilities and control features of these areas. The first approach suggests an integration of financial-type auditing and management-type auditing. The second seemingly recommends performing operations audits separately. It could be argued there is no line of distinction between the two approaches since every business operation is related to finance in one way or another. Actually, distinction between the two is probably a matter of emphasis and timing of reviews.

Extension of Financial-Type Audit

Table 19-2 indicates that when the auditor reviews petty cash transactions, he will make surprise counts, trace vouchers to reimbursement vouchers and test for approvals, etc. Although the auditor is not concentrating on fraud, he may, if the necessary precautions are used, detect its existence and take appropriate action. Extending this portion of a financial-type audit would determine the need for a petty cash fund or the amount provided if its use is found to be negligible or improper. If a large volume of small purchases is being made and the petty cash fund is not used more often for economy and effectiveness of operations, the reason should be determined.

The auditor can extend the financial-type audit to other areas. For receivables he would determine the soundness of issuing credit to customers, reasonableness of discount policy and procedure, adequacy of follow-up practices, adequacy of charges for goods and services to cover full costs and soundness of distribution channels.

For property (personal and real) he would examine policies, procedures and practices in acquisition, utilization, maintenance and storage, and disposal to determine whether the 3 E's are being practiced.

Questions such as the following would be appropriate: (1) What criteria are used to establish a new warehouse or procure EDP equipment? (2) Are adequate studies made prior to acquisition to justify need and location of these facilities? (3) Can transportation costs be reduced? With respect to operations costs, the auditor should determine whether duplication of effort and wasteful practices exist.

The logical question is: "How does the auditor become aware of matters to review when performing a financial-type audit?" Another question is "When should the auditor perform the extension work?"

To gain awareness, there are many possible benchmarks including:

• Review of vendors' invoices can result in an auditor finding that separate purchase orders are issued for like equipment, material or services. Substantial savings through quantity discounts as well as a savings in processing costs may be possible.

• Comparison of prior payrolls and number of employees when vouching expenses may indicate duplication of effort due to lack of coordination with other departments.

• Review of procurement may indicate large quantities of material ordered when inventory cards indicate large quantities on hand.

If the financial-type audit cannot be extended to management decision-making and operations, the matters can be documented for later consideration as a separate audit.

Separate Management-Type Audit

Various extensions and criteria of the financial-type audit have described how an auditor can detect ineffective, inefficient and uneconomical non-accounting matters. All of this points toward the possibility of savings and improvements if corrective action is taken. As mentioned, further inquiry can take place during the financial-type audit and/or the areas of weakness can be documented for subsequent audits.

In addition to this approach, the auditor can observe areas of weakness when touring plants and offices. His familiarity with overall operations and performance may disclose apparent areas of weakness. After appropriate survey and review, planned operations audits may be established.

In such audits, whether an extension of a financial-type audit or a separate management-type audit, the program of objectives and procedural steps would not be necessarily different. For example, if an audit were being performed regarding procurement of a particular item, consideration would be given to review of files, discussion with personnel in planning and engineering departments, if applicable, review of competitive bids, appraisal of vendors' prices, including the price effect of engineering changes, etc.

Auditor's Responsibility

In management-type auditing, the auditor's responsibility is no less important than in financial-type auditing. In fact, responsibilities are the same. Sufficient review and testing of specific cases, transactions or other units of operations are just as important in management-type auditing.

Just as in financial-type auditing, standards are generally not prescribed for determining the type of sampling to be used. Professional judgment plays an important role in selecting samples and evaluating results. The auditor must be independently satisfied with the work performed. If not, he must consider expanding the scope of detailed examination.

The audit staff should be independent and objective in examining and evaluating the performance of others in order to constructively contribute to better management. For some operations, management may have provided, as part of its control system, techniques for measuring or evaluating performance (including use of property and personnel). (This would be analogous to using predetermined totals of hours, for example, totals of payroll payments prior to computation and preparation of checks in a computer operation.) However, validity of such standards, as noted in Table 19-2, may, in itself, be questionable. Therefore, the basis for establishing such standards and their usefulness should also be reviewed.

If the organization does not have any internal standards or guidelines, they may be available externally. For example, the auditor may know criteria that will be useful for measuring and appraising operations and in arriving at supportable opinions, conclusions and recommendations.

It is the auditor's duty to consider all pertinent factors in evaluating performance where several criteria are involved. Even though he may determine, based upon tests, that management is complying with policies and procedures, weaknesses in management information systems may still exist. The auditor should also consider these weaknesses and recommend corrective action where savings can result.

Future Considerations

The profession has yet to come to full grips with the nature and scope of management-type auditing.

As John Carey says, accountants will find themselves drawn into the solution of management problems.[6] However, there are problems of equipping the profession to assume larger responsibilities implicit in the broadened concept of what professional accounting practice should be. Auditors should begin to broaden the scope of their services by increasing their competence in any phase which will help clients run their businesses better.

Although a full discussion of reporting standards is beyond the scope of this chapter, reporting problems must not be overlooked. To a large extent, reporting may be only a recitation of facts, with the conclusions, in many cases, axiomatic. For example, description of a wasteful operation together with a demonstration of the criteria, cause-and-effect relationship and significance should obviously lead to the conclusion that corrective action be taken. Recommendations will depend upon the circumstances involved.

An interesting reporting development is the auditor's opinion on financial statements. The auditor of the future may become the master of management information systems in all types of organizations and advise and assist in all uses of the information system. Carey says the attestation may extend beyond the balance sheet and income statements to all types of financial and economic data.[7] The independent audit may also embrace systematic examinations of the internal information system, organizational structure, planning and control functions and decision-making processes.

There are other interesting developments for future considerations. Edwin Caplan says that accountants (and auditors) have not considered to any significant extent the behavioral aspects of management accounting. He suggests a revitalization is needed which will make assumptions about the accountant's role in effectively using budgets, other accounting control techniques and understanding the interaction between these techniques and the motivations and aspirations of individuals to be controlled.[8] Fred Blum suggests that cost accounting should provide for "human values" and that there is a need for "social audits" of business to determine not only the "morale" situations but also how well or how poorly the business is satisfying the basic needs of its employees and the purposefulness and unity within the organization.[9] Without a doubt, these developments will have an impact on management-type auditing and indicate need for even further development of a conceptual frame of reference and standards.

Conclusion

Management-type auditing is an independent, objective, analytical and critical appraisal or examination of the manner and effectiveness of carrying out responsibilities. It may be regarded as an extension of the financial-type audit or conceived of as a separate audit.

A word of caution is in order. The auditor analyzes, evaluates and advises, but he does not direct. The organization under audit may accept or reject the findings and recommendations. It cannot be stressed too often that the most important single process in management-type auditing is developing findings that are significant, accurate and objective. What is important is that the audit work and reporting of findings be done independently, objectively and critically in order that a constructive contribution is made to better management. The result: Future business operations will improve.

Table 19-1. Objectives of Internal (Management) Control

Components and principles	Accuracy and reliability of data	Safeguards of assets and other resources	Control of operations-operational efficiency
Organization: Responsibilities should be divided so that no one person will control all phases of any transaction. Separate the accounting from the custody and operations. Provide direct lines of authority, delegation of specific duties, recognition of responsibilities and separation of incompatible duties.	This will assure cross-checks and thus accuracy and prevention of unintentional errors (commission or omission) by providing for one person's work automatically checking the accuracy of other groups.	This will assure disclosure of unauthorized and improper actions or disclose fraud by providing a pre-review or so-called administrative review (internal).	Variances from actual will be promptly disclosed without misrepresentation of the facts. Assets will be conserved through efficient, effective, and economical (profitable) operations.

Components and principles	Accuracy and reliability of data	Safeguards of assets and other resources	Control of operations-operational efficiency
· Accounting (records, etc.):			
Framework that can be fitted to assignments and adopted classifications that parallel organizational units and budgetary processes.	This will provide for accurate descriptions. Transactions will be suitably recorded and classified by means of an accounting manual and other media.	Accountability will be fixed through controlling accounts.	Appropriate summarization and interpretation of data will be facilitated for preparing financial and other statements and reports to assist in planning and setting standards.
Reporting:			
Prompt and accurate reports and memoranda on financial condition, results of operations, performance, forecasts, cash position.	This will provide reconciliations, confirmations and other documentary evidence.	Budget allotments will be compared to obligations to determine that antideficiency statute has not been violated and resources applied only to purposes designated by law and management.	Variances from actual will be provided. See organization.
Review:			
Independent internal review of operations, methods, systems, inspections.	Testing of accuracy, reliability.	Determine if assets are safeguarded and accounted for. Act as a deterrent. Uncover unauthorized and improper actions.	Appraisal of all other controls and verify compliance.

Table 19-2. Comparison of Objectives and Audit Procedures

Financial Reviews   Management Performance Reviews

(Note: Management is responsible for accounting, statements and operation.)

Financial (fiscal) reviews   Management performance reviews

Purpose is to render an opinion on financial statements—proper amount of testing (based on adequacy of accounting system and effectiveness of accounting control and internal "check") and verification work, with appropriate testing to support the independent opinion as to fairness with which financial position and results of operations are set forth.

Purpose is to determine and evaluate application of funds (in addition to receipts and disbursements of funds) with verification of authorized programs, activities and other purposes (missions)—based on effectiveness of administrative controls (in addition to accounting control and internal "check"), i.e., operational efficiency and compliance (total management control)—to determine whether they are performed effectively, efficiently and economically according to sound business policies and practices and sufficient testing to support findings of deficiencies and report thereon.

Auditing standards—general; field work and reporting standards that are generally accepted by the profession (see pronouncements). These standards are also applicable to management performance reviews (see right hand section of this sheet).

Auditing standards—specific criteria (as necessary) applicable to determine efficiency, effectiveness and economy of operations in accomplishing the results intended.

Audit Phase (Examples)

Petty cash

Objectives (audit responsibilities)	Audit procedures	Objectives (audit responsibilities)	Audit procedures
1) Determine that cash called for by records is on hand. 2) Determine that cash is fully accounted for.	1) Surprise count. 2) Examine transactions. 3) Trace cash vouchers to reimbursement voucher and inspect approvals.	1) Determine need for petty cash fund. 2) Determine reasonableness of amount. 3) Determine if full advantage is taken of making small purchases, etc.	1) Relate use with frequency of reimbursement and evaluate need for the fund as well as amount. 2) Examine other purchases to determine if full use is made. 3) Conclude benefits and protection of fund.

Receivables

1) Determine accuracy. 2) Determine validity. 3) Determine collectibility. 4) Determine whether all revenues and receipts from operations and amounts otherwise due are collected and accounted for.	1) Reconcile subsidiary records with controls. 2) Age and establish collectibility. 3) Test by direct correspondence with debtors.	1) Determine soundness of customers' credit. 2) Determine reasonableness of discount policy and procedure. 3) Determine adequacy of follow-up practices. 4) Combine tests with operations and determine adequacy of charges for goods and services to cover full costs.	1) Examine policies, procedures and practices by appropriate tests of transaction from beginning to end, noting weaknesses in the three E's. 2) Compare revenue with full costs and conclude as to adequacy of prices. 3) Obtain sufficient evidence regarding deficiencies.

Objectives (audit responsibilities)	Audit procedures	Objectives (audit responsibilities)	Audit procedures
Property (e.g., inventories and fixed assets)			
1) Determine clerical accuracy. 2) Establish physical existence and reasonableness of quantities. 3) Ascertain pricing and valuation. 4) Ascertain cutoff dates, treatment of "reserves" and balance-sheet presentation.	1) Observe the taking of physical inventory and make tests of counts or measurement to extent practicable. 2) Verify extensions, footings and total summaries and compare to subsidiary and controls. 3) Determine appropriate cutoffs for purchases and sales where applicable. 4) Obtain management certificates as appropriate.	1) Determine whether any important deficiencies resulted from defective accounting policies, procedures and practices. 2) Review procurement (acquisition) to determine that kinds, quality and quantity really needed are ordered and acquired; items are appropriately suited to activity; items are delivered when and where needed; prices are reasonable and by competitive bids (as appropriate), contracts are properly and adequately administered; outright purchase rather than lease (as appropriate), etc. 3) Review whether property is adequately used (including need for "spares" and inspections as to suitability), etc. 4) Review maintenance and storage to determine adequacy with objective to minimize unnecessary procurement and at least cost. 5) Review disposal determinations (or lack thereof) as to suitability, reasonableness of returns and disposition of proceeds, etc. 6) Review financing of acquisitions to determine whether it affects quantity and quality and kinds of procurements.	1) Examine policies, procedures and practices by appropriate tests of transactions from beginning to end, noting weaknesses in three E's. 2) Obtain sufficient evidence regarding deficiencies and report on corrective action needed. Include in the above stock levels, specifications, alternatives, actual with standards (also evaluate standards), agency's needs with others, use of appraisals as needed, need for warehouses and whether good management and custody practices exist and selection of size, etc., and selection of site.
Expenses			
1) Purpose. 2) Correctness.	1) Inspect records. 2) Test computations.	1) Determine need.	1) Review need and use.

ELLSWORTH H. MORSE, JR.

20 PERFORMANCE AND OPERATIONAL AUDITING

The terms "performance auditing" or "operational auditing" are usually used to distinguish between auditing of accounting and related records for the purpose of expressing professional opinions on financial statements and auditing that examines the operating, managerial or administrative performance of selected aspects of an activity or organization beyond that required for the audit of the accounts. The purpose of such extended auditing is primarily to identify opportunities for greater efficiency and economy or for improved effectiveness in carrying out procedures or operations. The objective is improvement in relation to the goals of the organization.

Unfortunately, such labels as performance auditing, operational auditing and financial auditing can cause confusion. The boundaries between them, even on a conceptual basis, are not sharp and clear. As good as our English language is, we have not been able to sharpen our terminology in many areas of accounting and auditing. Financial auditing requires the auditor to concern himself with many aspects of management or administrative performance and control. He cannot confine his attention to accounting records. The auditor of financial statements, if he is doing his job properly, will find himself on much the same ground as the so-called operational auditor.

The distinction—if one has to be drawn—is one of audit objectives. What is the purpose of the audit? The auditor of financial statements is usually engaged to do such work as is necessary to provide a report with an opinion on the financial statements. The so-called operational auditor, who is often part of the organization, makes examinations for the purpose of aiding management to do a more efficient and more effective job and, in private business, achieve more profitable results.

Some General Principles

The approach to be followed in making an operational or management audit is not much different, in concept at least, from that followed in a financial audit. These four broad steps would be performed for almost any type of audit:

(1) A preliminary survey of the activity being examined should be made to obtain necessary background.

(2) The basic charter or assignment of responsibility for the activity being examined should be studied to ascertain the authorized purposes and related authorities of the activity and any applicable restrictions or limitations.

(3) Pertinent parts of the management system should be examined by studying the policies established to govern the activities under examination, testing the effectiveness of specific operating and administrative procedures and exploring the problem areas or weaknesses encountered.

(4) Reports on results of the audit work should be prepared and submitted to those responsible for receiving or acting on the auditor's findings and recommendations.

Identification of Problem Areas

There are many techniques by which the auditor can identify problem areas warranting more penetrating examination. Here are some examples:

• *Survey work.* During the preliminary survey work through which practical working information is obtained on how an activity is supposed to function and on how control procedures are supposed to work, key features can be identified that appear to be difficult to control or to be susceptible to abuse. In a purchasing operation, for example, the following three steps may well be the key points:

(1) The determinations made of the quantities and the quality of materials to be purchased.
(2) The procedures followed in obtaining the best prices.
(3) The methods for determining whether the correct quantities and quality are actually received.

If, in relation to the total purchasing operation, the auditor concludes that these processes are the most critical from the standpoint of the need for good performance, he would be justified in concentrating his testing work on them.

• *Review of management reports.* The auditor's review of internal reports which management itself regularly uses to obtain information on progress, status or accomplishment of work can be valuable sources of information on possible problem areas suggesting audit attention.

• *Review of internal audit or inspection reports.* Internal audit or inspection reports can also be a valuable source of information on problem areas. Of particular interest to the auditor are those reports that bring to light important findings on which management has not acted. The auditor should inquire into the reasons and justification for inaction in such cases since these circumstances could throw light on weaknesses in the management system that have not previously been referred to top management for resolution.

• *Physical inspections.* Physical inspections of an organization's activities and facilities can be a useful way of identifying possible inefficiencies or problems that should be given audit attention. Examples are excess accumulations of equipment or material; idle or little-used equipment; employee idleness; rejections of product by inspectors (or customers); extensive rework operations; disposal of useful materials or equipment; and the like.

• *Test examinations of transactions.* A useful way to obtain a practical working insight into the efficiency of procedures is to pursue a number of transactions pertaining to the organization's operations completely from beginning to end. This kind of testing will provide the auditor with valuable information on the way the organization's business is actually transacted, on the usefulness (or pertinence) of prescribed procedures, on the capabilities of personnel involved, and on weaknesses in procedures or practices which could represent a drain on the organization's resources.

• *Discussions with officials and employees.* The auditor can also obtain valuable information on problem areas warranting audit attention through discussions with responsible officials in the organization and other employees concerned with the operations being examined. The degree of success in obtaining useful information in this way is in large part dependent on the auditor's reputation for independent and constructive inquiry. If he is regarded with fear because of overly critical reporting in the past, this source of information may not be productive.

Testing Effectiveness of Procedures and Practices

Testing the effectiveness of procedures and practices requires some preliminary review to learn how they work and to obtain a preliminary insight into their effectiveness and usefulness. On the basis of such testing, specific matters may be identified as problem areas or weaknesses needing further probing.

In his preliminary review work on management controls, the auditor should consider such factors as the following:

(1) Whether the policies of the organization comply with its basic charter or grant of authority.

(2) Whether the system of procedures and management controls is designed to carry out those policies and results in activities being conducted as desired by top management, and in an efficient and economical manner.

(3) Whether the system of management controls provides adequate control over the organization's resources, revenues, costs and expenditures.

Some of the specific factors that the alert auditor should consider in assessing the management control system and identifying problem areas warranting more detailed audit include the following:

(1) The use by management of standards or goals for judging accomplishment, productivity, efficiency or use of goods or services.

(2) Lack of clarity in written instructions which may result in misunderstandings, inconsistent applications, unacceptable deviations in what was wanted and the like.

(3) Capabilities of personnel to perform their assignments.

(4) Failures to accept responsibility.

(5) Duplication of effort.

(6) Improper or wasteful use of funds.

(7) Cumbersome or extravagant organizational patterns.
(8) Ineffective or wasteful use of employees and physical resources.
(9) Work backlogs.

Development of Audit Findings

When faulty conditions or practices are observed, further examination work will usually be necessary. First, the auditor should take up his preliminary observations with the responsible managers. If they are inclined to pursue the matters, the auditor may not need to go into them any further, at least at this time. If the managers are not convinced that they should do anything, the auditor should penetrate further. He should then examine specific cases, transactions or other units of operation in sufficient depth to reach valid conclusions, to report fairly on the results of the work and to support satisfactorily any recommendations made.

Developing specific findings is the heart of this type of audit. Essentially this process involves obtaining as much pertinent, significant information about each problem as is practicable and evaluating it in terms of cause, effect and possible courses of corrective action.

In developing his specific findings and conclusions, the auditor must do an adequate amount of analytical work and accumulate all appropriate evidential supporting material. He will need to:

(1) Identify specifically what the problem is—that is, what is deficient, what is defective, what is in error and the like.
(2) Determine whether the condition is isolated or widespread.
(3) Determine the significance of the deficiency in terms of costs, adverse performance or other effects.
(4) Ascertain the cause or causes for the condition.

(5)   Identify the persons in the organization responsible for the deficiency.

(6)   Determine possible lines of corrective or preventive action and formulate constructive recommendations.

The auditor should review his work and his findings with management officials responsible for the area being examined so that he will have the opportunity to obtain as much information as possible bearing on the problem and formulate his conclusions in the light of the detailed knowledge of the officials responsible for the performance being reviewed.

Relationship of Auditor to Management

The auditor should adopt the viewpoint that achieving efficient, economical and effective operations is a basic management responsibility. That responsibility must be discharged in the light of each organization's duties and authority. The entire structure of the management system of organization, operation and control should be designed to achieve this objective. The auditor should test the working of this control system, probe apparent weaknesses and issue a report on conditions found which includes conclusions and recommendations.

Standards for Judging Performance

In reviewing pertinent parts of the management system, the auditor should first ascertain how management officials themselves determine whether prescribed policies are being followed, whether authorized and prescribed procedures are effective, and whether they are being applied in an efficient and economical manner. This gives him a good starting point—and a perspective from the manager's viewpoint that is essential to acceptable audit results.

In addition, if the management has developed, as part of its control system, techniques for measuring or evaluating performance against predetermined objectives or criteria, the auditor should inquire into them to see whether he can apply them in his work. He should not use them blindly, however. He must be satisfied that they are logical and valid as a basis for judging performance.

If specific measures of internal performance are not available, the auditor has a much more difficult job of appraisal. He must then develop his own methods of examination and evaluation, utilizing all available pertinent facts and factors, in arriving at supportable opinions, conclusions and recommendations.

Under these circumstances, instead of trying to measure performance against precise standards, the auditor should try to ascertain whether waste is occurring or whether there is a less costly or more effective way to conduct the operations being examined.

The auditor may find, for example, that funds are not being prudently managed because of decisions to acquire unneeded goods or services. Or the procedures followed in determining whether materials and supplies are needed may be faulty and may lead to decisions to buy unnecessarily large quantities that cannot be fully used or cannot be effectively used except over a long period. In the latter case, storage and handling costs, as well as risks of obsolescence and deterioration are unnecessarily incurred.

The auditor must consider all pertinent factors in appraising performance. And to be effective and accepted as a constructive force, he must be fair, objective and realistic. Above all he must avoid making judgments and conclusions on performance based solely on hindsight.

Despite all the difficulties, however, if all significant factors are considered, judgments can be given by the independent auditor on the discharge of management responsibilties—judgments that can be of value in promoting improvements in management performance and that can be useful to third parties in connection with their evaluations of such performances.

Some GAO Examples

The U.S. General Accounting Office, which is an independent agency in the legislative branch of the federal government, has obtained considerable experience in expanding the scope of its audits of federal agencies beyond the boundaries of conventional financial auditing. In the federal government organization, the GAO is the independent external auditor of the individual departments and agencies, most of which also have internal audit organizations as a part of their management control systems.

The General Accounting Office is headed by the Comptroller General of the United States, who is appointed for a 15-year term—a significant factor in the manner of conduct and independence of operation of his office.

Auditing the affairs of federal agencies that spend something like $200 billion a year is a major part of the work of GAO, and it results in the preparation of hundreds of reports each year to the Congress (most of which are public) and to agency officials. They cover almost every kind of activity in which our government is involved.

Following is a sampling from some recent reports to illustrate the nature, variety and usefulness of a brand of auditing which concerns itself with identification of problem areas and ways and means of improving on them.

• *Maintenance.* The Navy and the Air Force spend about $5.5 billion a year to keep their aircraft in operation. The government has about $40 billion invested in these aircraft. The two military services, however, follow substantially different policies in determining when maintenance should be performed.

The auditors found that the Navy could reduce its

maintenance costs substantially if it followed Air Force practices. The audit report noted that had this been done for the F-4 fighter aircraft, the equivalent of about 40 planes could have been available to the Navy to perform missions over a year's time. The Department of Defense agreed in substance with the auditors' recommendations and the Navy undertook studies of the matter.

Another case involving maintenance relates to excess military aircraft. Such aircraft not needed by the military services are mothballed and stored. Many parts from such aircraft can be used in repairing operational aircraft instead of purchasing new parts. An examination of the program to reclaim usable parts revealed that the Navy could satisfy much more of its repair parts requirements from excess aircraft than it was doing and could accordingly cut back on purchases of replacement parts. Limited tests by the auditors showed that hundreds of thousands of dollars worth of additional parts could have been reclaimed.

• *Real property management.* The Department of State owns nearly $300 million worth of real property abroad and leases additional properties at rentals amounting to nearly $25 million a year. An examination of this program revealed that some parcels of real property were being retained even though high operating and maintenance costs made it uneconomical to do so. It was also found that the needs served by valuable properties could have been adequately met by acquiring less valuable properties.

The auditors pointed out that proceeds from the sales of valuable properties could be used to help finance other high-priority needs of the government. In this case, they also noted that lack of adequate accounting records for operating and maintenance costs was a contributing reason for uneconomical retention of the properties since no information was being reported to the management on what was going on.

The Department of State accepted the auditors' findings and agreed to improve its accounting system and to develop criteria for management use in evaluating utilization of owned property.

• *Personnel management.* The Department of Defense purchases tens of billions of dollars worth of weapons, support equipment and services every year. The single most important element in good procurement is the caliber of the people who do the work. An audit of the Defense career program for procurement personnel brought to light numerous problems. These included a need to update the program to keep it responsive to substantial changes in military procurement concepts over the years, lack of suitable career development of both civilian and military officers for procurement roles, need to elevate the status of procurement careers and positions, and need to attract qualified young people into these careers to eventually replace most of the aging work force. The auditors made numerous recommendations for strengthening this program, which should result in better procurement practices by the largest single procuring organization in the world.

Another case of faulty personnel management was found in reviewing the Army's practices in assigning project managers to major research and development projects. The review showed that most of the project managers were serving on important assignments for periods much shorter than required—in many cases for less than two years. Such tours were much too short in the light of the heavy responsibilities of such managers, which included planning, directing and controlling all project resources needed to develop and produce the item for which the office was created. Premature reassignments resulted in inefficiency because of the period of time required before successors could be found sufficiently knowledgeable about the projects to provide satisfactory leadership.

The Army agreed with the auditors' finding and the recommendation that it comply more closely with prescribed policy calling for longer tours.

- *Revenues from operations.* The Postal Service each year handles something like 9 billion pieces of second-class mail consisting of periodicals and newspapers.

It also loses money on this class of mail—over $400 million in 1968. GAO auditors found that because the Post Office tended to place almost complete reliance on information provided by publishers in determining the postage charges for their mail, it was losing substantial amounts of revenue.

As a result of examinations of mailings of hundreds of publications involving millions of pieces of second-class mail, they also found numerous cases of mail that failed to meet the prescribed requirements for second-class mail. In many cases, publications were found to have been ineligible for the lower postal rates for years. The agency's examinations of publishers' records were neither timely nor effective, and this resulted in failure to detect that some publications were improperly classified for second-class postage rates.

Recommendations were made to tighten the Postal Service's administration of these operations—an important need in the light of the annual postal deficit. The Postmaster General ordered a complete examination of all pertinent regulations and their administration.

Another revenue problem was found in the Veterans Administration. This agency rents to its employees government-owned housing at its field stations. The auditors examined the rentals being collected for about 15 per cent of the quarters and found that they were too low by nearly $600,000 a year. The standard of comparison in this case is the rental rates for comparable private housing in the same communities. This standard is prescribed by the Federal Office of Management and Budget. Recommendations for improving the situation were agreed to by agency officials.

- *Organization.* The Veterans Administration operates insurance field offices in Philadelphia and St. Paul. These offices administer over 5.5 million insurance policies. GAO auditors concluded that consolidation of the two offices was feasible and that such action would produce savings in operating expenses of over $1 million a year with no reduction in service to policy-holders. They recommended that the consolidated office be located at Philadelphia. VA officials agreed with the auditors' dollar estimates of costs and savings but did not express any view one way or the other on the recommendation to consolidate.

The foregoing are examples of how auditors can illuminate problem areas and point the way to cutting costs, increasing revenues and improving efficiency of operations. Audit work concerned with such matters is usually referred to as performance, management or operational auditing. But again these terms are not precise.

Auditing Results

The term "performance auditing" suggests that the full range of management's responsibilities is within the auditor's purview. This brings the further extension of his evaluations to the accomplishments of the organization or the effectiveness of its operations in achieving established or prescribed goals or objectives. This is a logical extension of the auditor's work.

Extension of audit scope is receiving considerable attention at present in the GAO and is of great importance in government operations where we have a national budget of over $200 billion with many competing claims for allocation of scarce financial resources to important national programs and purposes.

An important contribution can be made by auditors in determining whether or not governmental programs are accomplishing the purposes for which they were authorized, and whether or not alternative approaches might be more effective at less cost.

In this area, the concepts and techniques of systems analysis assume importance. Effective evaluations of complex governmental programs represent strong challenges to auditors, and they need to apply all the tools they can muster. The cost-benefit approaches and the sophisticated quantitative analytical techniques of the systems analyst add greatly to the auditor's abilities and need to be incorporated as appropriate in these examinations.

Some experience is being gained, but a lot more is needed. An example—again from GAO work—illustrates the scope and nature of such broadened evaluation work by auditors.

Examination of Pollution Control Program. Pollution of the nation's waters has become a matter of major national concern. The federal government in the past 13 years has made grants of nearly $1.5 billion to cities and other government entities to help finance the construction of something like 9,600 waste-treatment plants costing over $6 billion. A comprehensive GAO examination into the results of these expenditures in 1969 led to the following principal conclusions in a report to the U.S. Congress:

(1) The benefits obtained from the construction of municipal waste-treatment facilities were not as great as they could have been because many of the facilities were built on waterways where major industrial and municipal polluters located nearby continued to discharge untreated or inadequately treated wastes into the waterway.
(2) The construction grant program was being administered mostly on a "shotgun" basis—that is, grants were being awarded on a first-come, first-served or readiness-to-proceed basis. Little consideration was given to the immediate benefits to be obtained by the construction of specific treatment plants. No systematic approach was being followed to decide where applications of public funds would do the most good in helping to abate water pollution.

The auditors recommended that the federal agencies directly concerned require that the states, in establishing priorities for the construction of treatment facilities and in awarding grants, consider the benefits to be derived from construction in each case and the actions taken or planned by other polluters. They also recommended that the Federal Water Quality Administration use systems analysis techniques in planning for and carrying out water pollution control programs.

This recommendation is of interest because in making the study the auditors examined the degree to which the administering agencies used these techniques. GAO also engaged an engineering firm to assist in demonstrating the usefulness of systems analysis in developing and implementing plans to construct waste treatment facilities. The engineering firm, using data applicable to the Merrimack River and a mathematical model, estimated the construction costs of water treatment plants for various degrees of water quality for that river. Its report was incorporated in the GAO report to the Congress.

Conclusion

The hallmark of the effective auditor comes from what he accomplishes. Just being on the job usually has beneficial results in that his presence or prospect of showing up tends to stimulate better performance by the officials and employees of an organization.

The auditor's checks on compliance with prescribed policies and procedures that have been adopted to promote efficient operations and conserve resources can be a valuable protective service as well as a way to point up desirable changes.

The auditor's unending searches for better, less costly and more effective ways of doing things can make him a vital force in the management of any organization that has to be concerned with survival in the competitive struggle to obtain and make the most of scarce resources.

And, finally, the auditor's concern with providing independent expert evaluations of how well things are going, and of how better results might be achieved, points the way to an expanding future for the art and the profession of auditing. It could be a bright future. How bright depends on the profession's own performance.

21 ENHANCING PRODUCTIVITY THROUGH MORE EFFECTIVE USE OF HUMAN RESOURCES

Enhancement of productivity essentially is brought about by making changes in the way resources (inputs) are used, in order to improve the results (outputs) of human endeavor. The kinds of changes that enhance productivity fall into two basic categories: (1) those that are concerned with material changes, and (2) those that focus on the human resources.

On the material side, much attention has been devoted in the Joint Federal Productivity Project to the impact of technology on productivity: increasing automation, and the related kinds of changes in equipment, materials, and work processes that can increase the amount of goods produced by a given unit of labor. The typical emphasis is on work simplification, increased efficiency in terms of lower unit costs, and other indices that focus on the quantitative aspects of productivity.

Attention has also been devoted by the Joint Productivity Team Task Force to the question of more effective utilization of human resources as a means of enhancing productivity, but not to the same extent as is the case with material

Reprinted from *Measuring and Enhancing Productivity in the Federal Government*, Summary Report, Joint Federal Productivity Project, 1973.

resources. Up to now, the emphasis has been on relatively partial measures of manpower inputs, with only limited attention being given to the much larger question of organization, utilization and development of human resources within the "total system." Future efforts, therefore, must focus more attention on the human factors in the productivity equation.

This chapter discusses the work done to date that bears on the use of human resources and presents recommendations in respect to:

• First, alternatives to the application of arbitrary controls represented by personnel ceilings and average grade controls.

• Second, the need for more systematic research into organizational and motivational factors, and assistance to agencies in applying best practices to the solution of these problems.

Adverse Effects of Arbitrary Personnel Ceilings and Average Grade Controls

In our discussions with several hundred federal managers during the past two years, we have been told that managerial initiative and employee morale are sharply reduced:

• When arbitrary personnel ceilings make it impossible to maintain adequate service standards, or result in the accumulation of intolerable backlogs.

• When the requirement to reduce average salaries results in employing less qualified personnel who have higher attrition in the first year, and less promotion potential.

• When savings achieved are withdrawn and made available to less efficient activities.

• When mandatory personnel cuts are applied, equally, to those who have achieved greater efficiency and to those who have not.

The prevalence of these attitudes led us in Phase III to

inquire in greater depth among operating officials. We met individually with 50 managers in 11 different agencies, and sought candid, first-hand experiences on the difficulties that are caused by these practices.

These interviews were conducted by a consultant to the project team. They are summarized in the following paragraphs.

(1) *Personnel ceilings have major adverse effects on the efficient management of human resources. Across-the-board cuts and "freezes" are especially counterproductive.*

• Arbitrary cuts and freezes frustrate orderly planning and control of manpower and lead to costly circumventions such as excessive use of overtime, temporary hiring, and contracting out.

• Ceilings discourage the use of part-time personnel since such personnel are frequently counted as full-time positions.

• The inability to hire people because of a freeze or lack of authorized positions sometimes prevents the performance of work that was approved and funded.

• Reduction by attrition causes imbalanced staffing and leads to improper use of technical and professional employees.

• Managers resort to inefficient layoffs and rehiring just to meet the June 30 ceiling date.

• Ceiling reductions are incompatible with average grade reductions since attrition is heaviest at the lower grades.

To overcome these problems, the Defense Department has experimentally removed personnel ceilings at ten laboratories and permitted them to operate under a budget rather than a personnel constraint. This is known as Project Reflex. A GAO audit is being made of the experience in the three military departments. It appears that removing ceilings and allowing installation management to decide how to meet its mission—whether to obtain resources under contract, or to use a different mix of grades and staff talents, or to use overtime when prudent—contributes to better management.

The experiment has not been entirely successful in some activities because of the application of hiring freezes and grade de-escalation controls. However, enough experience has been gained to indicate that these experiments should be continued and extended. We agree that this is desirable, but feel that it should be done under closer review so as to document the results more carefully.

(2) *Arbitrary controls over average grade have additional adverse effects on the management of human resources.*
• They interfere with the progress of accurate job description and classification.
• They force recruitment of lower quality personnel than required for the level of work, increasing training cost and attrition and diminishing the number of people in the pipeline with promotion potential.
• They lower employee morale when earned promotions are delayed, especially in those cases covered by training agreements.
• They delay prudent management actions such as organization realignments.
• The impact is especially severe in organizations that have low turnover and no growth.

Conclusions and Recommendations

The joint task force is aware of the need to keep federal employment at the minimum, in numbers and salaries, required to conduct government operations. We believe, however, that year-end position ceilings, arbitrary across-the-board reductions, and grade de-escalation requirements are not effective manpower cost control mechanisms. Indeed, we believe they are, themselves, costly and dysfunctional, and impede rather than contribute to good manpower management. Preliminary findings of experiments in the Department of Defense lead us to believe that dollar controls are feasible to administer and bring good results.

We therefore recommend that OMB:

• Encourage large agencies (besides DOD) to experiment with removing personnel ceilings from components and allowing them to operate under budgetary instead of position controls.

• Remove ceiling controls from several smaller agencies for a test period.

• Give serious consideration, based on an assessment of these tests, to substituting dollar controls for position ceiling controls throughout the federal establishment.

It is the understanding of the joint task force that arbitrary controls over average grade will not be continued in fiscal year 1974, but that OMB will monitor each agency's average grade on a monthly basis in conjunction with turnover data. We think this is a wise decision.

We further recommend that:

• The monthly analysis of agency average grade and turnover data be supplemented periodically by information on productivity per man-year and data on unit labor costs. (Data gathered during Phase III on productivity trends in relation to labor costs showed that, in constant 1967 dollars, 133 of the 187 organizations analyzed had a higher rate of productivity improvement in terms of labor costs than in terms of man-years, indicating a more economical grade mix to handle the increased workload. On the other hand, there were 35 cases where the reverse was true. Each case, of course, should be analyzed on its own merits.)

The Need for More Systematic Research into Techniques of Improving Organizational Effectiveness and Employee Motivation and Application of Best Practices in Government Agencies

At the outset of Phase III, the joint task force noted the widespread public attention being given to worker job satisfaction.

In the July 3, 1972, report of the Joint Economic Committee, entitled "American Productivity: Key to Economic Strength and National Survival," this subject is discussed at some length, and the conclusion reached that "... more work needs to be done, both in developing statistics on worker attitudes and on documenting the relationship between attitudes and worker efficiency." The committee also spoke of the "number of cases where the application of human relations techniques has improved plant efficiency significantly."

It was decided to inquire further into these subjects during Phase III: (1) to determine which practices might be applicable to the federal government, and (2) to initiate a case study in at least one major agency as a first step toward establishing the experience base needed to evaluate these practices.

The OMB and CSC members of the joint task force subsequently researched the literature and visited several companies that had reported unusual successes in practicing one or more of the widely discussed techniques variously described as job redesign, job restructuring, job enrichment, participative management, organizational development, and similar phrases.

Concurrently, the Social Security Administration expressed interest in carrying out several carefully designed studies in "behavioral management" (defined by SSA as "management practices that deal more directly with the human factors in operations"). SSA had already begun to test a "Progressive Management Model" based on MBO concepts of two-way objective setting, performance review and positive reinforcement. Additionally, the agency agreed to conduct carefully documented and controlled studies of participative management, job enrichment and flexible work hours. A study of job enrichment has been started, in cooperation with the National Commission on Productivity and the project team.

In its exploration of these subjects, the joint task force encountered widely different views on the applicability of behavioral science techniques to productivity enhancement. They found little hard data on cause-effect relationships in the private sector that could be used by government managers to guide their decisions. Moreover, they were aware that the government environment, with its built-in constraints regarding pay, incentives, ceilings, etc., posed a more difficult setting in which to determine which techniques were useful and which were not.

The need for more reliable information on the costs, benefits, and risks of organization development in the public sector was recognized by the Executive Director of the National Commission on Productivity. In the spring of 1973, the NCOP contracted with the National Academy of Public Administration to conduct up to five additional controlled demonstrations in "productivity motivation."

By early spring, having gathered together a considerable body of information, both pro and con, concerning the applicability of organization development techniques, the joint task force believed it would be useful to provide a group of federal executives with a quick exposure to this topic to generate further inquiry and experimentation. This was accomplished at a conference held at Airlie House on March 18-20, 1973, at which selected consultants, industry and federal officials discussed their experiences.

As the Phase III effort came to a close, it was apparent to the joint task force that the experimental projects initiated in this phase would reach well beyond the scope and duration of the productivity project and that they required continuing official attention. Moreover, the data generated by these and other experiments needed to be gathered together, evaluated, and disseminated to the entire public administration community. Where appropriate, the new findings will also need to be incorporated into training programs so that productivity enhancing techniques can be widely institutionalized. Hence, the Phase III effort in this area is being brought to a conclusion with the publication of the proceedings of the Airlie House Conference and other related materials developed by the project team. The Civil Service Commission is the appropriate agency to plan and oversee these activities and to provide authoritative information and policy guidance to federal managers in these fields. The joint task force therefore recommends:

(1) That the Civil Service Commission should provide leadership, policy guidance, and technical assistance to all agencies on the personnel management aspects of productivity. This includes manpower planning and utilization, training, executive development, labor relations, pay and incentives, job design, personnel management research, and the integration of these functions with the overall productivity improvement program.

(2) That the Civil Service Commission proceed with its decision to establish and operate a clearinghouse to provide for the collection, analysis and dissemination of data concerning the motivation of productivity improvement through changes to employees jobs, incentives, the structure of work, and the work environment. An example of the kind of information proposed for this clearinghouse is shown in Special Report # 5.

Skills Improvement in Productivity

The joint task force would also like to call attention to the significant progress made during the past two years by the Civil Service Commission in incorporating productivity subjects in the curricula of a number of training courses and seminars. Training is now available to agencies in the following broad areas:

(1) Making better use of productivity information.

(2) Improving productivity by more skillful capital resource management.

(3) Improved work and systems design techniques.

(4) Improving executive decision-making through better investment analysis, cost estimating and cost-benefit analysis.

(5) Improving productivity motivation through job enrichment, job redesign and other organization development techniques.

RENSIS LIKERT

22 HUMAN RESOURCE ACCOUNTING: BUILDING AND ASSESSING PRODUCTIVE ORGANIZATIONS

The major source of the present-day apathetic and hostile attitudes of not only blue-collar workers, but also white-collar employees and supervisors, is the kind of management that focuses on short-range results—the kind of management that commonly used accounting methods encourage and reward. But when current financial reports are accompanied by dollar estimates of the change in the value of the human organization for the same reporting period, the kind of management that builds more productive human organizations will be fostered, because such management creates the will to work and at the same time contributes to employee health and satisfaction.

The resources to make these dollar estimates and to build these more productive organizations have been created by a half-century of social-science research. Tens of millions of dollars, provided largely by business, have been spent on this research. The resources it has developed are these:

• Knowledge of the key dimensions of a human organization.

Reprinted by permission of the publisher from *Personnel*, May, June 1973 by AMACOM, a division of American Management Association.

- Instruments for measuring these dimensions.
- Knowledge of the interrelationships among the human organizational dimensions.
- Knowledge of the relationship of each of these dimensions to performance results, both current and one or two years later.
- Evidence that there are, for all types of industry, consistent and dependable relationships between the human organizational dimensions and the end-result performance data.
- Knowledge of the nature and operating characteristics of a system of managing the human organization that, in comparison with the management system used by most firms today, is 20 to 40 percent more productive and yields better employee satisfaction and health.

To begin with the first point, the human organization of any enterprise (or segment of it) can be measured by a relatively small number of key dimensions, which fall into two classes—causal and intervening, or intermediate. Management can alter the causal variables, thereby producing changes in the intervening variables and, in turn, in the end-result performance data. These causal variables categories are organizational climate and managerial leadership. Policies and behavior at top managerial levels determine organizational climate variables, imposing constraints, either favorable or unfavorable, on what lower levels of managers can do. The elements used to measure the different dimensions of managerial leadership and organizational climate (causal variables) are shown below.

**Elements Used to Measure Human
Organizational Causal Variables**

Managerial Leadership

- *Support:* Friendly; pays attention to what you are saying; listens to subordinates' problems.

- *Team building:* Encourages subordinates to work as a team; encourages exchange of opinions and ideas.
- *Goal emphasis:* Encourages best efforts; maintains high standards.
- *Help with work:* Shows ways to do a better job; helps subordinates plan, organize, and schedule; offers new ideas, solutions to problems.

Organizational Climate

- *Communication flow:* Subordinates know what's going on; superiors are receptive; subordinates are given information to do jobs well.
- *Decision-making practices:* Subordinates are involved in setting goals; decisions are made at levels of accurate information; persons affected by decisions are asked for their ideas; know-how of people of all levels is used.
- *Concern for persons:* The organization is interested in the individual's welfare; tries to improve working conditions; organizes work activities sensibly.
- *Influence on department:* From lower-level supervisors, employees who have no subordinates.
- *Technological adequacy:* Improved methods are quickly adopted; equipment and resources are well managed.
- *Motivation:* Differences and disagreements are accepted and worked through; people in organization work hard for money, promotions, job satisfaction, and to meet high expectations from others and are encouraged to do so by policies, working conditions, and people.

The intervening, or intermediate, variables reflect the internal state and health of the organization, for example, the loyalties, attitudes, motivations, performance goals, and perceptions of all members and their collective capacity for effective interaction, communication, and decision making. These intervening dimensions are measured by the elements shown below.

The end-result dependent variables reflect the achievements of the organization, such as its productivity, costs, scrap loss, earnings, and market performance.

Elements Used to Measure Human Organizational Intervening Variables

Peer Leadership

- *Support:* Friendly; pays attention to what others are saying; listens to others' problems.
- *Goal emphasis:* Encourages best efforts; maintains high standards.
- *Help with work:* Shows ways to do a better job; helps others plan, organize, and schedule; group shares with each other new ideas, solutions to problems.
- *Team building:* Encouragement from each other to work as a team; emphasis on team goal; exchange of opinions and ideas.

Group Process

- Planning together, coordinating efforts.
- Making good decisions, solving problems.
- Knowing jobs and how to do them well.
- Sharing information.
- Wanting to meet objectives.
- Having confidence and trust in other members.
- Ability to meet unusual work demands.

Satisfaction

- With fellow workers; superiors; jobs; this organization compared with others; pay; progress in the organization up to now; chances for getting ahead in the future.

Performance—Determined by Quality of the Human Organization

Studies involving more than 200,000 employees and 20,000 managers or administrators in virtually all kinds of business and in governmental agencies, hospitals, schools, voluntary associations, and other organizations show that favorable scores on organizational climate and managerial leadership dimensions are associated quite consistently with favorable scores on the intervening variables and with high performance when trends over time are examined. Conversely, unfavorable climate and leadership scores are associated with unfavorable states of the intervening variables and poor performance results when the trends in performance over time are examined.

A smaller but rapidly growing number of studies demonstrates that these patterns of relationships exist also for changes in the causal variables—that is, improvement in the causal variables yields improvement in the intervening variables and, in turn, in performance results, whereas an unfavorable shift in the causal variables leads to a worsening in the intervening variables and in the end-result performance data over time, even though short-run increases often intervene. Moreover, the magnitude of the change in the causal variables is reflected in the size of changes in the intervening and end-result variables—large changes in the causal produce sizable shifts in the other variables. In widely different kinds of work, it has been demonstrated that changes in the human organization variables can cause from 30 percent to more than 70 percent of the total fluctuations in performance data such as productivity and costs.

Figure 22-1 shows the magnitude of the relationships among the human organizational variables and the relationships of the variables to performance data.

The width of each arrow is meant to be roughly proportional to the relationship between the variables connected by the arrow. The overall direction of causality is in the direction the arrow points—that is, the width of each arrow reflects the magnitude of the square of the coefficient of correlation (r^2) between the variables. The value of r^2 for each relationship is shown at the side of each arrow. Thus, for example, the .27 next to the arrow between managerial leadership and group process means that 27 percent of the variance in group process is accounted for by managerial leadership. Similarly, 67 percent of the variance in the job satisfaction of subordinates is accounted for by variations in organizational climate.

The arrows in Figure 22-1 are all shown as unidirectional, flowing from managerial leadership to the other variables and from the intervening variables to total productive efficiency. This is, of course, an oversimplification of the relationships, since there are feedback loops and some circularity among the variables. For example, the organizational climate of a unit is determined by the behavior of managers above the manager of that unit. This organizational climate is a causal variable for that unit; it provides limits—favorable or unfavorable—within which the unit's manager is free to exercise his own style of leadership behavior. Nevertheless, the arrows show the major flow of influence. Top managerial leadership determines organizational climate. These two variables are causal in character, determining the state of the other variables shown. These other dimensions are intervening variables, except for total productive efficiency, which, of course, is an end-result variable.

The magnitude of the relationships among the human organizational dimensions and end-result performance data is influenced greatly by the accuracy—that is, reliability and validity—with which the performance results are measured. Low correlations are often obtained because of inaccurate performance data. It is quite common for members of an operating unit, both supervisory and nonsupervisory, to protect themselves by deliberately reporting erroneous performance results. Their "adjustments" are known as the "fudge factor," and whenever the performance data, whether productivity costs, scrap, or other measurements, have been influenced by fudge factors or other alterations, they are correspondingly inaccurate.

These inaccuracies, or "noise," of course, lower the observed relationships—the coefficients of correlation—between the human organizational dimensions and the end-result performance variables, and are a common source of low correlations. Where the performance data are highly inaccurate because of fudge factors or other distortions, it is often useful to obtain an estimate of what the magnitude of the relationships between the human organizational dimensions and performance variables would be if the performance data were accurate. A statistical method called correcting for attenuation produces an estimate of what the coefficient of correlation would be if the performance data were highly reliable.

Any coefficients of correlation that have been corrected for attenuation should not, however, be used in computing changes in the value of the human organization. When evidence shows that computed correlations are substantially less than their true relationship because of errors and distortions in the performance data, management should take corrective steps, but such steps should not be punitive in any respect. Punitive action will increase hostilities and lead to greater, not lessened, use of fudge factors and even greater errors in the performance data.

Changes in the key dimensions of the human organization appear to be dependable indicators for forecasting changes in the productivity and financial performance of an organizational unit that the human organization will be able to sustain over substantial periods of time (in contrast with levels that can be achieved for shorter periods in response to punitive threats). Moreover, when changes in the human organizational dimensions occur, predictions can be made of the magnitude of changes that will occur subsequently in the output performance of that human organization, whether it be an entire corporation, a division, or a single unit. The accuracy of these predictions will vary, of course, from situation to situation and depending on several factors, such as the kind of work being done, but in each situation the relative accuracy of the prediction can be assessed by computing the probable error of the estimate. The prediction then can be interpreted and used in the light of its probable error.

Estimating Changes in Value of Human Organizations in Dollars

To estimate in dollars changes in the value of the productive capability of any human organization it is necessary to measure the key dimensions of that human organization at each time period, say, at one year ago (T1) and now (T2). Changes in scores on these dimensions from T1 to T2 can

Figure 22-1. Relationships Among Human Organizational Dimensions and to Performance

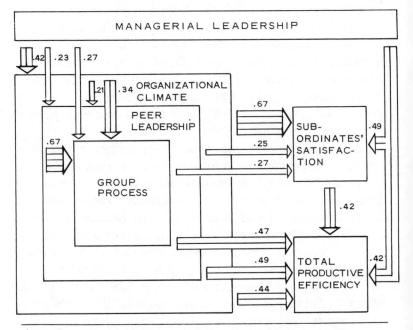

then be used to predict the change in the productive capability of that human organization. For example, if the causal dimensions of the human organization of a profit center showed a gain from T1 to T2 of one unit, the productive capability obviously increased. If, from statistical calculations, each unit of gain or loss in the causal scores is known to produce a corresponding shift in the productivity of the human organization that alters unit costs by $3.50, then improvement in the causal scores of one unit would yield a predicted improvement in total costs of $350,000 for a total production of 100,000 units. This estimate in dollars of the change in the productive capability of the profit center's human organization can be used to compute the change in the value of that human organization as an asset by capitalizing it at an appropriate rate. If 20 percent is used, the $1,750,000 increase in value of the human organization can be treated as an increase in the asset value of the profit center's human organization.

If the human organization of the profit center in our example had worsened, the decrease in asset value of the human organization would be computed in essentially the same manner. If, for example, there had been a decrease in the causal variable scores of the one unit from T1 to T2, the computations would show a predicted increase in annual production costs of $350,000 for 100,000 units. This would mean an estimated decrease of $1,750,000 in the asset value of the profit center's human organization.

Figure 22-2 shows the computational steps used in arriving at the dollar estimates; it is based on the following data about the plant in the example:

- The plant is one of 20 comparable plants engaged in essentially the same operation and using the same technology.
- For these 20 plants, the correlation between the causal human organizational scores and unit production costs is -0.70. (The correlation is negative, since the better the causal scores are, the lower are the unit costs.)
- The standard deviation in the human organizational scores is 0.25.
- The standard deviation in the unit production costs is $5.00.
- The plant has an annual production of 100,000 units; it had at T1 a causal human organizational score of 3.6; and it

had at T2 a causal human organizational score of 3.85. (The human organizational variables, shown on pages 264, 265, and 266, are measured on a scale of 1 to 5, with 5 being the most favorable.)

Figure 22-2. Translating Human Organizational Values into Dollars

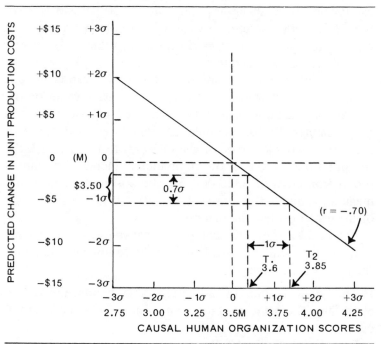

As the above data and Figure 22-2 show, the improvement in the causal human organizational scores is from 3.6 to 3.85, or +.25. This gain, when converted to standard scores by dividing the gain by the standard deviation in the human organizational scores, is +1.00 (+.25 ÷ .25 = +1.00). In turn, this gain of +1.00 is converted to an estimated gain in standard scores in the unit production costs by multiplying it by the coefficient of correlation (-0.70) between the human organizational scores and production costs (+1.00 X -0.70 = -0.70). Converting this reduction in unit production costs of -0.70, expressed in standard scores to dollars, yields an estimated reduction in unit costs of $3.50. This conversion to dollars requires multiplying the estimated reduction in standard scores by the standard deviation of the unit production costs (-0.70 X $5.00 = $3.50). The total annual reduction in costs is $350,000 (100,000 X $3.50), since annual production is 100,000 units.

The Most Profitable Way to Use Superior Managers

An important conclusion emerges from these human resource accounting computations: As a rule, it will prove more profitable for a firm to bring a below-average operation to average than to move an above-average operation to a very high level. This conclusion follows from two facts. First, an increase of one unit in human organization scores yields the same estimated improvement in cost savings and increased value of the human organization regardless of the original or final level of the human organization score at T1. (See Figure 22-2.) Second, an improvement in the human organization from below average to average can be maintained at this new level by a manager who has not yet become what I call a System 4 manager, but who is at least moderately skilled. (System 4 will be discussed in detail later on.) The increase in productive capability and asset value of the human organization is, consequently, retained.

On the other hand, when a human organization is built from above average to very good, it takes an excellent System 4 manager to hold it at this level. Under any less skilled manager, the human organization will regress toward its previous state, and the firm will lose this gain in productive capability and human asset value. There may be some circumstances, however, that would lead a firm to use a highly skilled System 4 manager to move an operation from an above-average level to a very high level. For example, the firm may wish to have a model of an excellent human organization to study its nature, operating characteristics, and potential.

Hidden Costs of the 1969-71 Recession

Changes in the productive capability of a firm's human organization cannot be assessed correctly unless periodic measurements of the causal and intervening dimensions of that organization are made regularly. Since most firms do not obtain these measurements, they are unable to detect the changes that are occurring in their human organizations, and, even worse, current profit-and-loss reports often encourage them to believe that changes are occurring that are the exact opposite of the shifts that actually are taking place. When profits go up, it is often assumed that the human organization has become more productive, but steps taken to maintain earnings or prevent losses may actually result in a decrease in the productive capability of the human organization, even though a short-range increase in reported profits is attained.

This has happened in many firms during the past few years. They have experienced a sizable, but often unrecognized, drop in the productive capability of their human organizations, a decrease now showing up in the difficulties of achieving high-quality production and low costs as markets again become firm. These unrecognized losses are a direct consequence of the cost-reduction moves that these firms made to meet the financial pressures caused by the recession. For example, a company manufacturing consumer durables had been growing rapidly and profitably as the market for its products expanded. The 1969-71 recession brought a pause in market expansion and exposed severe problems in inventory and production control, labor productivity, and a long accounts-receivable period. Overnight, profitability vanished, and the familiar action steps were ordered for the reduction of overhead personnel, for the reduction of inventory, and for a major effort to step up collections on overdue accounts; budgets were tightened, personnel were exhorted to reduce costs, and pressure was put on production workers to meet or exceed standards. The cost-reduction steps brought increases in reported earnings, but with a serious deterioration in the productive capability of the firm's human organization.

The Net Loss from Slashing Costs: A Case History

With these kinds of cost-reduction steps, the long-range costs typically exceed the short-range gains; it is clear that better cost-reduction strategies are needed, even in crisis. The experience of one plant of several hundred employees is a case in point. A management consulting firm that was brought in to carry out a cost-reduction program analyzed the staffing of each department in the plant against standards the consultants themselves established and found about a third of the departments appreciably overstaffed. For each of these departments, teams made up of persons from other departments, corporate or division staff, and the consulting firm were assigned to study the department and recommend ways to achieve labor savings. The manager of each affected department served as liaison, but no one from the department was on the team. After a plan for the labor savings was developed and approved, the managers of the affected departments were ordered to introduce the specific changes and achieve the designated savings, which totaled approximately $250,000 annually.

Measurements of the human organization of the plant were obtained before this cost-reduction program was started (T1) and again one year later (T2):

• The overstaffed departments where intensive cost-reduction efforts were undertaken were those that at T1 had the poorest management in terms of their human organizational scores. These departments were especially poor in terms of the causal variables (see Figure 22-3).

Figure 22-3. Relationship of Human Organizational Variables to Intensity of Cost-Reduction Effort—Major Indexes Profile

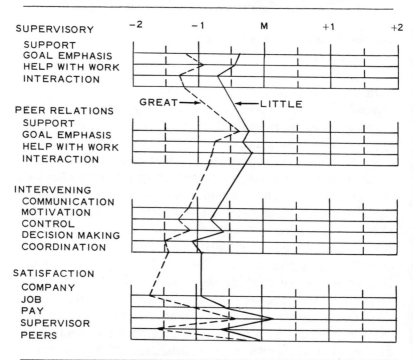

• The cost-reduction program treated the symptom of poor management by reducing overstaffing, but no effort was made to help the managers of the overstaffed departments learn how to manage their human organizations more effectively. After the overstaffing had been reduced, the

repeat measurements at T2 revealed that the managerial behavior as shown by the scores on the causal variables was actually worse than it was at T1. (See Figure 22-4.) There also was a general deterioration in the human organization from T1 to T2. Only two indexes showed an improvement from T1 to T2—peer help with work and peer team building, but, ironically, the increases in these scores occurred among nonsupervisory employees and reflected better teamwork

Figure 22-4. Human Organizational Variables in High-Effort Department Before and After Cost-Reduction Effort—Major Indexes Profile

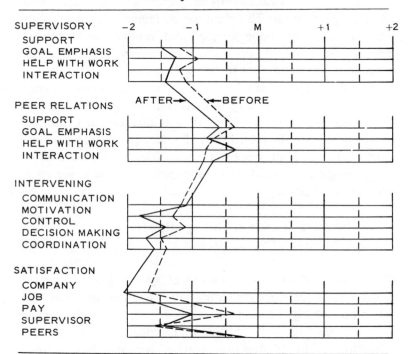

focused on *restricting* production, shown by the sizable drops in the motivation scores of the employees and unfavorable attitudes toward the company. Thus, treating the symptoms resulted in worsening the cause, poor management. In other words, a less productive organization emerged from the effects of the cost-reduction program.

• Computations based on the unfavorable shifts in the causal and other human organizational dimensions from T1 to T2 revealed that there had been a loss in the productive capability of the plant's human organization that would increase costs at least $450,000 annually, so, by treating symptoms, the cost-reduction program had achieved an annual savings in labor costs of $250,000, but at an estimated continuing annual cost of $450,000. The plant's actual experience over the past several years has confirmed the accuracy of the measurements of the human organization and of these predictions: The plant has sustained substantial costs of the kind that poor management produces—slowdowns, restriction of output, poor quality, excessive scrap, dissatisfied employees, and poor labor relations.

The conclusion should not be drawn from these findings that it is unsound to seek low costs or to take action when the economic survival of the firm is threatened. Quite the contrary. It is in the interests of all—management, consumers, employees, and shareholders—that efficient low-cost operating methods be used, but the question is how lower costs should be achieved.

Profitable Cost Reduction Through Highly Productive Human Organizations

Fortunately, there is a management system that achieves a much more productive human organization and has the capability of rapid action when it is necessary to reduce costs by methods that build, rather than worsen, the productive capability of the human organization—a system derived from the same research that has made possible dollar estimates of the changes in the productive capability of a human organization. This system is based on the principles and insights of the managers who are achieving the highest productivity and lowest costs and who have the most satisfied and healthy employees and the best labor relations. It is more complex than the usual management system and requires learning more effective leadership and problem-solving skills, but it produces human organizations that are about 20 to 40 percent more productive than average. Called System 4, it can be described by using the limited number of human organizational dimensions, both causal and intervening, discussed at the beginning of this paper. System 4 scores at the high, or favorable, end of each of the variables. By way of explanation, System 1 is exploitative-authoritative, System 2 is benevolent-authoritative, and System 3 is consultative; System 4 we call participative group.

To give an idea of the System 4 climate, characteristically, these factors are present:

• A great deal of confidence and trust is shown in subordinates.
• Subordinates' ideas are frequently sought and used constructively.
• A great deal of cooperative teamwork exists.
• The usual direction of information flow is downward, upward, and sideways.
• Subordinates are fully involved in decisions related to their work.
• Organizational goals are established by group action (except in crisis).
• Review and control functions are widely shared.

An effective means of enabling any firm or department to build a System 4 human organization is the survey feedback method. The human organization is measured and its scores on the causal and intervening dimensions are computed for each work group and for each of the larger units and then for the entire firm. Each manager, from the top executive down to and including first-level supervisors, is given the human organizational measurements of his work group and of the larger entities whose behavior and performance he is responsible for. Using System 4 as the desired model, each manager is encouraged and assisted to assess his own situation, to recognize his strengths and weaknesses, and, with the participation of his subordinate group, to plan and take the action needed to move his behavior and the human organization toward System 4. (For a description of this process and the coaching used, see *Improving Organizational Performance*, 1971, Rensis Likert Associates, Ann Arbor, Mich.)

In this process, not only are the human organizational dimensions used for analyses and problem solving, but the operating problems of the firm or department that are caused by inadequate human organization are also examined and solved by the relevant work groups. The focus is on task accomplishment, rather than on interpersonal process. When inter-personal obstacles develop, they are worked through directly, but only to the extent that they impede group effort to reach action on its central problems. As task problems are solved and procedures are established to handle them, roles and role relationships are changed. These, in turn, lead to improvement in interpersonal relationships and a more effective human organization. This cycle should be repeated at regular intervals, usually annually.

If the discrepancies between where an enterprise is now and where it wants to be are large, the change toward System 4 should be a gradual one, taken step by step. One huge leap should not be attempted, since most persons cannot successfully make great changes in their values, skills, expectations, and relationships in a short period of time.

The Relation of System 4 to
Performance-Improving Procedures

Many firms today are achieving appreciable improvement in performance by applying one or more procedures like management by objectives (MBO), positive reinforcement, autonomous teams, and job enrichment or redesign. But the gains that these firms are experiencing from the use of these procedures would be very much greater if used with System 4 management.

When MBO is used by a System 4 company, it becomes management by group objectives (MBGO). The objectives are set by the manager and his subordinates in group problem-solving meetings. Each subordinate knows both the team objectives and the objectives that he must attain. This team use of the MBO concept results in better understanding by team members of the responsibilities of each. Participation in setting the group's objectives heightens the motivation of each member to achieve the objectives and to help colleagues in attaining them. Each member expects each of the others, as well as himself, to do his best to reach the stated goals. Loyalty to other members is added to loyalty to the superior as a source of motivation. MBGO, consequently, is superior to MBO in achieving better understanding among members of the group of their interdependent objectives and relationships, mobilizing greater motivation among the manager's subordinates to reach the objectives and establishing better teamwork and coordination.

Positive reinforcement as ordinarily used involves reinforcing behavior by the manager, for example, by his giving recognition for a task well done. In a System 4 management, the positive reinforcement comes not only from the individual's manager but from all of the others in his work group. Reinforcement from one's teammates in a well-knit team adds substantially greater motivation and positive behavioral change than does reinforcement from the superior only. (Restriction of output, widespread in American industry, demonstrates the power of reinforcement by teammates.)

Job enrichment or the redesign of jobs is usually carried out with the involvement of the worker whose job is being changed, and often with the participation of other members of his work group. This involvement motivates the employee to do well on the new job, and if they have participated, those whose work is related to the changed job understand the changes and are able and willing to cooperate in coordinating their efforts. Job enrichment or redesign, when done well and with the full involvement of those persons whose work is affected, typically yields increased productivity and greater employee satisfaction, but it may boomerang in time, except in a System 4 atmosphere.

When job enrichment is carried out with the participation of those affected, they realize from their experience that their participation in decisions concerning this one part of their job has increased both productivity and their satisfaction. But if participation in matters affecting one aspect of their job yields such good results, most workers are likely to press to be involved in decisions dealing with all the other parts of their work life. Denying these requests of supervisory and nonsupervisory employees to be involved in decisions affecting them will make them dissatisfied and frustrated, so unless a firm is willing to shift to System 4, it should take a hard look before using any form of job enrichment that includes employee participation.

The reason that System 4 achieves substantially better results than other management systems from such procedures as MBO and positive reinforcement is its much greater capacity to mobilize high levels of cooperative motivation. For the same reason, it is capable of obtaining appreciably better results from the many other procedures that are useful in achieving improved performance, such as production teams and work simplification.

System 4 Improvements in Action

Moving the human organization of a department of about 200 employees in a large fabricating plant toward System 4 yielded substantial improvement in one year's time. Productivity increased 28 percent, scrap losses dropped to 25 percent of their previous level, and written grievances dropped from over 50 per month to an average of less than three per month. Other measures of performance and labor relations, too, showed comparable gains. This improvement effort was extended to the entire plant and within three years had yielded cost savings in excess of $5,000,000.

A sales region of a large consumer products firm was helped by means of the survey feedback method to move its human organization toward System 4. Over an eight-month period, the human organization scores were improved by about 20 percent, and sales as a percentage of quota showed an even greater increase. This region continued to improve its performance, breaking all previous sales records and selling a larger volume than another region that had a sales potential about one-fifth greater.

Comparable improvements in both the human organization and in performance are being obtained in other situations involving widely different kinds of work, but not every attempt to build more productive human organizations and achieve better performance succeeds so well. For example, a particular department may be part of a larger organization whose· top management does not want the management of the subordinate department to shift toward System 4. Or a manager may be so fearful of failing that he is unwilling to undertake the risk of trying to shift toward System 4.

To sum up, social science research has provided the resources to enable any firm or any manager to build a more productive human organization and achieve better performance. This research is also creating the methodology for estimating in dollars the value of the changes in the productive capability of any firm's human organization. As these dollar estimates become an integral part of the management information system of every well-managed organization, they will lead to sounder decisions based on more adequate information. Top managements and boards of directors will move much more rapidly than at present to the use of science-based management because of System 4's demonstrably greater capacity to achieve and maintain low costs accompanied by employee satisfaction and health.

SAMUEL J. BERNSTEIN AND LEON REINHARTH

23 MANAGEMENT, THE PUBLIC ORGANIZATION, AND PRODUCTIVITY

The current introduction of productivity-improvement programs at almost all levels of American government is
associated with the confluence of two major factors: the
sharply rising costs of providing public services and the
growing gap between these costs and revenues being raised.
To date, the various federal, state, and municipal attempts
that have been oriented toward measuring and increasing
productivity have met with only limited success (*Business
Week*, May 13, 1972). It is the purpose of this chapter to
report some of the operational or practical problems involved
in increasing productivity in the public sector. Our analysis is
based on participant observation in one such program.

We recognize that the specific conditions found in one
governmental bureau may not be symptomatic of conditions
in all governmental agencies. We feel, however, that an
in-depth analysis of the operations of a particular governmental bureau, based on a strong theoretical framework, will
highlight basic organizational productivity issues having

Reprinted from the July/August, 1973, issue of *Public Personnel
Management*, by permission of the International Personnel Management
Association, Inc. and the authors.

general applicability, and will provide organizational policy guidelines for improving employee performance in the public sector.

Following the open systems approach of Bennis, Schein, and Argyris, among others, we have taken the position that increased individual and organizational productivity—however measured—is a function of the level of integration of the four basic organizational components: the individual, the group, the organizational system and the public environment. The principal factors affecting each of these components as they impinge on the effective and efficient performance of the public organization are thus identified and discussed.

The Individual

• *Decision to join.* Although the public organization frequently is perceived to be overstaffed, it paradoxically suffers from an even more insidious problem of not being able to attract qualified candidates for middle and upper-range management positions that cannot or at times should not necessarily be filled from within the organization. At the municipal level this problem has reached such dramatic proportions that recruitment of qualified persons for even clerical and secretarial positions has become a difficult task. Hence, confronting every personnel officer in the public organization is the basic problem of getting the "right" people to join. The recruitment problem thus tends to further aggravate and complicate management's attempt to increase productivity in the public organization because the adequate manpower is just lacking.

Clearly there are many underlying conditions within the public organization that contribute to this recruitment problem and a discussion of each would be beyond the scope of the present chapter. However, there is a singular organizational factor that may be easily manipulated by management in order to improve the public organization's attraction for the right people at lower levels. This is the organizational rigidity that requires strict adherence to a 9 to 5, 40-hour a week work schedule by employees. By modifying this rigidity, particularly in metropolitan areas, through either the utilization of permanent part-time positions and/or "sliding time scales," two direct benefits may be expected. First, two important sources of committed labor are presently being ignored: namely, working mothers and the college and post-graduate student bodies. Both labor pools could be tapped within a flexible organization time setup. Their particular advantages for the public organization in terms of productivity may be said to be fivefold:

(1) They are more mature and thus tend to be more committed to their work.
(2) They provide a continuous supply from which the organization may draw potentially effective manpower.
(3) The continuous but less than full-time commitment provides the time necessary for these individuals to grow into the organization and vice-versa.
(4) Therefore a conversion process may be set in motion whereby these persons may take on full-time responsibilities when both the jobs and they are available.
(5) Continuity in the labor supply is built into the organization; hence, the potential for improved provision of public services is automatically enhanced without additional cost.

Second, at middle and upper-range management levels, a less rigid task framework coupled with a focus on project accomplishment fosters greater authority in the job and also greater responsibility. This increases the attraction of the public organization for creative persons seeking a challenge. In this context, the individual is permitted to view his various job responsibilities in terms of a project which he manages and is responsible for. Recent research in project management shows that this perception is related to more effective performance and satisfaction in jobs. *De facto* then, productivity should also increase.

The general form of the permanent part-time experiment involves assignments covering half or two thirds of a full day's work load, or two or three full work days per week. The form of the sliding time scale generally involves the abandonment of a strict 9 to 5 code. Instead, employees are permitted to pick their hours within broad time ranges as constrained by: (1) essential core times when it is necessary that he or she be in; and (2) an agreed-upon number of hours per week, measured in monthly time units.

• *Decision to perform.* In terms of an individual's productivity in an organization the essential issue to be addressed is the decision to perform. Three factors may be said to determine the response: (1) the individual himself; (2) the management; (3) the groups in the organization.

With respect to the individual, two organizational development techniques that have been effectively utilized in the private sector to stimulate performance may be adapted for the public organization. They are: (1) job enrichment; and (2) incentive systems. Job enrichment programs involve the varying of work tasks and the incorporation of staff into the decision-making process, known as "participatory decision-making." Incentive programs involve the use of reward programs—monetary or non-monetary—for enhancing competence in job performance. A noteworthy spin-off benefit that may flow from the utilization of these two programs together is employee cooperation with management for establishing more flexible organization formats. This in turn would lead to easier and more rapid shifting of organizational manpower from areas of decreasing demand to areas of increasing demand. The inability to freely shift manpower within public organization functions today is in part responsible for many presently built in backlogs in work flow.

Management, it may be said, seems to have succeeded in transmitting to public employees attitudes of loyalty to the organization, responsibility in fulfilling the assigned functions and fairness in dealing with the publics being served. However, by ignoring the changing nature of public requirements and demands for increased services, as well as job requirements, management has permitted employees to set lower productivity norms and to adopt at times defensive, and even restrictive postures with regard to organizational functions which may be restructured more effectively or even eliminated. In order to improve management's capacity to govern effectively inside the public organization, it is essential that two executive improvement programs be undertaken.

• *Management training.* This program ought to be carried out in conjunction with nearby academic institutions because its emphasis should be on the adaptation and application of new management techniques to the public sector in order to improve performance.

• *Organizational development.* In contrast to the former, organization development focuses on human relations aspects of public organization. Programs within this rubric have to emphasize the crucial role of management in integrating the needs of the various individuals and subgroups within the organization in order to establish organization contexts that permit pursuing organization goals without interference. To implement these programs effectively it is necessary that follow-on efforts be built into their structure and be placed under the aegis of the respective personnel officers of the different agencies or departments.

The Group

Survival is one of the major goals in organizational life. The vehicles for the search for survival or endurance are the informal groupings that tend to evolve in large organizations.

Where organizations are functioning less than efficiently, there is a tug of war battle between informal groupings in the organizations and productivity norms proposed by management. To minimize the impacts of groups sabotaging productivity improvement programs, project tasks are recommended. Specifically, this requires that work flow be split into separate projects and each project be assigned in a functional way to the different informal groups which exist in the organization. Because this proposal is not foolproof and does not cover all situations, an additional educational effort is required to effect a basic change in the attitude of work groups in the public organization. One issue that may be used to precipitate this attitude change is the presently ignored fact that, given continued increased public demands for services, productivity does not mean a consequent loss of jobs but rather a rearrangement of job functions for more effectively satisfying current and future growing public service needs.

The Organization

• *Managerial control.* In a profit-making enterprise, the objectives of the organization are met only when the product or service is sold, delivered and paid for. All other activities, such as purchasing, manufacturing and administration, are viewed as vital steps toward the goal but are not confused with the goal itself. Similarly, the function of government enterprise is to render a specific array of services to the community. It should be the responsibility of the governmental manager to see to the prompt and efficient performance of the service under his charge.

Due to the growing interdependence among governmental agencies, the processing of many activities requires the cooperation of two or more agencies. Our observations reveal that the conscientious manager diligently attends to the proper distribution of the input to his department, but less frequently follows up to the final disposition of activities directly under his control, and almost never pursues an activity which has been transferred to another agency for intermediate action. The efficient provision of the public service is thus delayed. Control systems must be designed where all pending activities are directly under managerial control, so they may be followed up easily and directly. One such system is discussed in the following section.

• *Coordination.* It has been indicated that the activities of government are becoming more interdependent (witness the Advisory Council for Inter-Governmental Relations). Many functions require the coordination of various federal and state agencies, of various state and municipal agencies, or of all three. The process is often complicated by the existence of public corporations with which separate relationships have to be established. Occasionally, the legislative statute that defines the function may provide for a coordinating body to mesh the efforts of the involved levels of government. However, when the coordinating body is not established by the statute, as is generally the case, the activity bogs down in an organizational morass, with everyone "passing the buck." It, therefore, should be the responsibility of agency heads to determine the extent of inter-agency coordination required by the organization and to take steps to set up a coordinating function with direct responsibility assigned to a department coordinator in each director's office. Locating this position in the directors' offices provides the necessary legitimacy for communicating with other agency or department heads in order to effect more immediate results in the form of better and more rapid communications, and thereby the provision of more effective service.

• *Systems.* In our dynamic environment, changes in laws and regulations, changes in organization policy, socioeconomic and population changes, and even technological changes all have a direct bearing on the operations of a governmental agency. It is thus startling to find systems and procedures in government bureaus that have not kept up with the times. Operations introduced 15 or 20 years ago are being followed today almost without change, regardless of their utility. By matching needs to resources and by flow-charting work procedures, we were able to recommend procedural changes in a small agency of 160 people which would result in a reduction of authorized staff of 20 percent, while increasing productivity and without basically altering organizational framework. It is evident that the addition of a qualified office systems analyst in government agencies could save his or her salary many times over by keeping job descriptions up-to-date, by instituting methods of work improvements, and by continuously adapting the agency's structure to changing needs. Such a position, clearly, is susceptible to strong internal political pressures and must therefore be carefully supervised by the agency head and the reporting system must be confidential within agencies or departments.

• *Computerization.* The major characteristic of government bureaucracy is the processing of forms and "papers." Nevertheless the information-processing capabilities of computers are not fully utilized. Public organizations, particularly at the local level, even today make only limited use of computers. To date, their primary use involves the preparation of payrolls for city employees and tax-collection, applications which are performed in "batch operations." Little consideration, however, has been given to developing "on-line" processing of administrative activities for improving information retrieval capabilities, statistical reporting, managerial control, as well as functional activities like personnel planning, welfare programs, land planning and usage registration, which is just beginning in the United States Department of the Interior, or even criminal justice applications so essential for improving the administration of justice today.

Our analysis revealed that adoption of these computer applications could reduce authorized clerical and administrative staff levels by an additional 20 percent with a more than commensurate increase in productivity payoff on hardware and software investment. The time estimated for achieving these returns falls between 12 to 18 months.

Reference is made at this point to an article that appeared in the *New York Times Magazine* (Sunday, October 22, 1972), entitled "Down and Out in New York," which reviews the steps being taken by the Lindsay administration to rationalize the welfare program and cut down on the abuses of the program. Referring to the modern management techniques, including computerization, being installed by the Department of Social Services, the author expresses doubts that these techniques can solve the welfare problems of the city, because of "the politics involved." This point punctuates the dangerous misinterpretation of the function of modern management techniques like computerization, and deserves clarification. The public organization plans and implements policies and at times even makes policies. It is the task of the administrator in the planning and implementing stages to be most expeditious and efficient. Thus it is in these areas where modern organizational management techniques and computer applications make their contribution. To criticize these organizational improvement techniques for policy shortcomings is equivalent to the ancient Greeks putting to death the bearer of bad tidings. Regardless of the policies adopted by an administration at any governmental level, computers can be a useful tool in administering public policies.

• *Manpower planning and utilization.* The heads of many departments, bureaus and agencies in government today joined the civil service during the Depression years and are at or near retirement age. Our observations have disclosed a dearth of middle management people, particularly at the local government level, trained to assume top management responsibilities. To avoid potentially serious problems of continuity, and to foster a smooth transition of leadership, a manpower planning program needs to be implemented by the directors of personnel in various agencies. This program should be all-inclusive, applying to all levels of employment, and emphasizing flexibility, so that management be given the power and ability to effect temporary and even permanent transfers of employees to areas of greatest need.

The Environment

Two institutions in the environment significantly influence the performance of the public organization. They are the civil service commission and the public service union. Their status stems from the rules and regulations promulgated by the commission and the work conditions negotiated by the union. The recommendations proposed for improving the competence of the public organization—flexibility in recruitment, changes in working conditions and hours, flexibility in transferring employees, incentive programs, manpower planning and utilization programs—are of concern to these two bodies, and must therefore be negotiated with them. Such negotiations may be difficult, but it is management's obligation to raise the issues. If the goal of improved productivity is shared by all parties concerned, it should be possible to implement the required organizational changes without violating the principles and objectives of either the commission or the public service union.

Conclusion

• *Implications.* Due to the size and complexity of the governmental bureaucracy, a major effort is required to effect improvements in productivity. This article has identified the principal factors to be considered in improving productivity, with regard to the major elements of the organizational system—the individual, the group, the organization and the environment. Particular emphasis was placed on showing the positive results which may be achieved from productivity improvement programs.

• *Summary of findings.* Our results may be summarized for the purpose of organization planning and development as follows:

(1) The source of potential candidates for government service should be expanded by adopting flexible working schedules.

(2) Incentive and job-enrichment programs should be instituted to increase the motivation of public service employees for improved performance.

(3) The rigidity of the governmental organization structure should be relaxed to permit managers to transfer manpower from areas of declining demand to areas of growing need.

(4) Enduring productivity improvement requires internal organizational efforts to streamline and update operational systems, to institute managerial control programs, and to expand the utilization of computer applications.

(5) To insure a smooth transition of leadership, manpower planning programs should be developed.

(6) The increasing need for inter-agency communication and cooperation should be met by the establishment of a high level coordinating function in each agency.

(7) Finally, public sector management should confront the task of negotiating needed patterns of change with the two major environmental institutions that are directly concerned, namely, the civil service commission and the public service union.

HARRY P. HATRY AND DONALD M. FISK

24 LOCAL GOVERNMENT PRODUCTIVITY IMPROVEMENT POSSIBILITIES

The National Commission on Productivity is concerned with helping governments to improve their productivity. It is not necessary nor desirable to await major improvements in productivity *measurement* before attempting to make improvements in productivity itself—particularly as we are somewhat pessimistic on moving ahead rapidly on improving productivity measurement.

In this chapter we present a sample of possibilities that appear to have potential in significantly increasing productivity at the local level of government and may merit testing if they are not already being tested. We have not attempted to make any evaluation of these possibilities nor to develop them in detail. Many, if not all, have potential drawbacks that also need to be evaluated. Even though some are currently being tested somewhere in the United States, the experiences need a systematic evaluation with adequate dissemination of the findings throughout the United States— even though crude measurement techniques have to be used.

We by no means intend this list as an exhaustive one, but

Reprinted from *Improving Productivity and Productivity Measurement in Local Governments*, prepared for the National Commission on Productivity by the Urban Institute, June, 1971.

only illustrative of the potential richness of ideas that might be of significance in improving local government productivity.

General Government

(1) Increase the innovation potential of governments by the following methods:

• Rotation of middle and upper level management among agencies within a government.

• More hiring from the outside at middle and upper management levels and perhaps even for non-managerial positions. A related need would be to broaden nationally the use of reciprocal certifications and develop pension plans permitting the transfer of experience and pension rights between cities for employees such as police, fire department personnel and city and county managers. These would reduce the incentive for an individual to remain excessive amounts of time with any single government.

• Improve the attractiveness of professional and management positions to bright, young people by, for example, the provision of adequate responsibility and opportunities for early promotion.

• Encouragement of more experimentation before launching full-scale programs.

• Use of "value analysis" ("value engineering") techniques. For example, ad hoc task forces with personnel from a number of agencies might periodically examine specific services for the purpose of "tearing each apart" and reconstituting them in light of community objectives including the need for greater efficiency.

• Provision of better salaries to attract persons with high level skills to come to local government and remain for reasonable amounts of time.

• Encouragement of active support and motivation by state

and local top level officials, including state and local government legislative bodies, to encourage new ideas and experimentation. This is usually vital to stimulate and develop the interest of lower levels of the government.

(2) Increase the ability of local governments to more effectively use modern technology.

Progress aimed at increasing the ability of local governments to more effectively use modern technology should be encouraged.

• Establishment of a national product evaluation center (e.g., consumer union) to examine commercial products and estimate the likely full costs and effects, and disseminate the findings throughout the nation.

• Creation of a national organization to develop performance specifications for government products needed throughout the country—with the specifications "modularized" to reflect major likely individual and regional differences. This would speed up the acceptance of new products and encourage market aggregation, which is badly needed to get science and technology applied to local government problems. It has been said that "Industry generally needs firm assurance of a large aggregated market for a fairly standardized product before it will invest in the research, development and manufacturing of a new product, especially one involving complex technology."

• Establishment of a national "Applied Research Center" to develop, test and demonstrate new products.

• Provision of an adequate dissemination system whereby information on useful science and technology, including information derived from the preceding items, would be rapidly and effectively disseminated to local governments throughout the country.

The recently formed Technology Application Program (TAP) of the International City Management Association is a start in these directions. Its program with NASA involves preparation by cities of initial performance specifications for a few hardware products; NASA is now investigating possible available science and technology that might satisfy these specifications. Some specific product needs identified by the cities in the project included short-range communication equipment to permit voice communication between firemen at the fire scene; improvement of traffic line paints to make them longer wearing, instant drying, and reflectorized but non-glaring; automatic fire hose pressure regulators so that firemen would not be needed for this during fire fighting; and electrical fault detectors to expedite location of faults in underground cable for maintenance activities. TAP is also planning to develop with National Science Foundation funding, a clearinghouse for science and technology information to local governments.

• Establishment of "system engineering" groups in the larger governments to develop useful technological applications.

(3) Improve local government planning and evaluation capabilities and procedures.

Adequate planning and evaluation capability is vital to major, long-range productivity improvements. Improved planning-budgeting systems such as PPBS are already being tried in a small number of local governments. Some of the needed elements are as follows:

• Consideration of a multi-year planning horizon when deciding on each year's program decisions. If governments continue to plan one year at a time, major changes will seldom be possible. It usually takes time to overcome inertia and implement major changes. It is, of course, necessary to make investments in one year in order to obtain returns in later years. However, the lack of systematic multi-year planning in many governments hinders the ability to effectively consider such options.

• Identification of citizen and community objectives and their systematic use for planning and budgeting purposes, rather than concentrating on internal activities such as workload measures and other immediate physical outputs such as miles of roads, numbers of hospital beds, and number of acres of parks—as is traditional.

• Provision for selective, systematic evaluation of current services and specific programs. Local government officials need to know how specific services are performing, especially major and new programs. They need information as to the total costs and impacts on citizens and the community, both the beneficial and negative ones. Little of this is done today except in a very haphazard and usually grossly deficient manner. This means that unproductive programs do not come to the surface readily. Improved measurement techniques are also needed to help in such evaluations. Local governments should try to put a certain percentage of operating funds, perhaps 1 percent to 3 percent, into program evaluation and analysis.

• Procurement of qualified, practical analytical personnel. The lack of such talent is a major limitation in undertaking systematic policy and program planning.

(4) Dissemination of information on successful or unsuccessful programs elsewhere in the country.

The transference of evaluative information on programs undertaken by one government to other city and county governments, if provided quickly, clearly and thoroughly, could be of great help. This could avoid potentially great waste resulting if one government has to learn information that it should have had available. Dissemination of "success stories" also would encourage others to use the latest tested ideas.

A clearinghouse, such as discussed under (2) for science and technology could be the nucleus here. Explicit provision should be made in any such clearinghouse for systematic program evaluation.

(5) Consideration of organizational consolidations or other joint arrangements to obtain "economies of scale."

It is commonly believed that certain economies can result

if done for larger units than individual cities or towns.

• The creation of *added* units of government such as special regional refuse disposal districts. This approach unfortunately proliferates governmental bodies.

• The creation of *larger* general units of government. If provision is made for retaining some decentralization of neighborhood services, this has considerable potential, if it can be achieved politically. Little systematic evaluation of such organizational arrangements has been undertaken thus far, perhaps reflecting the considerable problem with evaluation criteria such as the lack of adequate productivity data.

• Provision of joint purchasing arrangements or other joint activities, such as joint waste disposal sites, is a possibility for obtaining some of the potential benefits without requiring major organizational changes. Not only would joint purchasing permit price breaks through volume discounts, but also permit greater specialization by purchasing agents with potentially more informed purchasing, and might also help industry by providing larger markets for individual products.

(6) Increased use of the private sector—both businesses and citizens.

A number of possibilities are present.

• Greater use of private firms to undertake functions currently undertaken by the government. Private firms may, in some instances, be able to provide services at lower costs and without sacrificing quality. Private firms are often already doing solid waste collection. (As noted in Chapter 3, a recent New York City analysis indicated potentially large cost savings by switching part of its collection to private firms.) One city, Scottsdale, Arizona, has a contract with a private firm for fire-fighting (but uses city employees on call for certain fire-fighting duties). School districts have begun in a few instances to contract for some elementary educational services. Exploration of these and other "privatization" possibilities merit exploration and testing.

• Use of public funds as a carrot to attract citizen resources, such as in improving neighborhood conditions. For example, Arlington County, Virginia, recently has installed playground equipment with the citizens paying or donating the materials. This would serve to increase the output from public tax dollars.

• Attracting of citizen volunteers to certain activities, even in the larger local governments. It may well be that most local governments have not yet tapped opportunities for citizen volunteers for selected tasks such as recreational activities, certain health functions, various social services, schools aides, and even police functions. Regular, systematic attempts might be undertaken, perhaps through fliers and local radio and TV, to reach citizens with information as to what help is needed and whom to contact. Employee security and union concerns would need to be considered.

• Request citizens or businesses to do more on their own for certain services. For example, improved preparation of waste and its collection at curbside rather than at the "door" would ease the workload of the government and permit lowered costs. Another example would be to require burglary-prone businesses to maintain burglar alarm systems to reduce the need for police to monitor such facilities. Related to this would be government campaigns to the public to avert the need for corrective-type services, e.g., anti-litter campaigns, drug abuse control information and birth control information.

(7) Provision of added incentives and satisfactory working conditions to employees.

This is a major concern. In (1) we began by discussing the creation of an innovation atmosphere. Here we discuss more direct type of incentives. The discussion applies to management personnel as well as non-management.

• Use of formal incentive programs such as group bonuses. This is an often discussed but not widely used approach. The only common incentive program that we know occurs in the solid waste collection area, where collectors are permitted to go home as soon as they finish their collection routes without losing wages. Individual incentive systems seem to be frowned on by employees and their unions. However, group incentives might be worth considering. Group incentives such as bonuses to neighborhood police teams, to the personnel at individual schools, or to solid waste collection teams are possibilities. A major obstacle to such plans is the determination of the criteria whereby the bonuses would be distributed. There is no example to our knowledge of local governments permitting setting aside an amount of money for bonuses. Also, employees, the unions, and the public will mistrust any system that does not consider their views as to fairness and equity. Perhaps, if and when improved productivity measurement is undertaken, such as described elsewhere in this report, then formal incentives may be more feasible. However, even today it may be possible to work out incentive plans, at least in those jurisdictions where management-employee relations are good. These obviously would require considerable effort to work out, however.

• Provision of satisfactory, even pleasant, working conditions. Government employees, particularly blue-collar workers, often have many complaints about the basic working conditions, such as inadequate showers and toilets, protective clothing, drinking fountains, rest-break rules, canopies on open trucks for weather protection, etc. Such grievances, whether real or imagined, will fester and affect performance. In many cases the cost of correcting these is relatively small.

(8) Mechanization of revenue collection.

The use of mechanized operations for tax assessing to keep track of market sales and other factors affecting values. This would permit much more frequent updating of tax assessments to make revenue raising more productive and more equitable.

(9) Improvement of the capabilities of local government legislative bodies.

The continual entry of new councilmen in local government leads to the making of policy decisions by people of limited experience. Some initial improvements might be:

• Provision of training opportunities to new councilmen.

• Provision of research staffs to local government legislatures to help them examine and analyze policy issues.

(10) Improvement of labor-management relations.

It seems clear that in the years ahead the activity of local government employees and their unions will be aggressive in securing improved wages, working conditions, and employment security protections. The June, 1971, Labor-Management Relations Service newsletter of the National League of Cities, Conference of Mayors and the National Association of Counties reported that for the first 77 days of 1971 the number of strikes reported in the eastern half of the United States, 50, was more than double that tabulated for the same period in 1970, with sanitation, police and fire accounting for the great majority.

• Local governments will need to become more sophisticated in their bargaining with their employees and their unions. Full-time personnel, at least in the larger jurisdictions, are likely to be needed. Attempts to encourage increased productivity or at least preserve current levels will be needed. Some aspects of this were discussed in (7) above.

• More direct concern for government employees is probably needed. The desirability of improving working conditions was discussed in (7) above. In addition, explicit attention needs to be given to the welfare of employees displaced by new methods or new organizations, such as would result from some of the types of changes illustrated in this chapter.

(11) Increased training of employees.

Personnel at all levels and in all areas might benefit from periodic training programs aimed at updating or upgrading their skills. Even in the most "unskilled" areas, training aimed at improved performance might be useful to maintain and increase morale as well as productivity.

(12) Federal government procedures.

Two types of actions by the federal government on its own procedures may have particular impact on local government productivity.

• Simplification of procedures pertaining to state and local government application for, and administration of, federal grant programs. This could reduce the amount of time and effort spent on overhead-type activities.

• Improved use of federal demonstration-type programs to assure that demonstrations have a sufficient evaluation component. This would make available information as to the effectiveness, costs, and implementation difficulties of these demonstrations. An effective mechanism for dissemination of these results to other local governments is also needed.

Following are current practices or proposals that may increase productivity in specific local government services. While they represent views or judgments of experts in the separate fields, many of the activities remain controversial or of not fully proven merit.

Law Enforcement: Police

(1) Reallocation of policemen to assign them to times and locations more in accord with the workload (e.g., crime patterns and other calls). This potentially can increase police productivity in terms of response time, arrests, crime prevention and other police services without significantly increasing costs.

(2) Assignment of priorities to incoming calls so that important calls can be handled more quickly.

(3) Substitution of civilians for certain tasks currently done by policemen, including clerical, computer services, school crossing guards, police lab work, and meter maids. These may

reduce costs and provide better-trained individuals for these specialties.

(4) Assignment of detectives to geographical areas and times more in accord with the demand for their services, as measured by past experience.

(5) Mailing of summonses in some misdemeanor cases rather than sending patrolmen.

(6) Use of new technological devices such as walkie-talkies to expand the scope of action and flexibility of patrolmen and to permit them to receive information more quickly.

(7) Use of on-line computer systems to provide information such as data on suspects and automobiles. This might help to make the police more productive in the field.

Law Enforcement: The Court System

(1) Better scheduling of court cases to improve court productivity as well as that of other personnel such as police witnesses, prosecutors and juries. The time of all is frequently misused because of current practices arising out of the various uncertainties in hearing and trial times.

• Use of computerized procedures to schedule cases more effectively (based on such factors as severity of offense, likelihood of conviction, age of the case, whether the defendant is incarcerated, likely future availability of witnesses, and likelihood of repeated offenses by the defendant).

• Use of trained court administrators instead of judges for scheduling, court management, and other administrative practices.

(2) Improved procedures to save police time by calling police and other witnesses only when needed.

(3) Assignment of prosecutors to cases on the basis of factors such as listed in (1). This could potentially increase the productivity of the system, particularly in jurisdictions with large case backlogs. This is currently being tested in the District of Columbia.

(4) Setting of time limits for cases so that if the defendant

is not tried within the designated time period, say 60 days, the charges would be dropped. This forces the prosecution to act more quickly and discourages the granting of continuances.

Solid Waste Collection

(1) Too frequently solid waste collectors accompany the truck and its driver long distances to and from the disposal site. Possibilities exist for using waste collectors on other collections vehicles while letting loaded trucks and drivers go alone to disposal sites.

(2) Development of more mechanized sanitation trucks and easier to handle waste receptacles.

Health

(1) Use of paramedical personnel or physician assistants as substitutes for physicians to provide such services as portions of examinations, inoculations, teeth cleaning and even basic medical care in regions with scarce physician supply. (For example, HEW's MEDEX program is attempting to train returning armed forces medical corpsmen to become physician assistants.)

(2) Use of group, rather than individual, practice to provide more specialization and therefore more effective diagnosis and treatment, as well as to reduce total overhead costs.

(3) Use of prepaid medical fees rather than fee-for-service on the assumption that this will encourage physicians and medical staff to be more efficient (if it does not increase patient demand excessively).

(4) Use of computers for monitoring, diagnosis and prescription control as a substitute for manpower resources and to provide improved health care.

(5) Greater use of the telephone to save patient visits to the physician's office. It may be that a significant number of cases can be handled over the telephone through conversa-

tions between the patient and skilled personnel without requiring trips to the physician and the recurring tie-up of medical services.

Fire Protection

(1) Reallocation of existing fire fighting resources to increase productivity in some instances with little cost involved. The location of fire stations and amount of response to fires (e.g., number of vehicles) has been the subject of recent analyses. Operations research techniques have been used to develop mathematical models and simulations that aim at the selection of preferred locations for fire stations and at the number of vehicles to be stationed at individual stations or sent to respond to alarms of specific characteristics. (This includes work in New York City, the National Bureau of Standards, and the District of Columbia government.)

(2) Use of a chemical additive, "slippery water," to reduce the friction' of water in a hose, thereby permitting considerably greater water flow per minute or the use of smaller, lighter, easier to handle, hose. New York City has been experimenting with this and has identified significant possibilities for productivity increase through its use.

Education

(1) Use of schools twelve months per year and more hours per day, in part, perhaps, for other than educational purposes such as for community recreation. This could lead to more productive use of capital facilities.

(2) Use of various types of computer-assisted instruction, programmed learning equipment and perhaps cable TV to increase productivity.

(3) Adoption of school "accountability" procedures to provide measurement of individual school performance, using criteria such as achievement criteria. Such procedures are

receiving considerable current interest. The ability of individual school superintendents and principals to undertake annual assessments of a school's strengths and weaknesses and in comparison with other schools in the school district could provide information and incentives for increased performance.

(4) Use of performance contracting for elementary schools. Private companies might be able to provide improved education for which payment is based on improvement in student achievement levels. Some such experiments are currently being tried.

25 FACTORS THAT HAVE CAUSED PRODUCTIVITY CHANGE

Background

Productivity measurement would be rather meaningless if it consisted only of gathering statistics and adding up the results.

The important questions are what do the indices reveal and what are they used for after they are developed? Explaining the cause of change—so that the future may learn from the past—may be the most valuable use of productivity measurement in the federal sector.

The relevant questions are:

- Is the change that occurred a result of planned action to improve either quantity or quality of performance or is it simply a happenstance?
- What are the positive and negative factors that caused the result?
- What will be the probable future trend under present practices?
- How can the trend be influenced now?
- Specifically, how can future productivity trends be

Reprinted from *Measuring and Enhancing Productivity in the Federal Government*, Summary Report, Joint Federal Productivity Project, 1973.

optimized in relation to cost-effective service, accuracy of output, or other meaningful quality criteria?

Two Overall Cautions Voiced by Agencies

Throughout this project, the agencies have voiced concern that overall productivity measures may be misused, particularly in the budget process or at high levels of Government where an intimate understanding of their meaning may not exist.

One source of agency concern is in the internal OMB instructions that assume that productivity is rising and will continue to rise. Instructions to budget examiners state that productivity gains of at least 2.5 percent are expected.

The joint productivity team's findings for the five-year period ending June 30, 1972, covering a sample of 60 percent of the civilian work force, indicate that the average annual rate of gain was 1.7 percent, with the highest year reaching 2.8 percent. Between 1971 and 1972, about half of the organizational elements increased and about half decreased. The data outlined in the remainder of this chapter will help give insights into the reason for productivity change and why it is unsound to assume that productivity is rising and will continue to rise. The internal OMB instructions should be revised accordingly.

A second concern of the agencies is that the productivity index must be analyzed more from year to year and must be associated with other indicators of performance, particularly indicators of effectiveness and quality change.

What Has Caused Productivity Improvements?

As shown in Table 25-1, 98 factors were reported on questionnaires or identified in workshop discussions. For ease of analysis, these were grouped into (1) human factors, (2) management factors, and (3) workload factors.

Table 25-1. What Has Caused Productivity Improvement?

Human factors (27)	Management factors (54)	Workload factors (17)
• Increased efficiency of personnel	• Improvement through capital investment	• Workload increases
• Acquisition of skilled personnel	• Automation	• Workload stability
• Job enrichment–job restructuring	• Procedures simplification	• Workload predictability
	• Organization improvements	• Reduction in complexity
	• Affirmative improvement program	• Reduction in quality

Human Factors

These 27 factors indicated that productivity improvement had resulted from:

- Increased personnel efficiency.
- Acquisition of skilled personnel by the activity concerned.
- Improved motivation of personnel, often through job redesign or upgrading.

Management Factors

These 54 factors, which were recurring, presented a very high percent of the organizational elements whose productivity improvement was significant.

- *Improvement through capital acquisition.* This includes computerization, other forms of mechanization, or newly improved facilities. This factor is not surprising because, since 1965 the number of general-purpose computers has grown from 2,412 to about 6,000 and from $1 billion of direct in-house operating costs to over $2 billion, not including military and intelligence-type applications.

• *Procedures simplification.* Such improvements are associated with mechanization and computerization in all instances but are also present in labor-intensive activities (such as those involved in grant processing) when paperwork simplification has been a factor in improved productivity. A prime tool of simplification, which will be illustrated later in this chapter, is the application of statistical-sampling techniques.

• *Organizational improvements.* When this is cited as a contribution to productivity, it usually involves either improved human factors or more efficient assignment of work. An interesting case was the Export-Import Bank's decision to organize its staff by type of loan, rather than by geographic location to obtain better use of personnel and the benefits of specialization.

• *Work attitude.* In many cases a positive attitude toward improvement—on the part of both management and employees—causes productivity gains.

Workload factors

These 17 factors, although mentioned somewhat less frequently than the human and management factors, indicate that the inherent nature of the workload causes improvement or decline in productivity. The workload characteristics which favorably influence productivity change are:

• Workload increases often enable an organization to get more production per employee.

• Workload stability enables better planning of work and staffing.

• Workload predictability, even when on the downturn.

• Reductions in complexity, usually resulting from procedures simplification. However, in five cases noted, the customer did more of the work, such as preparing packages for mailing.

- Reductions in quality. However, only three elements identified downgraded quality as having been a primary factor in productivity improvement.

Factors That Caused Productivity Decline

Table 25-2 shows there were 77 causes cited for downturns in productivity. Using the same categories as above, the joint productivity team found that these comments were divided as follows:

Table 25-2. What Has Caused Productivity Declines?

Human factors (12)	Management factors (20)	Workload factors (45)
• High turnover	• Phase-in of new	• More complex adp
• Loss of skilled	facilities	requirements
employees	• Reorganization	• Rapid drop in
• Drop in employees'	• Lag in workforce	military forces
efficiency	adjustments	• Increase in output
• Increase in nonpro-	• Outmoded facilities	complexity
ductive time for	• Uneconomic	• Quality increase
training	contracting	• Change in character
		of work

Human Factors

These 12 factors, less than half of those mentioned in connection with productivity improvements, indicated that productivity decline had resulted from:

- High turnover.
- Loss of skilled employees.
- Drop in organization efficiency.
- Increase in nonproductive time for training.

These factors are all of a pattern; most likely, they are

associated with other causes for which management is responsible.

Management Factors

These 20 factors were about one third of the number cited as contributing to productivity increases. These factors, which occurred in rather isolated situations, involved:

• Loss of productive effort while phasing in new facilities or equipment.
• Loss of productive effort during transition brought about by reorganization.
• Lags in adjusting personnel strength upward or downward during periods of rapid workload change. This is an understandable problem and is particularly a phenomenon present in the buildup and phasedown of Vietnam workloads.
• Outmoded facilities.
• Uneconomic contracting. This reason was at the top of the list of problems seen by the union representatives with whom the members of the joint productivity team met.

Workload factors

These 45 negative factors exceeded the positive factors by almost 3 to 1. This suggests that deteriorating productivity will frequently involve workload factors not fully under the control of the manager or the employee.

The principal workload factors include:

• More complex data-processing requirements. A current case is the increased demand on the Internal Revenue's tax return processing centers for transcription of data for revenue sharing and other external uses. The number of items that must be examined on each tax return rose in 1 year from 131 to 148.
• The rapid drop in military forces, down 1.2 million men

from the Vietnam peak. The impact on supporting services and facilities has been substantial. The lead times involved in reducing the overhead structure of military bases is such that the rapid force reductions may cause very costly productivity penalties.

• Increase in output complexity. Although there were three cases cited of quality downgrading, there were 22 cases cited where upgrading quality or output complexity cuased productivity to drop below the 1967 level—and many more cases where productivity gains were depressed. The most notable functional area is health care operations where productivity per man-year declined in every organization reporting.

• Change in character of work. Although more general, this refers to those situations where work outputs have changed significantly. In the large military depot complexes, part of the work is being devoted to rebuilding stocks which have become depleted and to rewarehousing, that is, repositioning stocks within the premises. The traditional measures of requisitions processed (customer orders filled) do not reflect this type of work.

NOTES

Notes to Introduction

1. *Measuring the Productivity of Federal Government Organizations*, Washington, D.C.: Government Printing Office, 1964, p. 3.
2. *Ibid.*, p. 3.
3. Thomas D. Morris, William H. Corbett, Brian L. Usilaner, "Productivity Measures in the Federal Government," *Public Administration Review*, XXXII (November/December 1972), p. 759.
4. *Guidelines for Evaluating Work Measurement Systems in the Federal Government*, Washington, D.C.: GAO-OMB-CSC (July, 1972), p. 1.
5. *Measuring and Enhancing Productivity in the Federal Sector*, Washington, D.C.: CSC-GAO-OMB (June, 1972), p. 32.
6. *Measuring the Productivity of Federal Government Organizations*, p. 5.
7. *Proceedings of the Workshop on Effectiveness Measurement*, Washington, D.C.: OMB-CSC-GAO (November, 1971), p. 1.
8. Ralph C. Bledsoe, et al., "Productivity Management in the California Social Services Program," *Public Administration Review*, XXXII (November/December 1972), p. 800.
9. For example, see Richard E. Winnie and Harry P. Hatry, *Measuring the Effectiveness of Local Government Services: Transportation*, Washington, D.C.: The Urban Institute, 1972, and *Improving Productivity Measurement and Evaluation in Local Government, A Four Part Study*, Washington, D.C.: National Commission on Productivity, 1972.
10. *Proceedings of the Workshop on Effectiveness Measurement*, p. 34.
11. Bledsoe, et al., "Productivity Management in the California Social Services Program," p. 802.
12. See citations in note 9 above.

13. Morris, Corbett, Usilaner, "Productivity Measures in the Federal Government," p. 757.

14. *Measuring and Enhancing Productivity in the Federal Sector*, Chapter 3.

15. Damon Stetson, *Productivity: More Work for a Day's Pay*, Washington, D.C.: Labor-Management Relations Service, 1972, p. 3.

16. John W. Kendrick, "Public Capital Expenditures and Budgeting for Productivity Advance," *Public Administration Review*, XXXII (November/December 1972), p. 804.

17. *Measuring and Enhancing Productivity in the Federal Sector*, p. 58.

18. *Analysis of Productivity–Enhancing Capital Investment Opportunities*, Washington, D.C.: GAO-OMB-CSC (September, 1973).

19. *Improving Productivity Measurement and Evaluation in Local Governments, Part IV: Procedures for Identifying and Evaluating Innovations–Six Case Studies*.

20. *Auditing*, Washington, D.C.: OMB-CSC-GAO, 1972, a compendium prepared for the Joint Project Team.

21. George Gustafson, "Management-Type Auditing," *Internal Auditor* (November/December 1970), reprinted in *Auditing* compendium pp. 14-21.

22. Chester A. Newland, "Personnel Concerns in Government Productivity Improvement," *Public Administration Review*, XXXII (November/December 1972), p. 807.

23. Patrick J. Lucey, "Wisconsin's Productivity Policy," *Public Administration Review*, XXXII (November/December 1972), p. 798.

24. Morris, Corbett, Usilaner, "Productivity Measures in the Federal Government," p. 757. Also see *Behavioral Science and Organizational Productivity: An Annotated Bibliography*, Washington, D.C.: OMB-CSC-GAO, 1973.

25. *Measuring and Enhancing Productivity in the Federal Government* Washington, D.C.: OMB-CSC-GAO-BLS (June 1973), pp. 57-64.

Notes to Chapter 4

1. In May, 1972, I outlined a number of "objectives" for dealing with Wisconsin's fiscal situation in the 1973-75 biennial budget. At the top of the list was productivity improvements, discussed here. Other related policies included: (1) *Low priority programs.* Each agency was directed to list programs or activities that comprise 10 percent of its budget which, in the view of the agency, are the lowest priority services; they were also asked to provide an impact statement on each program so that it could be assessed against the priorities of other departments. (2) *User fees.* Agencies were asked to carefully evaluate current charges for special services provided by state government and consider the advisability and practicality of initiating charges for some services now being delivered free. (3) *Increased federal aids.* Wisconsin ranks 45th among the states in the percentage of federal aids received on a per

capita basis. Although to some extent this ranking is unavoidable (because of federal aid formulas), agencies were asked to examine their policies and a general review of state procedures in this area was initiated. (4) *Building moratorium.* A moratorium was announced on new facilities, which will allow only absolutely essential building or remodeling to be done, and, where possible, the shutting down of old and costly facilities.

2. Sig Gissler, "Productivity in the Public Sector: A Summary of a Wingspread Symposium," *Public Administration Review,* Vol. XXXIII, No. 6 (November/December 1972).

3. Harry P. Hatry and Donald M. Fisk, *Improving Productivity and Productivity Measurement in Local Governments,* Washington, D.C.: National Commission on Productivity (June 1971), p. 4.

Notes to Chapter 11

1. U.S. Bureau of the Budget, *Measuring Productivity of Federal Government Organizations,* 1964.

2. These concepts along with our findings of the current status of productivity measurement over the full spectrum of local government services are presented in an earlier report to the commission, "Improving Productivity and Productivity Measurement in Local Governments," by Harry P. Hatry and Donald M. Fisk, The Urban Institute, June, 1971.

Notes to Chapter 15

1. T. Morris, et al., "Productivity Measures in the Federal Government, *Public Administration Review,* Vol. No. 6 (November/December 1972), p. 753.

2. F. C. Thayer, "Productivity: Taylorism Revisited (Round Three)," *Public Administration Review,* Vol. No. 6 (November/December 1972), p. 833.

3. E. Shanahan, "In Midst of Boom, Federal Spending Is Key Issue," *New York Times* (January 7, 1973), Section F, p. 19.

4. *First Annual Report of the National Commission on Productivity* (March, 1972), U.S. Government Printing Office: 1972 0-459-873, p. 6.

5. V. Ridgway, "Dysfunctional Consequences of Performance Measurement," *Administrative Science Quarterly,* 1, No. 2 (September, 1956).

6. H. Levinson, "Management by Whose Objectives," *Harvard Business Review* (July-August 1970), p. 125.

7. P. Seimiller, "Responsibilities of Labor and Management" in *Collective Bargaining Today,* Washington: Bureau of National Affairs, 1970, p. 43.

8. G. T. Allison, *Essence of Decision,* Boston: Little, Brown and Company, 1971. See summary, pp. 256, 257.

9. A. Weber, "Stability and Change in the Structure of Collective

Bargaining" in *Challenges to Collective Bargaining*, Englewood: Prentice-Hall, 1967, by the American Assembly, Columbia University, p. 20.
10. *Ibid.*, p. 78 (J. Steiber).
11. McKinney's *1972 Session Laws of New York*, St. Paul: West Publishing, 1972, p. 678.
12. Agreement between the State of New York and the Civil Service Employees Association, Institutional Services Unit. See Articles 7, 6 and Article 8. Dated 6/21/72.
13. Supplemental Agreement of December 26, 1972 between New York State and the Civil Service Employees Association.
14. A. Raskin, "Two Views of Collective Bargaining" in *Challenges to Collective Bargaining*, Englewood: Prentice-Hall, 1967, by the American Assembly, Columbia University, p. 173.
15. U.G. Foa, "Interpersonal and Economic Resources," *Science*, Vol. 171 (January 1971), p. 345.
16. "New Evaluation System Sought by Civil Service Commission," *Washington Star News* (December 26, 1972).
17. B. Agnew, ed., "Productivity Still Has a Bad Name," *Business Week* (January 6, 1973).

Notes to Chapter 16

1. Bureau of the Budget, *Measuring Productivity in Federal Government Organizations*, Washington, D.C., U.S. Government Printing Office, 1964.
2. U.S. Civil Service Commission, General Accounting Office, Office of Management and Budget, *Measuring and Enhancing Productivity in the Federal Sector*, Washington, D.C., mimeograph edition, June 1972.
3. See John W. Kendrick, "The Treatment of Intangible Resources as Capital," *Review of Income and Wealth*, Vol. VIII, No. 1 (March, 1972).
4. The reader is referred to a listing of the advantages and disadvantages of the alternatives to capital budgeting contained in Appendix J of the report cited in note 2.

Notes to Chapter 19

1. Accounting, Research and Terminology Bulletins, Final Edition, "No. 1, Review and Resume," American Institute of Certified Public Accountants, Inc., 1961, p. 9.
2. Robert K. Mautz, "The Nature and Reliability of Audit Evidence," *The Journal of Accountancy*, May, 1958, p. 43.
3. Robert N. Anthony, *Management Accounting, Text and Cases*, Richard D. Irwin, Inc., 1956, p. 2.
4. "Readers' Problem Clinic," Fredric E. Mints (ed.), *The Internal Auditor*, March, 1960, p. 64.
5. Eric L. Kohler, *Auditing, An Introduction*, Prentice-Hall, Inc., 1947, pp. 45-51.

6. John L. Carey, "The Integrated Accounting Service," *The Journal of Accountancy*, November, 1965, pp. 63-64.

7. *Ibid.*, pp. 61-64; also, January, 1967, p. 48.

8. Edwin H. Caplin, "Behavioral Assumptions of Management Accounting—Report of a Field Study," *The Accounting Review*, April, 1968, pp. 342-362.

9. Fred H. Blum, "Social Audit of the T Enterprise," *Harvard Business Review*, March-April, 1958, pp. 77-86.

CONTRIBUTORS

Walter L. Balk is Associate Professor of Public Administration at the Graduate School of Public Affairs, State University of New York at Albany

Samuel J. Bernstein is Associate Professor of Public Administration at Baruch College, CUNY

Dan Cordtz is Associate Editor of *Fortune*

Donald M. Fisk is a Senior Research Associate at the Urban Institute

George A. Gustafson is Assistant Professor of Accounting, California State College

Herbert L. Haber is former Director of Labor Relations for the City of New York

Patrick E. Haggerty is Chairman of Texas Instruments, Inc.

Harry P. Hatry is Director, State-Local Research Program, the Urban Institute

James D. Hodgson is a former Secretary of Labor

John W. Kendrick is Vice-President and Director of Economic Research, The Conference Board

Rensis Likert was Director of the Institute for Social Research at the University of Michigan and is Board Chairman of Rensis Likert Associates

John V. Lindsay is a former Mayor of the City of New York

Patrick J. Lucey is Governor of Wisconsin

Ellsworth H. Morse, Jr., is Assistant Comptroller General, U.S. General Accounting Office

Leon Reinharth is Assistant Professor of Organizational Sciences, Newark College of Engineering

Herbert Stein is a former member of the President's Council of Economic Advisers

Richard E. Winnie is a former Consultant to the Urban Institute

INDEX